The Political Power of Global Corporations

THE POLITICAL POWER OF GLOBAL CORPORATIONS

JOHN MIKLER

polity

Copyright © John Mikler 2018

The right of John Mikler to be identified as Author of this Work has been asserted in accordance with the UK Copyright, Designs and Patents Act 1988.

First published in 2018 by Polity Press

Polity Press
65 Bridge Street
Cambridge CB2 1UR, UK

Polity Press
101 Station Landing
Suite 300
Medford, MA 02155, USA

All rights reserved. Except for the quotation of short passages for the purpose of criticism and review, no part of this publication may be reproduced, stored in a retrieval system or transmitted, in any form or by any means, electronic, mechanical, photocopying, recording or otherwise, without the prior permission of the publisher.

ISBN-13: 978-0-7456-9845-8
ISBN-13: 978-0-7456-9846-5(pb)

A catalogue record for this book is available from the British Library.

Library of Congress Cataloging-in-Publication Data

Names: Mikler, John, author.
Title: The political power of global corporations / John Mikler.
Description: Cambridge, UK ; Medford, MA : Polity Press, 2018. | Includes bibliographical references and index.
Identifiers: LCCN 2017023460 (print) | LCCN 2017036603 (ebook) | ISBN 9780745698489 (Mobi) | ISBN 9780745698496 (Epub) | ISBN 9780745698458 (hardback) | ISBN 9780745698465 (pbk.)
Subjects: LCSH: International business enterprises–Political aspects. | Business and politics. | International relations.
Classification: LCC HD2755.5 (ebook) | LCC HD2755.5 .M55 2018 (print) | DDC 322/.3–dc23
LC record available at https://lccn.loc.gov/2017023460

Typeset in 10.5 on 12 pt Times NR
by Toppan Best-set Premedia Limited
Printed and bound in Great Britain by CPI Group (UK) Ltd, Croydon

The publisher has used its best endeavours to ensure that the URLs for external websites referred to in this book are correct and active at the time of going to press. However, the publisher has no responsibility for the websites and can make no guarantee that a site will remain live or that the content is or will remain appropriate.

Every effort has been made to trace all copyright holders, but if any have been inadvertently overlooked the publisher will be pleased to include any necessary credits in any subsequent reprint or edition.

For further information on Polity, visit our website: politybooks.com

For Kara, Annika, and Erin

CONTENTS

Acknowledgments	ix
Tables and Figures	xiii
Abbreviations	xv
1. Introduction: The Global Corporate Takeover	1
2. Theorizing Global Corporations' Power	23
3. Geographical Concentration	51
4. National Institutional Embeddedness	73
5. Private Authority and the Potential for Private Governance	102
6. Conclusion: Three Implications	131
Notes	147
References	153
Index	183

ACKNOWLEDGMENTS

Over lunch one Arctic winter's day in 2013, while I was on sabbatical as a Visiting Fellow at Durham University, David Held suggested I should write a book on the political power of global corporations. My *Handbook of Global Companies* was on the verge of being released, and he thought I might be in a good position to say something about the topic. "You know: theory, framework, key examples, that kind of thing," he said. It seemed like too big a topic for one book, and while I was flattered to be asked I was less than enthusiastic about the possibility of writing it at the time. Without his encouragement I doubt I would have taken on the task, and the idea grew on me until four years later the result is this book.

On the way, the central themes emerged primarily as a result of discussions with students. For me teaching is a joy, and actually my main source of intellectual stimulation. I hope it is for my students as well. It seems wrong to single out any individuals, yet I feel I owe Harry Maher a debt of gratitude. He took my senior undergraduate globalization subject in 2015, and in one tutorial I found myself responding to his well-informed critique of neoliberal globalization with the exclamation: "I don't need neoliberalism, I don't need to talk about markets, market forces and marketization to understand the power of the world's major corporations! I know who they are, I know their *names*, I know where they come from, I know where they go to, and I know what they do!" Everyone laughed at how surprisingly (including to me) worked up I had got. Some agreed with my impassioned response while others disagreed, but at that moment I realized what had to be at the core of a book on the political power of global corporations: an explicit focus on them as political actors, and re-territorializing them as reflecting geopolitical patterns of power rather than stressing their transnationality.

There are so many people to thank in the writing and completion of this book, I am bound to leave somebody out. I hope they will forgive me if I do.

Before the invitation to write this book and the 2015 "eureka" moment mentioned above, I have found the work of Stephen Wilks and Doris Fuchs hugely influential. They are not the only ones to speak truth to the political power of global corporations, but for me they do so with flair and clarity. They are nothing less than the inspiration behind this book.

For making the project a possibility, and enabling it, Louise Knight, Nekane Tanaka Galdos, and all the team at Polity cannot be thanked enough for their support, advice, and encouragement at every stage.

So often the focus for academic research is on sources of funding, when what is most valuable is time. I am grateful to the University of Sydney for granting me a six-month sabbatical to complete the book in 2016. I am also particularly appreciative of the understanding and support of Colin Wight and Simon Tormey as respective Heads of the Department of Government and International Relations and School of Social and Political Sciences.

For reading and commenting on drafts of the entire manuscript I am grateful to my wife, Kara, and Ainsley Elbra. Ainsley also deserves thanks for her research assistance, and especially her remarkably extensive knowledge of the literature on private governance, as well as its practice. For their invaluable advice and suggestions, I am grateful to Linda Weiss, Nicola Phillips, Graeme Gill, Tony Payne, Tom Hunt, Genevieve LeBaron, Adam Barber, Damien Cahill, Jason Sharman, Richard Eccleston, Anika Gauja, Rodney Smith, Madison Cartwright, Tabitha Benney, Shahar Hameiri, Stephen Bell, Andrew Hindmoor, Elizabeth Thurbon, Wes Widmaier, Karsten Ronit, Susan Engel, Susan Park, Matthias Hofferberth, Delphine Rabet, Hannah Murphy-Gregory, James van Alstine, Duncan Wigan, Aynsley Kellow, Jan Fichtner, David Held, Eva-Maria Nag, Caner Bakir, Fred Gale, Laure Astill, Lyne Latulippe, Alison Christians, and Stewart Jackson.

For their stimulating discussions and insights that have informed, and indeed changed, the book's contents, Sophie Roberts, Brian Coughlan, Imogen Fountain, Rob Clark, Rachel Holden, Danny

Bielik, Ellis Zilka, Gillian Ramsay, Sundran Rajendra, Jill Greatorex, Chris Anastopoulos, Ken Engsmyr, and Teresa Moffett deserve thanks. And of course, the Wednesday-night tennis crew: Paul Thurloe, Belinda Mullen, Jim Leeper, Joanne Corcoran, Lachlan Habgood, Paul Sanderson, and Ben Clarke. Not only have they been supportive and offered their opinions, but they have put up with my post-match diatribes on a weekly basis when they had every right to feel entitled to enjoy a quiet beer. My thanks also go to friends in the corporate world for their insights, advice, and suggestions, particularly Stephen Ferris, Ian Taylor and Rob Grierson. Our long discussions, which I tell colleagues constitute fieldwork, are always a pleasure. To friends and family I have not named, please know that without your love and support completing this project would have been impossible.

Special thanks must go to two people in particular. First, Neil Harrison, with whom I have collaborated on several pieces of research previously, and whose challenging emails and mind-expanding Skype discussions at strange hours (due to him being in the United States and me in Australia) have greatly informed the way I have come to see corporate power over the years. This book has gotten in the way of further collaboration, while helping to inform the contribution I hope to make when we next do so. Second, my colleague Diarmuid Maguire, who not only provided advice on this book, but who has also provided intellectual stimulation, challenging critiques of my ideas, recommended reading, mentoring, and above all else great friendship over the last ten years. He is retiring as this book is published, and the University of Sydney's Department of Government and International Relations will be greatly diminished as a result. So will my lunchtimes.

Finally, none of this would have been possible without the care and support of my family. As always, my wife, Kara, deserves my thanks for her support in so many other ways besides reading drafts. Every time I commence a new project she knows what she is in for but comes on the ride anyway. My daughters, Annika and Erin, have likewise done a sterling job of putting up with me while consumed by writing. Annika, now fifteen years of age, has broadened my appreciation of science fiction to embrace the excellent young adult literature that imagines some of the most dystopian corporate-dominated futures. Erin, at ten years of age, continually challenges me by exclaiming in response to my often turgid dinner-time political pronouncements: "Yes, but what can we *do*?" For both, and no doubt others of their generation, the idea that big corporations from, and with, powerful countries rule the world seems obvious. In addition, they always remind me of the need to be positive as well as relevant. I hope that this has rubbed off on the contents of the book. As I say in the concluding chapter, it is neither the first nor final word on the subject, but it is my take on it, and I hope it proves useful to the reader.

John Mikler
April 2017

TABLES AND FIGURES

Tables

1.1: Top 20 Nonfinancial Global Corporations' Sales versus States' GDPs and Expenditures, 2013	9
2.1: IPE Theories and the Three Waves of Conceptualizing Globalization	29
3.1: Top Ten Headquarters of FT Global 500 Corporations	56
3.2: Nationality and Transnationality of the World's Top 100 Nonfinancial Corporations, 2013	57
3.3: Top Ten Headquarters of FT Emerging 500 Corporations, 2015	61
3.4: Nationality and Transnationality of the World's Top 100 Nonfinancial Corporations from Developing Countries, 2013	61
3.5: FDI Stocks	65
3.6: FDI Flows	67
3.7: FDI Stocks as a Percentage of GDP in Industrialized States, 2013	69
4.1: LMEs versus CMEs	80
4.2: State Intervention/Control in Corporate Affairs in Industrialized States	92
4.3: State Intervention/Control in Corporate Affairs in the BRICs versus Industrialized States	97

5.1: Global Corporations' Headquarters, World's
  Most Admired Companies, and Soft Power, 2015   122
5.2: Fortune 500 World's Most Admired Companies
  Ranked by Key Attributes, 2015   123
5.3: Confidence in Major Companies, the Government,
  and Charitable or Humanitarian Organizations   128

Figures

1.1: Government Expenditure   13
1.2: Tax on Corporate Profits   14
1.3: OECD Average Share of Taxes in Total Tax Revenue   15
2.1: The Norm Lifecycle   34

ABBREVIATIONS

BRICs   Brazil, Russia, India, and China
CFCs   chlorofluorocarbons
CME   coordinated market economy
CSR   corporate social responsibility
EU   European Union
FDI   foreign direct investment
GDP   gross domestic product
GFC   global financial crisis
ICANN   Internet Corporation for Assigned Names and Numbers
ICC   International Chamber of Commerce
IPC   Intellectual Property Committee
IPE   International Political Economy
ISO   International Organization for Standardization
LME   liberal market economy
M&As   mergers and acquisitions
MNC   multinational corporation
MNE   multinational enterprise
NGO   non-government organization
TNC   transnational corporation
TNI   transnationality index
TPP   Trans-Pacific Partnership
TRIPs   Trade-Related Aspects of Intellectual Property Rights
UK   United Kingdom

UNCTAD	United Nations Conference on Trade and Development
US	United States
USTR	US Trade Representative
VOC	varieties of capitalism
WBCSD	World Business Council for Sustainable Development
WTO	World Trade Organization

1 INTRODUCTION: THE GLOBAL CORPORATE TAKEOVER

Global corporations are "in charge." This is a widely held view, and it is not unusual for it to be expressed with negative sentiments given that they are often portrayed as "the dark lords of globalization" (Micklethwait and Wooldridge 2003, 168). Indeed, the impact and ongoing fallout from the 2007–2008 global financial crisis (GFC) has only increased fears that states no longer govern in the interests of their citizens, but in the interests of these powerful entities over which they have little control. Such fears are reflected in much contemporary science fiction, which has produced a dystopian oeuvre that imagines futures in which states are powerless and societies are at their mercy. For example, Margaret Atwood's *Maddadam* and William Gibson's *Sprawl* trilogies are set in near futures where to all intents and purposes governments are non-existent, and global corporations perform all functions once associated with the state, but in a manner that presages the collapse of civilization.[1]

Why commence a book on the political power of global corporations with reference to science fiction? I do so to highlight that what is widely accepted and acknowledged in popular culture is relatively less analyzed in the politics and international relations literature. Most debate has been framed in more abstract terms. Rather than the political power of global corporations, the power of *markets* versus states is most often stressed (e.g., Schwartz 2000), and the early globalization literature in particular revolved around the manner in which impersonal market *forces* increasingly dominate states' economic, social, and political agendas. As the redoubtable Susan Strange put it, "Where states were once the masters of markets, now it is markets which, on many crucial issues, are the masters over the governments of states" (Strange 1996, 4). Even if global corporations embody the power shift away from states this entails, they were seen as being motivated by *market imperatives*. Therefore, the marketization of all economic relations is what is usually stressed as mattering politically, because market forces and market imperatives do not produce governance in the sense of control over national destinies. To quote Strange (1996, 14) again, "What some have lost, others have not gained" and the resulting "diffusion of authority away from national governments has left a hole of non-authority, ungovernance it might be called." In other words, the state governs and no other actor can govern like a state.

Pitched ideological battles have been fought on the basis of these claims. Pro-market liberal commentators have celebrated the demise of states, or at least their diminished relevance, and the rewards to be reaped from a world in which markets are global and free (e.g., Bhagwati 2004; Wolf 2004). Critical voices, particularly Marxists, have bemoaned this prospect, seeking instead alternatives to the structural basis for the capitalist class relations underpinning globalization (e.g., Kitching 2001; Coburn 2011). Between the extremes there has often been a metaphorical throwing up of hands in acceptance of the proposition that states can only function (rather than rule) in a passive, facilitative role as the places where global market imperatives are played out by the global corporations that act on the basis of them.

I do not think it goes too far to caricature these debates as akin to a study of scientific phenomena: irresistible global market forces that impact on states like political "meteors" on the surface of the Earth. This seemed what the earliest pronouncements regarding globalization verged on, such as those of Ohmae (1990), who proclaimed the world had become "borderless," and Fukuyama (1992), who declared "the end of history" at the conclusion of the Cold War. Their claims were essentially that international relations as traditionally conceived no longer mattered in a world of laissez-faire capitalism and the inevitability of neoliberal market deregulation and privatization that went with it. It was as if the very shape of the world were being altered to resemble one large market with national and regional variations erased. This view underscored Levitt's (1983, 101) pronouncement that "the earth is round, but for most purposes it's sensible to treat it as flat. Space is curved, but not much for everyday life here on earth." It was the end of geography because nationality, national differences, and national preferences were being "leveled" by globalized markets. Thomas Friedman agreed, although he used a fashion rather than geographical analogy to famously declare that all states had to don neoliberal "golden straightjackets" (Friedman 2000, 87).[2] They could try wearing other political "clothes," but not only would they be unfashionable, they would suffer the consequences of the global market punishing them for so doing, inflicting economic and social pain they could ill afford to bear.

Those familiar with the globalization literature will no doubt retort that rather than the views of the early globalists (or "hyperglobalists," as they are sometimes more pejoratively called) being mainstream, though I would contend that actually they are in most contemporary journalism and popular commentary, all serious globalization scholars now study the transformation of the exercise of state power rather than its annihilation. The analysis of politics and power in a globally interconnected world is not predicated on the globalists' zeal for the inevitability of free market capitalism writ large on the world as if it were some kind of force. Most serious scholars recognize that the debates surrounding this vision have often been ideologically motivated, and often hyperbolic in tone. Yet, in recognizing that globalization instead entails a process of political transformation, the more nuanced globalization literature still often returns to the analysis of markets versus states as it considers the question of "who governs" in a globalized world. For example, while the governments of nations remain very much drivers of the processes and outcomes of governance (e.g., see Weiss 2003; Drezner 2007; Bell and Hindmoor 2009), the marketization of all aspects of society and state functions is often said to have produced a neoliberal form of the state (e.g., see Harvey 2005). If not this, then states themselves are seen as having embraced markets as a policy choice rather than having it thrust upon them (e.g., Tiberghien 2007; Thatcher 2007). Indeed, there has been a vast literature since Vogel's (1996) *Freer Markets More Rules* that examines the marketization of states' functions as a process of reregulation, as opposed to neoliberal deregulation.

As a starting point, it is surely not unimportant to consider whether states or markets "rule," how a more economically interconnected world drives the embrace or rejection of this viewpoint, and the extent to which this embrace or rejection is real (i.e., inevitable) or ideological (i.e., chosen). However, the intention of this book is to challenge the abstraction involved in a focus on markets that risks obscuring the role played by global corporations. These key actors have gone somewhat "missing" in the impassioned debates about the political pros and cons of neoliberal globalization. While the state has remained "in" as the subject of most analysis—in terms of its demise, continued relevance, transformation, and so on—by comparison a more acute understanding of the rise of global corporations has been left "out." For example, because global corporations can operate multi- or transnationally there is debate about the extent to which states serve as "merely the handmaidens of firms" (Strange 1997, 184; see also Crouch 2004). What this means from a corporate as opposed to a state perspective is relatively less clear because while states are reasonably well drawn in terms of their institutions and ideologies, and, it may be noted, so too is the role played by civil society and civic groups (e.g., see Keck and Sikkink 1998, 1999; Scholte 2011, 2002), corporations are all too often more simply sketched as mechanisms of profit maximization. Yet global corporations perform a crucial and central role in determining the global distribution of economic wealth, global development outcomes, global economic processes, and the fate of the polities of nations. How they do so is relatively understudied from a political power perspective. It is as if they are a residual category of political actor with assumed rather than studied motivations.

The result is that even as they criticize it, those with a political eye on the economy and economic processes seem largely to accept the mainstream neoclassical economic assumption that firms maximize profits by combining capital and labor, and then consider the resulting economic, political, and social impacts produced. They accept that such decisions occur in markets that are now increasingly globally interconnected, while states are territorially grounded, and largely leave it at that. Of course states' ability to serve the interests of their citizens may be undermined by an ideological embrace of the neoliberal "inevitability" of global markets, and there are certainly many fine and complex analyses of the institutional embedding of neoliberalism in national, regional, and global governance (e.g., Teeple and McBride 2011; Cahill 2014). Even so, the result is often a rather disembodied and de-territorialized analysis that focuses on the power of globally mobile *capital*, and the way assumed corporate *interests* are served that clash with citizens' aspirations. Korten (2015) suggests global corporations now potentially "rule the world" given the size and scope of their operations, and there have been calls for more political analysis of how they do so (e.g., see Harrod 2006; Kollman 2008; Zadek 2013), but it is easy to form the view that the literature remains "utterly deficient" (Fuchs 2005, 771). Indeed, unfortunately it seems the case that "instead of mountains of scholarly achievement, we have a few oases in an arid landscape" (Wilks 2013, 2).

My intention is to further develop these oases or, if you like, to do some "landscape gardening" so as to facilitate further contributions to them. As such, this book has two aims. First, to explicitly re-embody global corporations as political actors with complex identities and strategies to be examined, rather than assumed in more abstract terms. As they embody the power wielded *in*, rather than *by*, markets, they should be the focus for analysis. Second, to re-territorialize global corporations as political actors produced by their home states and regions, rather than the "globe." The territories in which they operate are the places from which they institutionally derive their power and, politically, not just where they still primarily act but also *from which* they act. These two aims lead to the book's central point: that as political actors from, and located in, specific states and regions, global corporations' political power flows from their ability to construct their identity and interests in others in territorially defined political contexts. The arguments in respect of re-embodying and re-territorializing global corporations are presented below, followed by an outline of the chapters to follow that will demonstrate this central point.

Re-Embodying Global Corporations

In 1970 there were just 7,000 global corporations—i.e., parent firms associated with foreign affiliates beyond the borders of their home states (Clapp 2005). There are now over 100,000, with nearly 900,000 foreign affiliates (UNCTAD 2011). Whether conceived as multinational corporations (MNCs), transnational corporations (TNCs), or multinational enterprises (MNEs), a global dimension to almost all the world's major corporations is now taken for granted. MNCs are defined as such because they invest, produce, and sell their products and services in more than one national jurisdiction. Seeing them as TNCs goes beyond them operating in several jurisdictions to passing through/across borders as if these were irrelevant. The MNE term, most often used in the international business and management literature, encompasses aspects of both in the sense that modern business involves the management of supply chains and coordinating networks of operations across several national jurisdictions. Global MNEs are regarded, somewhat tautologically, as those which operate on a global scale. There is no agreed definition of what this means, but one interpretation is that these are corporations with at least 20 percent of their sales in each of at least three continental markets (*Financial Times* n.d.).[3] In all cases the result is at least a regional, if not purely global, conception of their operations, with this increasingly the norm as they come to operate "as if the entire world (or major regions of it) were a single entity" (Levitt 1983, 92).

It follows that state sovereignty is weakened, because no individual government has jurisdiction over all the activities of any global corporation. Even if they were to agree to share sovereignty to regulate corporate activity, which is highly challenging as evidenced by the case of the European Union (EU) as perhaps the only example of this working in practice, in the absence of global government nothing less than global governance is required to regulate the activities of global corporations.[4] If this does not eventuate, the alternative is neoliberalism under which markets are seen as effectively ungovernable. This view was popularized by Margaret Thatcher, with her "TINA" principle (i.e., that There Is No Alternative to the market), and subsequently embraced to one degree or another as an inevitability by leaders of all political persuasions, including Bill Clinton, whose 1992 presidential campaign was noteworthy for the unofficial slogan "it's the economy, stupid." The choice, if one accepts this view, is between being "neoliberal or neo-idiotic" (Chang 2008, 27), so that all states in a more economically interconnected world must accept that "your economy grows and your politics shrinks" (Friedman 2000, 105).

It similarly follows why it may be thought inevitable that global corporations must be in charge. This is because they are, first and foremost, usually defined as "market actors" (e.g., Broome 2014, 92–111). In addition, the neoliberal ideal that markets should be dominant in economic, political, and social affairs, and that they should be completely unfettered, is related to the power that global corporations enjoy. The argument that this should be the case, that it is *right*, is important because it suggests that global corporations should be *legitimately* in charge. It is not a new argument. As liberalism came to be entrenched as a conservative rather than a radical idea, those propounding the virtues of markets versus states as well as their inevitability made such statements as "the state is just about through as an economic unit" and that "all governments (will) acknowledge the truths of political economy and liberalism (will) be carried throughout the globe" (Kindleberger 1969, 207). In a similar vein Vernon (1971, 3) famously declared that the spread of global corporations meant "concepts such as sovereignty and national economic strength appear curiously drained of meaning."[5] A long line of liberal scholars who saw the state as needing to act to bring this about, and ultimately neoliberally inspired world leaders who appeared to embrace the need for the state to get out of the way, therefore laid the foundations for accepting what for many is now the conventional wisdom. This is that states should surrender their power to the freedoms and competitive imperatives of global markets, thereby enjoying the benefits of global trade and investment rather than engaging in war for territorial conquest.

Thus, arguments in favor of markets and market actors being in charge predate the rise of global corporations. The aim of those making them was to promote individual freedoms over the power of authoritarian states, and therefore they attacked the power of the state in favor of free and competitive markets populated by merchants, entrepreneurs, and small- to medium-sized enterprises. The genesis of this idea was of course in the post–Industrial Revolution writings of the Father of Liberalism, Adam Smith. His reference to the governing power of the market's "invisible hand" was an allegorical one. In alluding to it he was attacking the visible hand of the state. The invisible hand of the market was therefore "code" for individual freedoms, particularly the freedom of individuals to act in their self-interests. An individual who is free to do so is "led by an invisible hand to promote an end which was no part of his intention" (Smith 2003 [1776], xvii), and all individuals acting to maximize their own gains cumulatively produce better outcomes for society than when those in positions of authority seek to impose their will on them, even when they presume to do so in the common (i.e., national) interest. As such, the invisible hand of the market produces better outcomes for society than the visible hand of the state, or, as Ricardo put it, the "pursuit of individual advantage is admirably connected with the universal good of the whole" (Ricardo 1962 [1821], 81).

Whether or not one accepts this, the reality today is that advantage is pursued through global corporations. This is not done on the basis of market competition, but via global control of the markets for their products and services. It is not the state of affairs Adam Smith promoted. Far from liberal capitalism and the modern global corporation being synonymous, he actually derided the joint-stock company as "antiquated and inefficient" by comparison to sole-traders and owner-managers (Micklethwait and Wooldridge 2003, 6; see also 42–43). As well as being against the form of the modern global corporation because it divorced shareholder ownership from management control, Smith disliked it as a way of organizing economic activity because of the tendency for markets dominated by such firms to produce monopolistic rather than competitive markets. The world he imagined was one of individual merchants "preferring the support of domestic to that of foreign industry" (Smith 2003 [1776], xvii), but according to Nolan et al. (2002) by the end of the twentieth century no more than five global corporations controlled each of the world's major industries, with around a third of these having one corporation accounting for more than 40 percent of global sales. There may be over 100,000 global corporations, but the reality is that very few of these dominate the global economy.

As Crouch (2011, 49) observes, there has been a "corporate takeover of the market" by these enormous entities, which do not so much compete in markets as they control them. The result is that the visible hand of the state has not been replaced by the invisible hand of Smith's market forces, but by a visible handful of corporations. This evokes Chandler's (1977) notion of the visible hand of management. Focusing on US corporations, he contended that increasingly they were administratively coordinated rather than market coordinated, and that a managerial hierarchy in enterprises of great size and scope was better suited to strategically administering their operations than market competition. This management hierarchy is a source of power, and over time it alters the very structure of industry sectors in favor of the corporations that administer them, and ultimately the economy as a whole. His observations made in the 1970s in respect of the American economy would seem to resonate in respect of a contemporary global economy-dominated global corporations.

A basic measure of their size is given by their annual revenues. In 2015, the Fortune Global 500 companies together had sales totaling US$31.2 trillion (Fortune 2015a).[6] Given that the size of the global economy was estimated to be US$73.5 trillion in the same year (World Bank 2016), this means that they effectively accounted for nearly half of it. In fact, Table 1.1 shows that the world's twenty most global corporations have sales greater than the combined gross domestic product (GDP) of the bottom 138 states, and some are larger than middle income states such as Algeria and Portugal. It could be argued that such statements are problematic, though, because as GDP is a value-added measure of national output, a corporation's value added rather than its sales should be used for comparative purposes. Thompson (2003) estimates that many corporations' value added is between 20 to 30 percent of their turnover, so that the sales figures quoted in Table 1.1 overstate their relative size by a factor of three to four. However, arguments for statistical accuracy on the basis of like-for-like measurement risk missing the point that global corporations are not unitary actors. Instead, they are enmeshed in global networks which they coordinate. For example, Walmart does not own *any* manufacturing operations but contracts over 100,000 suppliers that produce the products it sells (LeBaron 2014; Walmart 2013; Walmart 2017). Other corporations like Apple, Gap, and Nike also produce no goods themselves. Instead, their core function in the production process is

Table 1.1: Top 20 Nonfinancial Global Corporations' Sales versus States' GDPs and Expenditures, 2013

Nonfinancial Corporations (ranked by sales)[a]	Sales (US$ million)	State (ranked by GDP)		GDP[b] (US$ million)	State (ranked by expenditure)		Expenditure[c] (US$ million)
(1) Walmart Stores Inc.	476,294	(27)	Taiwan	511,280	(12)	Australia	555,877
(2) Royal Dutch Shell PLC	451,235	(28)	Austria	428,456	(13)	India	506,405
(3) Exxon Mobil Corporation	390,247	(30)	Thailand	387,253	(14)	Netherlands	399,496
(4) BP PLC	379,136	(31)	Iran	380,348	(15)	Mexico	354,112
(5) Volkswagen Group	261,560	(42)	Finland	268,281	(18)	Belgium	285,657
(6) Toyota Motor Corporation	256,381	(43)	Greece	242,306	(19)	Saudi Arabia	282,602
(7) Glencore Xstrata PLC	232,694	(44)	Pakistan	232,757	(20)	South Korea	272,830
(8) Total SA	227,901	(48)	Portugal	224,983	(21)	Norway	226,365
(9) Chevron Corporation	211,664	(50)	Czech Republic	208,796	(22)	Poland	222,048
(10) Samsung Electronics Co. Ltd.	209,727	(51)	Algeria	208,764	(24)	Austria	218,256
(11) Apple Computer Inc.	170,910	(54)	Romania	191,598	(25)	Switzerland	215,782
(12) E.ON AG	162,573	(55)	New Zealand	184,752	(26)	Denmark	191,712
(13) Daimler AG	156,641	(56)	Ukraine	179,572	(27)	Indonesia	174,607
(14) General Motors Co	155,427	(57)	Kuwait	175,788	(28)	Finland	154,508
(15) Eni SpA	152,313	(58)	Vietnam	170,565	(29)	Israel	119,765

Continued

Table 1.1: *Continued*

Nonfinancial Corporations (ranked by sales)[a]	Sales (US$ million)	State (ranked by GDP)		GDP[b] (US$ million)	State (ranked by expenditure)		Expenditure[c] (US$ million)
(16) Ford Motor Company	146,917	(59)	Bangladesh	161,763	(30)	United Arab Emirates	118,308
(17) General Electric Co	142,937	(60)	Hungary	133,424	(31)	South Africa	116,071
(18) Cargill	136,654	(61)	Angola	124,169	(32)	Greece	115,776
(19) Hon Hai Precision Industries	133,362	(62)	Morocco	103,836	(33)	Portugal	112,651
(20) GDF Suez	118,561	(63)	Slovak Republic	97,743	(34)	Iraq	112,556
Top 20	4,573,134	Bottom 138		4,504,235	Bottom 166		4,402,553

Sources: UNCTAD (2014a); IMF (2015).

[a]This lists the corporations with the most foreign assets, which is one possible measure of globality in the sense that it indicates corporations with operations across many national jurisdictions. Of these, the ones with the highest sales are listed.
[b]Current prices
[c]Total general government expenditure

the contracting and logistical management of their global supply chains. As such, the sales these global corporations report are a close approximation of the value added in the global production processes they oversee, and serve to demonstrate the magnitude of the economic impact and influence of their operations.[7]

Comparing sales with states' GDP may even underestimate their relative size. A comparison with national expenditure is probably more accurate because a state's budget is analogous to a corporation's sales, these being an indicator of how much it has spent on purchasing labor, resources, investments, goods, advertising, corporate image-making, lobbying, consultants, and so on, in order to produce a desired surplus. In essence, corporate sales are an indicator of organizational budget, rather like a state's budget, and, this being the case, Table 1.1 shows that the sales of the world's 20 most global corporations are greater than the combined expenditure of the bottom 166 states. In addition to rivaling the world's major states on the basis of their national expenditures, it is noteworthy that by comparison to the US$4.6 trillion in sales accounted for by the global corporations listed in Table 1.1, in the same year the United Nations had a budget of US$5.1 billion (United Nations 2012). Perhaps more pertinently, given that it describes itself as "the only global international organization dealing with the rules of trade between nations" (WTO n.d. a), the World Trade Organization (WTO) had a budget of just US$210 million (WTO 2016).[8] Therefore, they are much larger than not only many of the world's most powerful nations, but also the international organizations that are so much more the focus of international relations studies because they are supposed to make "rules for the world" (Barnett and Finnemore 2004).

Why, then, do we still hear so much regarding neoliberal globalization and the marketization of all aspects of our societies and polities? Why are we so often told that, regardless of what we might desire as citizens, global economic imperatives determine what is feasible? One answer to such questions would be that it is politically advantageous for global corporations to cast themselves in the image of market actors, and for this to be widely accepted. As J. K. Galbraith (1977, 191) observed:

> The service of the accepted image of economic life to the political needs of the business firm—the large corporation in particular—is, in fact, breathtaking. In broad concept it removes from the corporation the power to do wrong, leaves with it only the power to do right. Are prices too high? The corporation is blameless. Prices are set by the market.

Are products deficient in safety, durability, and design? Are they really needed? They only reflect the will of the sovereign consumer. ... One sees how great are the political and social advantages of this image of economic life.

Seeing global corporations as market actors operating on the basis of global market forces serves their interests by shrouding the political power they actually possess. It also potentially de-territorializes where they possess and wield it.

Re-Territorializing Global Corporations

If it is accepted that markets are increasingly global, and that the firms operating in it are market actors that are similarly global in their operations, then it would seem to follow logically that while less economically powerful states are weakened more than others, nonetheless the sovereignty of all states is undermined. The question then becomes the extent to which this happens. If states are forced to reinvent themselves in the image of the global market, and are driven by the same market imperatives that motivate global corporations as market actors, then politically states must "shrink" in terms of both their size and influence in order to accommodate rather than modify market forces (e.g., see Mann 1997). Yet although such arguments may logically follow, as discussed above it is problematic to conceptualize global corporations simply as market actors driven by market imperatives. It is similarly problematic to see states as shrinking away to irrelevance.

The data actually indicate the opposite is the case. Figure 1.1 shows government expenditure in the G7 major advanced states has grown from 37 to over 40 percent of GDP in the last fifteen years. After the GFC it seemed plausible that the future could be, or even must be, one in which "the role of the state will be larger and that of the private sector will be smaller" (Altman 2009, 2–3), and all the groupings of states shown did increase their expenditure considerably following it, particularly those in the G7. But the data also indicate that government expenditure over a longer period of time has not universally declined. Instead, it has risen markedly in Latin American and Caribbean states, to reach levels comparable to the non-G7 advanced economies which on average have maintained expenditures of between 30 to 35 percent of GDP. Government expenditure remains much lower in Sub-Saharan African states at between 20 to 25 percent of GDP. Rather than universally falling as a share of GDP, the reality is that

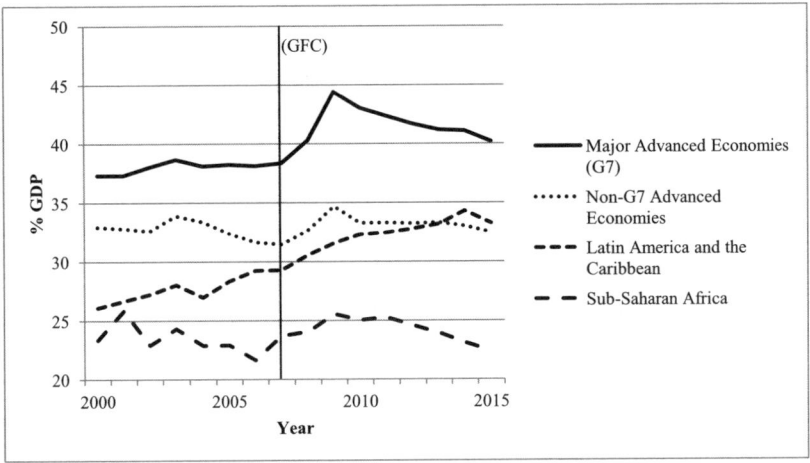

Figure 1.1: Government Expenditure
Source: IMF (2015). The data represent averages of expenditure as a percentage of GDP for the countries in each group, rather than expenditure as a percentage of GDP for all counties in this group combined.

government expenditure has been rising, steady, or fluctuating depending on states' income levels, stages of development, and policy choices in response to economic conditions.

Perhaps more surprisingly, economically powerful states have also raised corporate taxes as their economic interdependence has increased. In 1980, taxes on corporate profits accounted for 2.3 percent of GDP on average across all OECD states, increasing steadily thereafter until 2007 when they accounted for 3.7 percent. They slumped in the aftermath of the GFC but have since recovered to around 2.8 percent on average. For example, the US increased its take of corporate taxes after the GFC from 1.4 percent of GDP in 2009 to 2.2 percent by 2015 (OECD 2016a). Figure 1.2 also shows that there is considerable variation between the major OECD states in the percentage of tax revenues accounted for by tax on corporate profits. For example, there is a marked trend to falling corporate taxes as a share of total tax revenue prior to the GFC in the case of Japan, but, for the other states shown, only the impact of the GFC appears associated with a lower share of revenue from taxes on corporate profits. There is a very mixed picture both before and after, while for the OECD on average there is a trend over time to an increase in the share. In short, tax on corporate profits

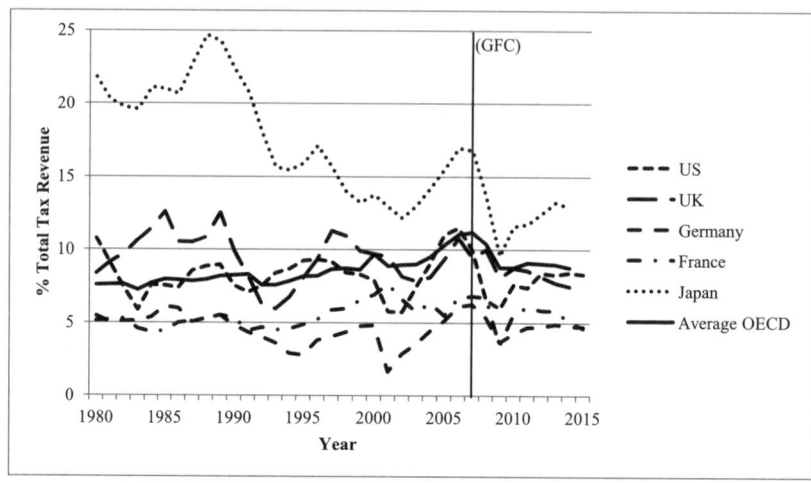

Figure 1.2: Tax on Corporate Profits
Source: OECD (2016a)

seems more a matter of national policy choices and economic conditions than global market imperatives.

Total tax as a percentage of GDP has similarly increased steadily across all OECD states on average, from around 30 percent in 1980 to 34.3 percent by 2015 (OECD 2016b), and Figure 1.3 shows that the tax burden has not shifted away from corporations. The share of corporate tax in total tax revenue increased across OECD states over the 1990s, and despite falling after the GFC is currently around 8.8 percent on average, higher than in the 1980s. Trends in the share of corporate taxes versus other sources demonstrate that personal income taxes as a share of total tax revenue have fallen, while social security contributions have increased so that the two have converged to have a similar share of the total. Other components of taxation have remained relatively stable. Therefore, the share of corporate taxes in total tax revenue also seems determined more by national policy decisions than dictated by global market imperatives. To the extent that corporate taxation as a share of total taxation rises or falls, this again seems more a reflection of underlying economic conditions, given that the only time a steep fall occurs in tax revenues is with the impact of the GFC.

These observations in respect of government expenditure and corporate taxation have been made before. For example, five years prior

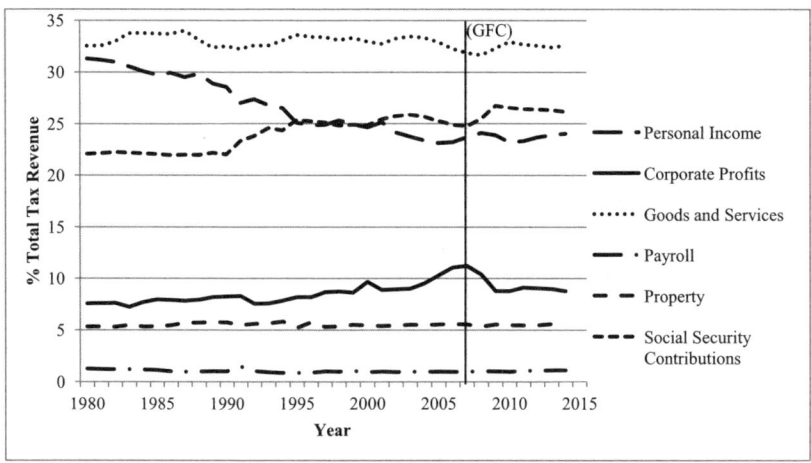

Figure 1.3: OECD Average Share of Taxes in Total Tax Revenue
Source: OECD (2016a); OECD (2016c); OECD (2016d); OECD (2016e); OECD (2016f); OECD (2016g)

to the GFC, Weiss (2003) noted that economically powerful states had increased corporate taxation over the period their economic interdependence had intensified, and that evidence was lacking they had shifted the burden of tax from capital to labor. So can we simply say that economically powerful states rather than global corporations are still in charge? This is not so straightforward. The size of governments in economically powerful states is increasing and their ability to tax corporations seems undiminished, but their *role* may have altered. Progressive Marxist scholars like Cahill (2009, 14) believe that since the GFC there has been "no sign of a broad based commitment by policy makers to dismantling the political and economic power gained for capital through neoliberalisation" (see also Crouch 2011; Cahill 2014). If this is the case, government expenditure and corporate taxation may be growing in order to serve corporate interests. In a sense, global corporations have "outsourced" aspects of their operations to governments, with the former paying the latter for the services they desire. Indeed, Wade (2010) suggests the reason why Washington Consensus policy settings have endured in the face of the worst global economic crisis since the Great Depression is that they serve the interests of powerful elites in advanced industrialized states—i.e., both corporate *and* political leaders. This dovetails with arguments by the likes of Braithwaite (2008) and Jordana and Levi-Faur (2004), who consider the way the increasing concentration evident within industrial sectors, and the growth in size and influence of the corporations comprising them, have led not to the demise of the state but to a reorientation of its role. Markets that are highly competitive and made up of many small enterprises are hard to regulate, but faced with global markets controlled by "mega-corporations" it is more efficient for states to reach agreement on rules for their operation rather than imposing arm's-length regulations on them. Contrary to "the neoliberal fairytale" (Braithwaite 2008, 4) of the demise of the state in the face of the rise of the importance of global market forces, instead there has been a reorientation of corporate–state relations.

Given industries dominated by a visible handful of global corporations, it would seem that a better question than whether states are politically diminished by the activities of global corporations is the extent to which they, versus these corporations, set the agenda. The reality is that there are large, powerful global corporations and large, powerful states, and they may be acting together rather than in opposition to one another. As Haufler (2006, 89) notes, only with Adam Smith's *Wealth of Nations* "does a separation between public and private economic affairs start to be widely discussed," but such distinctions are far from clear-cut in reality. As Dicken (1998, 467) puts it:

> Nation states, whilst essentially political institutions, have become increasingly involved in economic matters, arguably as increasingly competitive economic actors. Transnational corporations, though fundamentally economic in function, have become increasingly political in their actions and impact.

The hybrid forms of authority produced in the process mean that Milton Friedman's (1970) dictum that "the business of business is business" seems to hold in some cases and for some issues. But increasingly, it is also the case that the "business of business is government" as corporations perform public roles while powerful states maintain considerable discretion to determine how they should do so (e.g., see Haufler 2001; Porter and Ronit 2006; Büthe and Mattli 2011; Green 2013). Therefore, it can be argued that states are increasingly operating in the interests of global corporations, or equally that these corporations increasingly serve states' interests as they perform functions at their behest or on their behalf. A simple ruling one way or the other is virtually impossible. What can be said is that the relationship between states and global corporations is what matters, rather than an ideological commitment to some artificial boundary between the two.

It also suggests a need to re-territorialize our understanding of global corporate power. Perhaps the most compelling reason to do so is that corporations increasingly have interests and operate beyond national territorial boundaries, with all the problems this raises for regulating and controlling them, given that they are outside the scope of international law and are still subjects only of national laws, yet are fundamentally transnational in nature (e.g., see May 2006). Nevertheless, despite over sixty years of a supposedly global neoliberal agenda, it remains the case that economically powerful states still account for 80 percent of world output, 70 percent of international trade, and up to 90 percent of foreign direct investment (FDI) (Chang 2008, 32). More accurately, it is the corporations from these states that do so. The FT Global 500[9] are responsible for at least 80 percent of the world's stock of FDI, around 70 percent of world trade, and 30 percent of the world's GDP (Rugman 2000; see also Bryant and Bailey 1997). They are not placeless entities. Just ten states are the headquarters for 84 percent of them. The US alone accounts for 42 percent (*Financial Times* 2016). With the emergence of Brazil, Russia, India, and China (collectively known as the BRICs) as economic powers it may no longer be as true as it once was that "a statistical profile for the current corporation indicates that it is predominantly Anglo-American" (Harrod 2006, 27–28), but it remains the case that the home bases of the world's largest corporations are like a map of global economic power, hence the close correlation between the national economic and corporate data.

Declaring corporations with international operations and interests as global is therefore problematic. Measuring the extent to which they are is even more so, but one widely used measure is the United Nations Conference on Trade and Development's (UNCTAD) transnationality index (TNI). It calculates corporations' transnationality as the arithmetic mean of three ratios: foreign assets to total assets; foreign sales to total sales; and foreign employment to total employment. According to UNCTAD (2014a), the average TNI of the world's 100 most transnational corporations on the basis of their foreign assets is 60 percent.[10] But although on average they have more of their interests and operations abroad than at home, and while some corporations are indeed highly transnational, many that one might have expected to be actually are less so. For example, as the world's largest retailer, Walmart is often taken as the emblematic case of a global corporation, yet has a TNI of only 36 percent. This is not to say that its impact on global markets is irrelevant, and nor should its impact be ignored in particular states such as China where many of its products are manufactured. However, Walmart is clearly an American company. Furthermore, corporations' TNIs may overstate their globality, as the aggregated data on their assets, sales, and employment may considerably abstract from the actual geographical spread of their operations. Many that have high TNIs are more accurately regional than global in their operations and interests, and some are more accurately binational than transnational (e.g., see Rugman and Verbeke 2009).

Those adhering to the globalization thesis will surely respond that while corporations' national and regional operations remain important, their nationality matters less than it used to, and that there is an inevitable process of transnationalization under way. They contend that corporations are increasingly challenging and undermining the governments of the nations where they are headquartered, and that all states must focus on competing to attract their investment. Activists like Jeremy Brecher decry the social and environmental impacts produced as "wages and social conditions tend to fall to the level of the most desperate" in the resulting "race to the bottom" (Korten 2015, 241). In economic policy terms, the global production networks that corporations control compromise the ability of national governments to implement independent monetary policies, and lead them to curtail nationally focused industry policies in favor of fiscal incentives for global corporations (Held et al. 1999, 276–279). Yet such claims are widely contested on the basis that there is also evidence of a "race to the top" as global corporations help to spread newer technologies and higher standards as they invest abroad (Vogel 1995; see also Braithwaite and Drahos 2000; Drezner 2001). There is also evidence that economically powerful states dress themselves in neoliberal "clothing" in order to make rules in their national interests. An example of this is to be found in OECD member states negotiating free trade agreements that allow them to support their global corporations in the guise of investment in science and technology through publicly funding research and development, while depriving developing countries from protecting their infant national industries through more traditional subsidies and tariffs (e.g., see Aggarwal and Evenett 2014). In the case of the US specifically, Weiss (2014) identifies a "security network state" through which the role of the defense establishment in meeting security imperatives has underpinned its technological superiority, while Block and Keller (2009, 475; see also Block 2011) claim that "the US has created a decentralized network of publicly funded laboratories"—i.e., essentially the architecture of a hidden developmental state.

Given the lack of clarity on whether global corporations undermine or promote states' interests, nevertheless there are three responses to make in respect of arguments either way that do not so much negate as qualify them. First, the changes so far have been extremely gradual. The average TNI for the world's top 100 most transnational MNCs grew from 52 to 60 between 1993 and 2014 (Dicken 2007, UNCTAD 2014a).[11] At this rate, it will be another 30 to 40 years before their average TNI reaches 75 percent. Second, global trends mask national specificities. For example, the average TNI of the 22 US firms in the world's 100 most transnational corporations is just 50, meaning that the global corporations headquartered in the world's most economically powerful state retain half their sales, assets, and employment at home. By comparison, the sixteen corporations from the UK, which has the second-highest number of corporations in the top 100, have an average TNI of 71 (UNCTAD 2014a). Such differences suggest something American and British about the profile of these corporations as opposed to their globality. Third, while the trend toward greater transnationality has been steady, albeit gradual, it is by no means clear that it is irreversible. Indeed, the average TNI of the world's 100 most transnational corporations was actually slightly higher in 2013 than 2014 at 61 percent (UNCTAD 2013a). This may simply reflect movement in and out of the list of particular corporations with differing profiles, and it may be contended that this should not be overstated by comparison to the more general trend for corporations to construct increasingly elaborate global supply chains to benefit from the lower standards, lower wages, more flexible conditions, and general financial benefits of internationalizing their operations. However, as the opportunities for efficiencies/exploitation shrink with the development of the states in which these companies have invested, and as the cost of oil and carbon emissions ultimately must be factored into corporate strategic decision making, global strategies may become less attractive (e.g., see Anon 2011). This may at least produce a rationalization of global supply chains, even if it does not involve a wholesale consolidation of operations in corporations' home states.

There are geographical patterns to global economic power that encompass both states and their global corporations. Rather than making generalizations about corporate behavior and impacts based on notions of transnationality and global market imperatives, the reality is that where corporations are based, make their key strategic decisions, hold their assets, employ their workers, and generate their revenue are factors that remain important in the exercise of their political power.

Conclusion

To the extent that markets exist, corporations make and control them rather more than they compete in them. Therefore, they are best seen as political actors with economic motivations, and it is problematic to focus on markets as the "places" where this occurs. The risk is a disembodiment of the power they wield. As I have previously argued (Mikler 2012), a good deal of what Hay and Marsh (2000, 6) term the "globaloney" written about globalization results from focusing on concepts like "the market" rather than on actors like global corporations, and assuming the actions of the latter are synonymous with the imperatives of the former. Global corporations should be more central in debates about where political power resides in an economically globalized world. The purpose of this introductory chapter has been to establish the basis for doing so. In the chapters that follow, these themes will be further explored theoretically, empirically, and by employing illustrative examples.

Chapter 2 further develops the re-embodiment of global corporations as political actors. Like states, their power may wax and wane (e.g., corporations like Pan Am and Lehman Brothers are now but a memory), but, while ascendant, how they control their markets and their agendas vis-à-vis states is salient to the political power they wield. A framework for understanding how they wield their power instrumentally, structurally and discursively, drawing on the work of Fuchs (2007), is explained. In addition to demonstrating the links between these three "faces" of their power, links are also made to debates about conceptualizing globalization and, relatedly, the main international political economy (IPE) traditions. The purpose in so doing is to demonstrate that global corporations' political power does not just arise from them exercising leverage in light of the material wealth they possess and the economic processes they control, but from the way in which they construct themselves as legitimate self-governors. As such, the case is made for why discursive power is their goal, as it reinforces other aspects of their political power by increasing perceptions of their legitimacy. This *discursive legitimacy* potentially frees them from the shackles of externally imposed regulation and grants them the "right" to set agendas.

Chapter 3 expands on the re-territorialization of global corporations' political power. Where they are based, where their interests lie, and where they invest are analyzed to demonstrate that they are more accurately national and regional, rather than global political actors.

While they certainly act globally, and have global interests, global corporations' headquarters remain a key aspect of their identity. Contrary to expectations that a more globalized economy produces more diffusion in both the operations and nationality of global corporations, the data are shown to indicate ongoing and increasing concentration in established economically powerful states and regions, such as the US, EU, and Japan. Although the rise of the BRICs suggests this should change, as new global corporations take their place on the world economic stage, what is also shown is that the geographical patterns of power produced by the existing global corporations are being reproduced by the new global corporations from these emerging market economies. For example, while the US dominates as the headquarters for the established global corporations, China does so for the newer emerging ones. While different states are involved, the same concentrated geographical patterns of their operations and interests are evident.

Because of the national and regional concentration of global corporations shown in Chapter 3, the national institutional contexts in which corporations are embedded are the focus of Chapter 4. Drawing on the comparative capitalism literature, the extent to which there is pressure for institutional convergence or divergence in the relationship that global corporations have with their home and host states is considered. This is done by considering the established industrialized triad of the US, EU, and Japan, as well as the BRICs with a particular focus on China. Building on the literature that considers the relationship between business and government in developed and developing states, in addition to continuing variations in the institutional basis for corporate-state relations found in industrialized states, it is shown that in all cases states and their global corporations, whether established or emerging, operate *together*. To the extent that they do so differently, this helps to shape expectations of what is "natural" or "inevitable" in how global corporations wield their power.

Given the power they wield, where they wield it, and the institutional contexts in which this occurs, Chapter 5 considers how global corporations themselves attempt to translate their power into influence, and thence private authority. They do so in order to increase their material returns, but beyond this the argument is made that they do so in order to enhance perceptions that they are legitimate private governors, either freed from state regulation or as equal partners with states. To this end, there is a focus on the growth of, and controversies surrounding, corporate social responsibility (CSR) and the growth of private standards and private governance such as through the International Organization for Standardization (ISO). It is shown that, contrary to their desire to be seen as possessing the discursive legitimacy to self-govern, public perceptions of their right to do so are weak by comparison to that of governments and non-government organizations (NGOs). There is also evidence that more "traditional" concerns such as serving shareholders' interests strategically dominate their agendas.

Chapter 6 concludes the analysis and discussion in the foregoing chapters with a focus on why the existence of global corporations does not produce a dysfunctionally neoliberal world in which markets and market imperatives take precedence, but one in which political processes and governance are a function of global corporate power. Political power in a more economically interconnected world is a more complex matter than can be revealed by the relations between states, and the extent to which the balance is tipped more or less in favor of global corporations versus states and their citizens depends on the power they wield, and how they wield it. This largely turns on the extent to which they are perceived as being legitimately in charge, and whether economically powerful states and their citizens accept this to be the case. Therefore, it depends on whether they find it desirable to grant their global corporations more or less political power than they already possess as a result of their size, market control, and economic influence. It also suggests a refocusing and greater emphasis, both theoretically and empirically, on the political power global corporations possess in world affairs.

2 THEORIZING GLOBAL CORPORATIONS' POWER

Much of the disembodied debate around global corporate political power alluded to in Chapter 1 reflects the way the main IPE traditions stress the role of the state versus the market, in the process casting corporations as market actors. The intention of this chapter is to address the relative theoretical absence of global corporations in IPE, by comparison to states and a rather abstract focus on global markets, and in the process to integrate the major IPE traditions with how globalization is conceptualized from a corporate perspective. This is done as the starting point for understanding, and also integrating, theories of the multi-faceted nature of the power global corporations wield.

In the first section, global corporations are located in the three main IPE theoretical traditions: nationalist, liberal, and Marxist. Assuming readers are broadly familiar with these, the import of the traditions for global corporations is discussed, before relating them to how globalization is conceptualized. With reference to the constructivist challenge to the main IPE traditions, the point is then made that the political power global corporations wield should be seen in terms of whether they are perceived as legitimately in charge. This is because, depending on the degree to which a particular IPE tradition ideationally dominates the others, it frames the manner in which globalization is conceptualized, and by implication the political power global corporations are seen as entitled to wield. This has bearing on the extent of ideational, and indeed ideological, support for global corporations' interests and agendas.

The discursive power that gives rise to, and in turn reflects, political legitimacy is usually seen as the third of three faces of political power. In the second section, the three faces of the power global corporations possess are related to the IPE theories and globalization debates outlined in the first section. In so doing, it is demonstrated that global corporations possess and use the instrumental and structural forms of their power, with these enhanced if they are perceived to possess legitimacy as the result of their discursive power. This involves them purposively seeking to create their interests in other actors, particularly states, and for their interests to be accepted as desirable by society more broadly. If the discursive aspects of global corporate power are tied up with the ideational aspects underpinning conceptualizing globalization, then potentially the global economy may be made in the image of their interests. This is because ultimately their discursive power allows them to shape and institutionalize norms that support their interests. As such, global corporations are not neutral players in the construction of their legitimacy.

The extent to which global corporations are truly "in charge" is a complex question, but the conclusion reached is that the answer to it turns on the extent to which they are perceived to possess the necessary discursive legitimacy to be so. They pursue this goal as they wield their political power relationally with states and the international organizations to which states belong. That is to say, their power is national, and perhaps regional (e.g., in the case of the EU), before it is global because it must be normatively and institutionally embedded in key territories if it is to be produced, and reproduced beyond them. But if global corporations are to construct their political legitimacy to the extent that they rival governments not just as a result of their lobbying efforts, relations with policy makers, and economic dominance, it is through their ability to discursively leverage their instrumental and structural power to create and sustain institutions conducive to serving their interests.

Locating Global Corporations in IPE and Globalization Debates

As Watson (2008) notes, the main theoretical IPE traditions are seen as existing in a trichotomy of nationalist, liberal, and Marxist approaches. Nationalism may be taken to include neo-mercantilism and economic nationalism, both of which inform the developmental state literature. Liberalism includes classical liberalism as espoused by the likes of Adam Smith and the classical economists, embedded liberalism in national and international regulatory regimes, and neoliberalism as a new form of liberal ideology, or a radical extension of it, since the 1980s. For Marxism, neo-Marxist traditions such as World Systems Theory, Gramscianism, and critical theory may be included. These traditions have bearing on the conceptualization of globalization. The extent to which one theoretical tradition or another, and likewise a particular conceptualization of globalization, is believed to be more or less accurate is also related to ideologies and beliefs that give rise to norms that become widely accepted to the point they are institutionalized. The IPE traditions, the conceptualizations of globalization that are related to them, and the ideational basis for these have implications for where, and how, the political power of global corporations is theoretically located and conceived.

IPE Traditions

Nationalist accounts in IPE see the state as the key unit of analysis interested in economic wealth for the relationship it has with power and sovereignty (e.g., see Viner 1948). Therefore it is natural, and essential, that the state should be in charge of guiding and promoting economic development. This is exemplified by the developmental state literature that sought to explain the rapid economic rise of East Asian states after World War II as a function of state strategic guidance and economic coordination rather than free markets (e.g., see Johnson 1995; Evans 1995; Weiss and Hobson 1995; Weiss 1998; Woo-Cumings 1999). There is also a literature that considers the manner in which some states continue to coordinate economic activity once developed, rather than leaving this to the invisible hand of market competition, with this exemplified by Continental European and East Asian states' varieties of capitalism (e.g., see Schmidt 2002; Streeck and Yamamura 2001, 2003; Walter and Zhang 2012a). More on this is discussed in Chapter 4, but for now the point is that in general states are seen as having an interest in strategically intervening in and directing their economies in the national interest. Beyond their borders, an economically interconnected world provides opportunities for powerful states to dominate and control the terms of trade faced by weaker developing states. The former protect their industries and entrench their economic and political power over, and in relation to, the latter by making sure that the global economy serves their twin power and wealth aims. Therefore, powerful states are those with the capacity to control and direct their corporations to ensure they serve the national interest. Weaker ones must develop the institutional capacity to do likewise. If this is not as feasible in the case of global as opposed to national corporations, it follows that even the national interest of economically powerful states is undermined as they can no longer control them as readily. Weaker developing states likewise have their policy autonomy undermined not so much by more powerful states as by the global corporations that have slipped these states' territorial boundaries.

Liberal accounts start with an attack on the state in order to refocus analysis on markets and market actors which rationally and efficiently maximize profits. Neoliberal accounts see this as inevitable in addition to desirable, given that global market forces cannot, as well as should not, be denied. As noted in Chapter 1, there is a particularly acute political zeal in the neoliberal endeavor to attack the power of the state to relocate it in markets, with this attack particularly evident as the Cold War drew to an end with triumphal pronouncements of a homogeneously capitalist world. As Harvey (2005, 11) explains, where liberalism was once "embedded" in the sense that "entrepreneurial and corporate activities were surrounded by a web of social and political constraints … the neoliberal project is to disembed capital from these constraints." Jones (2014) refers to the agents of this political project in its early years as "the outriders": think tanks and influential elites who helped to shape the neoliberal agenda prior to its mainstream political embrace in the 1980s. Whether states are involved in creating and underpinning a liberal world such as through embedding liberalism in international agreements and organizations (e.g., the Bretton Woods institutions), or getting out of the way to accede to the imperatives of a neoliberal one, it is evident why an obsession with globally free markets has come to dominate debates in IPE. It is similarly evident why a belief that global corporations as market actors should be free to act in their self-interests flows from such a perspective, and why, as noted in Chapter 1, it suits global corporations that this view is as widely propounded and accepted as possible.

Where liberals see economic opportunities maximized by the efficiencies of free markets, Marxists see maximized exploitation and alienation. Their focus on class relations defined by the capitalist mode of production leads them to see the capitalist class, or *bourgeoisie*, who control the means of production subordinating those who do not in an endless search for greater profitability.[1] The state is co-opted to do the bidding of the capitalist class, resulting in the institutionalization of regulations and policies that serve their interests at the expense of the public good and democratic processes. This happens at all levels: locally, nationally, and globally. As Marx and Engels (1967 [1848], 83–84) put it in their *Communist Manifesto*:

> The bourgeoisie has through its exploitation of the world market given a cosmopolitan character to production and consumption. ... All old-established national industries have been destroyed or are daily being destroyed. They are dislodged by new industries, whose introduction becomes a life and death question for all civilized nations, by industries that no longer work up indigenous raw material, but raw material drawn from the remotest zones; industries whose products are consumed, not only at home, but in every quarter of the globe.

The global corporate takeover they predicted produces not the enrichment of all. Instead, "accumulation of wealth at one pole is, therefore, at the same time accumulation of misery, agony of toil, slavery, ignorance, brutality, mental degradation, at the opposite pole" (Marx 2007 [1867], 709). This is how the world comes to resemble the dystopian futures imagined by science fiction authors mentioned in Chapter 1: a world of increasing inequality, underpinned by governments that are either powerless or acting in the interests of a "transnational capitalist class" (Sklair 2001). It produces the global class relations neo-Marxists identify: a world characterized by wealthy "core" states versus poor periphery states and regions, increasingly unequal as a whole as well as in its parts, and, without intervention, prone to crisis and ultimately doomed to violent collapse (e.g., see Wallerstein 1984, 2004; Piketty 2013).

An overdelineation of the boundaries between the traditions does not necessarily help capture the reality of international economic relations, though. For example, Eric Helleiner points out that states may pursue liberal policies for nationalist reasons. He calls this "liberal economic nationalism" (Helleiner 2002, 320). By this he means that while a set of measures such as subsidies and tariffs to protect domestic industry may be taken as examples of nationalist economic policy, so too liberal policies may serve the national interest of strong states whose corporations are in a position to outcompete others in global markets and therefore no longer need protectionist measures (see also Chang 2002). In other words, states may follow a liberal agenda out of nationalist intent when economically ascendant, while being less inclined to do so when economically challenged. Nevertheless, the boundaries are heuristically useful, including for the global corporate power implications they suggest in that corporations may be framed as serving the interests of powerful states (nationalism), replacing states (liberalism), or serving elites occupying the transnational capitalist class (Marxism).

Waves of Conceptualizing Globalization

These different frames are also related to how globalization is conceptualized, which Martell (2007) identifies as having occurred in three "waves": the initial pronouncements of the globalists who predicted the demise of states, the rejection of their analysis by the skeptics who asserted that states remained in charge, and a more pragmatic middle ground occupied by the transformationalists who study the altered role of the state in a more economically interconnected world. The political implications of these conceptual waves are shown in Table 2.1, along with how they may be related to the IPE traditions and the implications for global corporations. Given that the waves of theorizing globalization are historically sequential, with only the most extreme commentaries now embracing a purely globalist or skeptical account, most mainstream analysis is in the transformationalist vein. This is why the shaded cell in Table 2.1 is emphasized.

Transformationalist accounts stress neither the continued centrality of states nor their demise, but their political transformation. This view recognizes that globalization is a dynamic concept, so that it is more a set of processes than an outcome: it is a process of "ization" rather than an "ism." As such, the globalist and skeptical accounts are theoretically possible, and may be realized in reality. And each of the IPE traditions views and explains them in different ways, so that it is not just a matter of which of them is "correct" so much as it is a matter of which unit of analysis is central: the state (nationalism), the market (liberalism), or class (Marxism). As no theoretical interpretation is necessarily right, so no particular outcome is necessarily inevitable. What transpires depends on the interactions states have with each other as well as with non-state actors, and these interactions may produce outcomes that both enable and constrain them in different ways and across different dimensions. Crucially, states' political agency often depends on them cooperating with each other in order to retain and enhance it in a globalized world, as well as with non-state actors such as global corporations that are themselves both agents of, and subject to, the political transformations under way.

This is the central point made by authors such as Held et al. (1999), Dicken (2007), Scholte (2005), and contributors to collections such as Hay and Marsh (2000) and Held and McGrew (2002 and 2003), which

Table 2.1: IPE Theories and the Three Waves of Conceptualizing Globalization

	Globalists	Skeptics	Transformationalists
Politically	If global governance is not possible, neoliberalism is inevitable. All states have their sovereignty attacked, and the difference is only a matter of degree.	Nation states remain central, as do regional blocs. International power relations remain important (i.e., relations between states) and give rise to inequality, but states retain political agency.	Politics is globally transformed. Nation states remain important but are reconstructed in how they act in an economically interconnected world. A key aspect of this is their need to share sovereignty in order to retain and enhance it.
Theoretically	Nationalists: States lose the capacity for economic policy autonomy. The result is the demise of neo-mercantilism, economic nationalism, the developmental state, and state-guided forms of capitalism in general.	Nationalists: Powerful states remain in charge, and states remain the unit of analysis for understanding global economic relations. Liberals: The promise of neoliberal globalization needs to be pursued for the benefits that will inevitably flow. States should shift power to the market as a policy choice.	Nationalists: States share sovereignty with corporations and other non-state actors in the national interest. Liberals: Neoliberal globalization is imperfect, but the extent to which it exists depends on the role states can play in facilitating it.

Continued

Table 2.1: *Continued*

	Globalists	Skeptics	Transformationalists
	Liberals and Marxists: Markets are in charge and market relations determine outcomes in an economically interconnected world. For Marxists, the class relations underpinning capitalist relations of production that drive global markets determine outcomes.	Marxists: Socialist states, and states that present alternatives to the neoliberal globalization orthodoxy, are possible and must be promoted.	Marxists: Capitalism is global, but states have the opportunity to choose whether or not to embrace it, and to what degree. They should choose to reject it for other forms of economic governance.
Corporately	Corporations are in charge, and states must accede to their demands.	States are in charge, and corporations attempt to influence them. This may or may not serve the national interest.	States and corporations are "entangled," sharing sovereignty and authority with one another, to potentially mutually serve each other's interests.

Source: The "politically" row is based on Martell (2007, 177), but otherwise the table is original.

are emblematic of the transformationalist literature that rejected the epochal change prophesized by the globalists at the end of the Cold War, as well as skeptical claims that little had changed. Theirs is also an institutional and relational conception of globalization through which political agency is continually reconstructed as a result of the interactions between state and non-state actors at all levels: locally, nationally, regionally, and globally. At their core, I would contend they are drawing on Mann's conception of infrastructural power: "the institutional capacity of a central state ... to penetrate its territories and logistically implement decisions" (Mann 1993, 59). A state's territories could be narrowly conceived as those defined by its borders, but with globalization he finds that "the transnational and the national have surged together" (Mann 2000, 41). In other words, the conception of the national interest must now encompass global spaces. This leads Weiss (2006, 173) to make the point that, rather than questions of which actors are in control, as is stressed by liberals and Marxists and animates much of the debate between globalists and skeptics, in reality "global and national networks of interaction are not competing for space, but are intertwined."

Thinking in terms of networks helps in comprehending that it is not that disembodied market "forces" have taken over, that states are "dead" and so on, but that in a more economically interdependent world there are more actors involved, and that there is the need for an actor-centered analysis in understanding the intertwining of national and global networks. This includes analyzing the power dynamics inherent in the mutual *entanglement* of global corporations with states. I have previously argued (Mikler 2011, 2012) that this somewhat abstruse term is useful, as it does not imply one actor or the other is in charge, nor that they necessarily serve each other's interests, although depending on the issue this may be the case, and depending on one's perspective it may be desirable.[2] For example, for Weiss (2006, 2010) successful states are those with the capacity to engage in "governed interdependence" via, among other relations, state-business alliances that operate on the basis of "reciprocal consent"—i.e., for the two to be mutually intertwined on the basis that they serve each other's interests, but with the state strategically in the governing lead. One does not necessarily have to accept that this must be the case, as it could equally be contended that corporations, rather than states, must strategically be in the lead, or that the class relations underpinning capitalist relations of production make this inevitable—i.e., a more liberal or Marxist rather than a nationalist rendering of the relationship. As per the pluralist approach to understanding the exercise of power in liberal democracies, on which there is also a considerable literature, it could simply be contended that a range of interests and demands is articulated by various actors, including corporations, and that governments weigh and balance these in order to negotiate compromises in the public policy process (e.g., see McFarland 2004; Lang et al. 2008). Whatever the case, it means that the starting point for understanding political power relations needs to be an analysis of shared sovereignty (on the part of states) and private authority (on the part of corporations, global or otherwise), and the national and global institutional contexts in which this happens.

Furthermore, it should be acknowledged that corporations are the legal creations of states. Their very existence as actors separate from states arises because states give them license to be so. Limited-liability publicly listed corporations, with shares traded freely on a stock exchange, which comprise the vast majority of global corporations, were created in the nineteenth century as "a power center that was within society yet independent of the national state" (Drucker 2011, 170; see also the contributions in Parkinson et al. 2000). This is another reason why the view that they are market rather than political actors has become so widely accepted: because states legally created them in this image. It is not the intention of this book to delve into the legal construction, requirements, and privileges of corporations, but simply to make the point here that they require the legal support of states to exist in their current forms, and to be free to pursue their interests. Therefore, rather than state sovereignty and corporate private authority being shared, it is more accurate to say that it is the political power that arises from both, that is, with the latter originally dependent on the exercise of the former. As states and corporations share their power, they transform the nature of their sovereignty and private authority.

This has some interesting implications. Although there is a theme in much of the globalization literature that stresses the inevitability of the neoliberal state, with this involving a ceding of state sovereignty to non-state market actors through a process of deregulation and privatization, it is little acknowledged that the corollary of this is a "publicization" of corporations as they assume the mantle of responsibility for performing functions that were once seen as the preserve of states. In other words, their private authority potentially becomes more public, rather than remaining as purely private as it once was. This is the focus of Chapter 5, but for now the point is that global corporations may act on behalf of "their" states not just nationally, but globally, and therefore states may utilize the territorial reach of global corporations to serve their national interests and enhance their sovereignty. The interests of one, or the other, or both, may be served in the process. Whatever the outcome, the state remains as a locus of political power, but does so in relation to its global corporations.

The Power of Ideas

There are also normative implications as to what the outcome *should* be. Depending on one's viewpoint, global corporations must either be controlled and guided to serve the national interest (nationalism), or freed to promote growth and opportunity for all (liberalism), or curtailed/eliminated to emancipate the oppressed (Marxism). As Gilpin (1987, 25) notes, the main IPE theoretical approaches are therefore more accurately "three ideologies." This is why the constructivist challenge to them stresses the power of ideas in creating as well as reflecting structures of power. The clearest explanation is given by Finnemore and Sikkink (2001, 393), who see constructivists as having a "focus on the role of ideas, norms, knowledge, culture and argument in politics, stressing in particular the role of collectively held or 'intersubjective' ideas and understandings of social life." As such, "(a) human interaction is shaped primarily by ideational factors, not simply material ones; (b) the most important ideational factors are widely shared or 'intersubjective' beliefs, which are not reducible to individuals; and (c) these shared beliefs construct the interests and identities of purposive actors" (see also Adler 1997; Price and Reus-Smit 1998; Ruggie 1998; Wendt 1999; Amin and Palan 2001; Hay 2006). Therefore, the extent to which either a nationalist, liberal, or Marxist perspective is regarded as self-evident depends on both the interests *and* the ideological standpoint of the observer. The same may be said for the waves of conceptualizing globalization. This is not to say that there is not an empirically observable reality in support of the perspectives, but that widely held intersubjective beliefs are the "filters" through which this evidence is explained and assessed.

The "norm lifecycle" in Figure 2.1 demonstrates the manner in which such beliefs are brought to bear in global power relations. In stage 1, norm entrepreneurs advocate a new approach that embraces a new way of seeing a particular issue. By raising the profile of a new norm, a tipping point is reached, after which it is taken up in stage 2 by states, international organizations, and other actors who intervene to promote and construct rules flowing from its implementation. This leads to the new norm "cascading" through other states and international organizations. Finally, by stage 3 norms are so habitualized that they become part of how actors in professions, the bureaucracy,

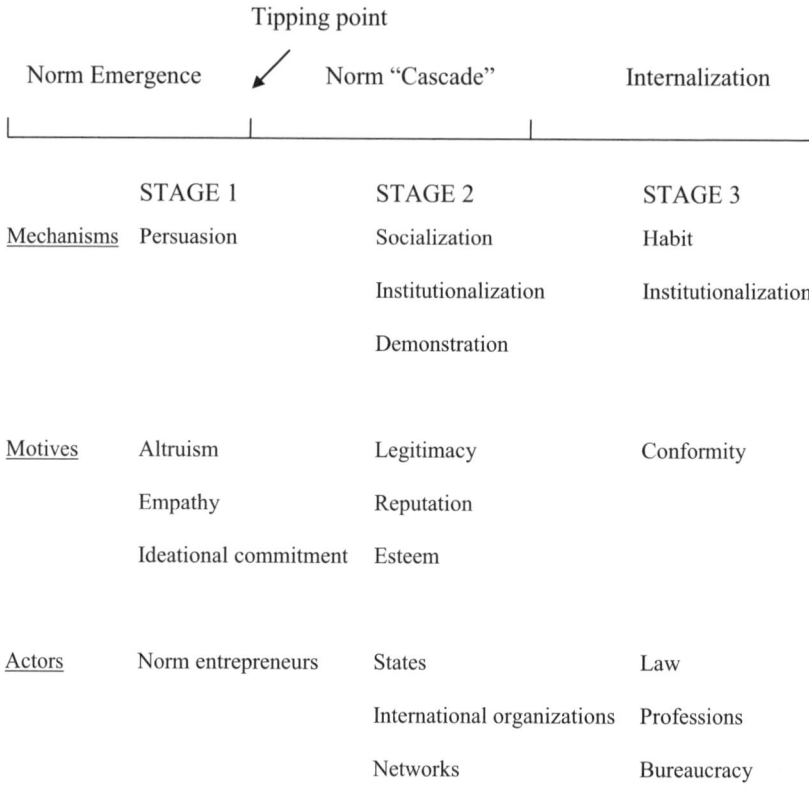

Figure 2.1: The Norm Lifecycle
Source: Based on Finnemore and Sikkink (1998, 896–898)

and the public at large behave, almost without them knowing that they are there. To put it technically, they become institutionalized. If one accepts this perspective, then the nature of globalization and the form it takes are produced by an "ideas game." As Bell (2013, 115) puts it:

> Ideas can have real effects and the impacts of globalization become almost a self-fulfilling reflex. If policy makers believe a "golden straightjacket" exists, then, in effect, it exists.

Likewise, if global corporations are able to persuade states and their societies that they possess not just the ability but also the right to exercise their power, then we may as well say they do indeed have the right to do so. In this sense, ideas about them both reflect and shape the political power they possess. Whether and how this happens means we need to understand the way global corporations purposively wield and enhance their power.

Three Faces of Power

A "three faces of power" framework as suggested by Fuchs (2007; see also Fuchs and Lederer 2007; Levy and Egan 1998) is useful for unpacking the complexity of the political power global corporations possess, and how they are relationally entangled with states in wielding it. Conceiving political power in these terms is not new, though relatively speaking her application of the framework to global corporations is. For analytical purposes their political power may be seen as instrumental, structural, and discursive. In this section, her framework is reprised, with examples in respect of each of the faces of power provided, in order ultimately to draw links with the main IPE traditions and waves of conceptualizing globalization discussed above.

Instrumental Power

Instrumental power focuses on the direct influence of one actor on/over another in order to achieve a desire outcome. As per Dahl's (1957, 201) definition, this means, "A has power over B to the extent that he can get B to do something that B would not otherwise do." This is about leverage exercised to achieve a desired end (i.e., it is instrumentally motivated) between purposive actors (i.e., it is exercised relationally). It is related to the concept of hard power in traditional realist conceptions of international relations, which sees an anarchical world where coercion creates either a balance or imbalance between states to produce stability or conflict. States clashing on battlefields in order to increase their territory, or invasions for the purpose of increasing command over lands, peoples, and resources, dominate thinking here. But more contemporary arguments downplay the colonialism and militarism that previously characterized international relations by arguing that because of globalization we live in a more pacified world where states no longer act so aggressively. Instead of nationalist sentiment predominating, they now pursue liberal goals of free trade and borders open to FDI, with global corporations a key vehicle in driving expanded global markets and therefore the economic benefits of all. The result is that we live in a world in which "the original backbone of the nation state is turning to jelly" (Mann 1997, 492), hence the positive liberal account of the globalists in which power has been ceded by states to global market forces.

However, if we reanimate such debates to focus on the actors, then we see that the field on which instrumental power relations are played has shifted from interstate to include state-corporate relations. For global corporations, we see it most in their efforts to directly lobby and influence states. For example, along with the UK the US is one of two global financial hubs, and the financial sector regulatory reforms the US enacted in the aftermath of the GFC gave rise to extensive lobbying by major banks. In particular, the Dodd-Frank Wall Street Reform and Consumer Protection Act, passed in 2010, incorporating a series of regulations designed to prevent a recurrence of factors that produced the crisis,[3] resulted in expenditure of at least US$100 million each year by the US financial industry since its introduction aimed at limiting is impact (Weisman and Lipton 2015). In the year after it was introduced lobbying was so intense this amount was spent in the first half of the year alone (Protess 2011). This includes expenditure by industry associations like the American Bankers Association, Financial Services Roundtable, and Securities Industry and Financial Markets Association, which collectively spent US$126 million from 2010 to 2015 (OpenSecrets.org 2015a,b,c).[4] Individual corporations also lobbied heavily on their own behalf, such as J. P. Morgan Chase, which spent US$37.5 million over the same period (OpenSecrets.org 2015d). Their lobbying intensifies during elections. Over the 2013–2014 US election cycle, Wall Street banks and financial institutions are estimated to have spent more than US$1.4 billion, the equivalent of US$1.9 million per day, making them America's largest source of campaign contributions and second-largest spender on lobbying (Americans for Financial Reform 2015).

Large sums of money are spent on achieving outcomes for the corporate sector in other states too. For example, the UK's Chartered Institute of Public Relations estimates that the public relations industry is worth around £6.5 billion, of which approximately 30 percent is focused on private sector lobbying to influence "public affairs." The motivations for this are described by Parvin (2007, 10) in the following terms:

> If lobbying, in its widest sense, did not produce commercial results and consequently improve profits, then it is reasonable to assume that it would not be carried out at all. Businesses make their investment in the expectation that they will see a worthwhile return and it is this

interaction between the political process and profit that fuels scepticism about the role and influence of lobbying.

In other words, the instrumental motivation behind the relations fostered by lobbying and public relations is the achievement of enhanced material outcomes.

The expenditure of such large sums of money may simply be the "tip" of the lobbying "iceberg," though. Real instrumental power comes not so much from the expenditure of funds as having access to, and influence over, those in power. Although access and influence may be bought, it is the relations rather than the financial resources deployed that matter most. Corporate representatives with the right connections are in the most powerful position to secure the outcomes they desire, and their access and influence are not as transparently evident. Nevertheless, it may be inferred. For example, Wilks-Heeg et al. (2012) find that forty-six of the top fifty publicly listed corporations in the UK have a member of parliament as either a director or shareholder. This leads Jones (2014, 71) to conclude that "British business and political elites are not distinct entities: they are deeply intertwined." They are mutually entangled to such an extent that Moran (2008, 74) sees the directors of British corporations as "incorporated into the policymaking elite."

The corporate-state connections evident in the UK may be found in all states to one degree or another (e.g., see Coen 2009). They often come to light when contentious public policy issues arise. For example, an investigation by Davies (2015) found that the major industry associations and corporations in Australia promoting the expansion of coal seam gas exploration, the subject of heated debate due to its potential environmental impacts, extensively employ former members of parliament and political staff from all the major parties, "many of whom had a role in the regulation of the industry before jumping the fence to industry." Also "a few … have come back the other way, moving from senior jobs in the major gas companies to senior advising roles in ministers' offices." The connections are so extensive there is effectively a "revolving door between politics and the mining sector," and they probably reflect deeper corporate-state relations that have previously been suggested. Notable among these are allegations that the fossil fuel industry, including corporations in the mining sector, have such extensive access to government that their officeholders wrote Cabinet Submissions with the aim of reducing efforts to address climate change. Those involved called themselves "the greenhouse mafia" (Pearse 2007; Hamilton 2007).

Corporate–state relations are so globally widespread that the "revolving door" analogy for government–business relations has been widely used (Levy and Egan 1998, 342; see also Newell 2000; Newell and Levy 2006; Falkner 2008; Sell 2009; Tienhaara 2014). Examples such as the role played by the Australian greenhouse mafia reflect the powerful position large corporations are in for "providing governments with expert advice, technical reports and position papers, and assisting decision makers directly with policy formulation and the writing of legal texts" (Vormedal 2008, 43). Less euphemistically, they are in a position to capture states' regulatory agencies (e.g., Weidenbaum 2004; Carpenter and Moss 2014). They can then influence international negotiations and international agreements on issues like climate change, so that influencing national regulatory agendas should be seen as part of their broader strategy to serve their global interests. Likewise, the banks lobbying US law makers are obviously not simply US-focused in their interests, nor in their operations. They know that what happens on Wall Street affects their global interests and, as the GFC demonstrated, the global economy. Similarly, the British corporate elites entangled with policy makers are not solely focused on British markets for their financial returns. The purpose of their lobbying is to co-opt their government to act in their interests, both nationally and abroad. A good example of this in practice was David Cameron arguing in 2011 as UK Prime Minister at a summit in Brussels against the EU's proposal for a financial transactions tax along with a raft of other new regional financial regulations. At the time, this was seen as Cameron effectively acting as a lobbyist for the British financial sector, in the sense that his representations were a "bid to safeguard the City" despite polls indicating British support for the regulations in the context of post-GFC fiscal austerity measures (Curtis 2011).

Because there is an international dimension to most major corporations' interests and operations, there are therefore international implications for state–corporate relations. However, there is growing acceptance that due to global economic interconnectedness corporations are increasingly active in representing and lobbying for their interests across and between states. In this regard, Mattli and Woods (2009, 9) suggest that "the view that most regulatory issues start out as domestic problems before globalization makes them international issues underplays the fact that a good deal of transnational regulation is motivated by uniquely transnational problems; and that transnational institutional structures may offer privileged access to some actors, biasing global regulatory outcomes in ways difficult to comprehend from a purely domestic perspective." This is evident in the case of the EU, described as a "microcosm of globalization" (Weber 2001, 4) for the supranational institutions that characterize its governance and the interconnectedness of its member states. Fuchs (2007, 85) dubs it "the world's largest playground for interest groups," and in this regard authors like Coen (2009) and Ronit and Schneider (1997) find that the overwhelming majority of EU lobbying is corporate, by comparison to that focused on social, labor, and environmental issues.

At the global level, one of the most cited examples of corporate lobbying is in relation to the WTO's agreement on Trade Related Aspects of Intellectual Property Rights (TRIPs). Approximately a dozen US global corporations formed the Intellectual Property Committee (IPC) with the purpose of "globalizing enforceable intellectual property standards" (Braithwaite and Drahos 2000, 71) by presenting a powerful united front in lobbying governments involved in the international negotiations.[5] Corporate executives from these firms also directly engaged their European and Japanese counterparts to press for a TRIPs agreement with their governments (Sell 1999). Through coordinated representation of their interests it is claimed they effectively "made public law for the world" (Sell 2003, 96) that enhanced their intellectual property rights globally, thereby safeguarding their investments and operations across multiple jurisdictions. In the process, they increased their revenues by raising the price of patentable knowledge. At the time the agreement was signed, its full implementation was estimated to have increased patent payments to US-based global corporations alone by US$19 billion a year (Wade 2003, 624; citing World Bank 2002). Therefore, states signed the TRIPs agreement, but in so doing were acting on behalf of global corporations which reaped the rewards.

There are many other examples of corporate lobbying around international negotiations, particularly in respect of the environment. The key role played by the major chemical manufacturers in international negotiations to ban the use of ozone-depleting gases such as chlorofluorocarbons (CFCs) is often cited.[6] The corporations that controlled the global market for CFCs were initially against international efforts to do so, but in 1986 the US-based chemical manufacturer DuPont strongly backed global restrictions when commercially viable alternative gases became available. This enabled the US government to reverse its opposition to an international agreement to phase out CFCs. It is widely accepted that the backing of such global corporations was central to the signing and success of the resulting Montreal Protocol, still one of the largest international environmental agreements (e.g., O'Neill 2009; Hale et al. 2013). In a similar manner to the WTO TRIPs agreement, Tienhaara et al. (2012, 51) find that DuPont and other major chemical companies "came to shape regime evolution and helped to speed up the phase-out of ozone-depleting substances." Conversely, the Global Climate Coalition, which operated from 1990 to 2002, successfully lobbied to stave off international agreements for reducing greenhouse gas emissions. Among other things, it funded studies that suggested the science was inconclusive, or the economic costs prohibitive (e.g., Beder 2002; Levy and Rothenberg 2002; Ihlen 2009). Like the Australian greenhouse mafia, its membership comprised the world's major producers and users of fossil fuels, including automobile manufacturers, the mining industry, and oil and gas companies. But increasingly, rather than lobbying to oppose international environmental agreements, global corporations seek to shape them. For example, the World Business Council for Sustainable Development (WBCSD) and the International Chamber of Commerce (ICC) are regularly represented at international environmental negotiations (see Orsini 2011; Bauer et al. 2012).

Examples abound of the way corporations lobby governments both nationally and internationally in support of their interests. From them, a key observation may be made in respect of their instrumental power. This is that there is a fundamentally territorial aspect to it. As global as their interests and/or operations may be, if their power is expressed instrumentally then it must be expressed *somewhere*. This is also the case for international organizations and intergovernmental groups as these remain comprised of states and operate on the basis of negotiations and agreements between them. Likewise, the fora where the negotiations are held must be the focus of their lobbying and representations. Such territoriality is potentially less the case for the expression of global corporations' structural power.

Structural Power

Structural power emphasizes the manner in which issues are organized "in" and "out" of politics via political actors' agenda-setting capacity. As Bachrach and Baratz (1962; see also Strange 1988) put it, "A devotes his energies to creating or reinforcing social and political values and institutional practices that limit the scope of the political process to public consideration of only those issues which are comparatively innocuous to A." To do this requires underlying control of processes and resources. Global corporations certainly possess such control through their size and market dominance. Just 10 percent of the world's public companies generate 80 percent of all profits, and the largest of them—firms with more than US$1 billion in annual revenue—account for 60 percent of global revenues and 65 percent of global market capitalization (Dobbs et al. 2015). It is not unusual for the top four firms to account for around 40 percent of all revenue in major industrial sectors (Anon 2016a), given that, as noted in Chapter 1, they tend to control the markets for their products and services more than they compete in them. They are therefore in a strong position to punish or reward states for the provision of favorable investment conditions. More than just possessing a command over resources to lobby policy makers, or having close relations with them, their global economic dominance puts them in a "privileged position" by comparison to other non-state actors like non-government organizations (NGOs) to get what they want before they need to ask for it (Tienhaara 2014, 166; see also Lindblom 1977; Frank 1978; Cox 1987).

Their size and market dominance means they are often household names synonymous with the products they produce worldwide. For example, it makes less sense to conceptualize a global market for smartphones than it does to consider the major corporations that make them, such as Apple and Samsung. Together, these two companies have accounted for 40 to 50 percent of global smartphone sales for the last four years. The operating systems and platforms that support them—iOS versus Android operating systems, and App Store versus Google Play for the applications that run on them—mean that the decisions they make in respect of their core businesses have flow-on effects to other industries and industry sectors. Although there are corporations that make smartphones which compete with Apple and Samsung, 81 percent of the 1.3 billion smartphones sold worldwide in 2014 used the Android operating system and therefore ran applications bought from Google Play (IDC 2015; Statista 2015). The result is something of an illusion of choice for consumers with two types of phones on offer from global corporations that dictate the environment and terms on which content to support them is offered by others.

Another example is the automotive industry. Its major firms are best conceived as vast conglomerates rather than entrepreneurial enterprises. The top ten automotive manufacturers in 2014 accounted for 71 percent of global motor vehicle production. The top three alone—Toyota, Volkswagen, and General Motors—accounted for 33 percent (OICA 2014). This handful of global corporations controls an industry that accounts for 4 to 8 percent of GDP and 2 to 4 percent of the labor force in OECD countries. The industry's importance is then further magnified in particular states and regions. In the US, car manufacturing employs 14 million people either directly or indirectly in component suppliers and related industries, contributes 6 percent to private sector GDP and as much as 20 percent in some regions. In the EU, the car industry accounts for 9 percent of manufacturing value added and directly or indirectly employs over 12 million people. In Japan, 7.1 million people are employed by the industry directly or indirectly, and it accounts for 11 percent of total manufacturing output (UNEP and ACEA 2002; UNEP 2002). Given its importance to the world's most economically powerful states and regions, it is not surprising that a variety of industry support and state bailout programs was put in place for the industry following the GFC. For example, in the US, public funding of US$51 billion was provided to General Motors to prevent its collapse, which would have seen the loss of 1.2–2.6 million jobs and US$35–105 billion in tax revenues (Healey 2013; McAlinden and Menk 2013). Instrumental power may have been a factor in these measures, but it is also the case that in structural terms General Motors was too big to be allowed to fail.

The structural power possessed by global corporations is therefore particularly evident in times of crisis. Like the American car industry, the bailout of the UK's banks and the US financial industry's toxic assets, along with the financial guarantees and the various fiscal and monetary stimulus measures put in place by various states, constitute the contemporary emblematic example of the support given to a highly concentrated industry sector dominated by enormous global corporations on the verge of collapse. In a study of the financial sector rescue programs of Australia, Canada, France, Germany, Italy, Japan, the Netherlands, Spain, Switzerland, the UK, and the US, the Bank of International Settlements finds that "governments became crucial during the crisis, as traditional sources of funding for financial institutions dried up" (Panetta et al. 2009, 1). The estimated combined expenditures of these eleven states on various packages totaled €5 trillion (US$7 trillion). If other states are included and the timeline extended to include not just the immediate impact of the GFC but ongoing problems such as the Eurozone crisis thereafter, much more than this has been spent on the various fiscal and monetary policy measures taken. But at the time, this represented 19 percent of these states' combined GDP. For those states most severely affected, the outlays were much larger, such as the UK's, which represented 44 percent of its GDP (Panetta et al. 2009; see also Langley 2015). At the core of the measures to shore up the global financial system was the need to protect the interests of a handful of banks. On average, 70 percent of the banking market in OECD countries is accounted for by their largest three banks (OECD 2014a; see also Beck et al. 2005), while globally fourteen banks dominate foreign exchange rate markets, and ten dominate global options markets (OECD 2011). The concentration in economically powerful states' banking sectors has actually increased since the GFC (IMF 2012), to the point that in 2015 the top three UK and US banks together boasted assets of US$12.5 trillion, while the top ten in the world had combined assets of over US$25.9 trillion (Banks Around the World 2015). This means that these top ten banks' assets are around 140 percent the size of the entire US economy and 35 percent of the global economy (World Bank 2016). If they fail again the impact will be felt globally, and, as before, they will need to be bailed out.

Beyond global corporations being big and possessing resources comparable to or greater than states, this last example highlights the way they control global economic processes and create the economic interconnectedness that is the foundation of globalization. Increasingly, the industrial intersectoral divisions between them are being broken down, so that the industry concentrations within sectors are becoming evident *across* them. Three of the world's largest companies by market capitalization are Apple, Google, and Microsoft. Together they are valued at US$1.4 trillion (*Financial Times* 2016). While they were once reasonably accurately thought of as firms producing IT hardware and software, increasingly they are involved in retailing, manufacturing, and information services provided through their affiliates and the global supply chains and operations they strategically coordinate. They are increasingly not just in charge of the markets for their products, but the global networks between industrial sectors. As such, these corporations' operations do not just span the globe, but also the virtual and physical worlds, and they are increasingly in a position to provide their products and services to consumers regardless of price competition. This is because "the more things are connected to each other and to the companies in charge of the networks that control them, the harder it will be for insurgents to get a foothold in the market" (Anon 2016b, 9).

This is enhancing the tendency for global corporations to dominate trade and investment relations. Even by the 1990s, 60–70 percent of trade in manufactured goods between OECD countries was intra-firm rather than inter-state in nature (Bonturi and Fukasaku 1993; see also Karliner 1997). Today, global corporations are estimated to be responsible for 80 percent of global trade (Dobbs et al. 2015). Trade occurs on the basis of competition between the suppliers of intermediate goods and services to them, rather than on the basis of Ricardian comparative advantage between states. No wonder, then, that the former Director General of the WTO, Pascal Lamy, invited corporate leaders to take the initiative in crafting international trade and investment rules in the following terms:

> It no longer suffices that you trade while relying on governments to craft the regulatory framework for you in the WTO through which your trade relations would take place. You must provide the "evidence," through your trade experience, of what is actually happening on the ground, and must guide us in how to make things better (WTO 2011).

He would seem to be in agreement with James Enyart, former Director of International Affairs for Monsanto, who is on the record as having stated that "the rules of international commerce are far too important to leave up to government bureaucrats" (Sell 2003, 96).

As a result of their control of international trade and the relations underpinning it, it follows that global corporations can play their suppliers off against one another, and strategically organize their operations in a manner they find most desirable. They can also play states off against one another. In a globalized world characterized by high capital mobility, they do not need to just react to states' natural endowments, but may proactively impose economic costs and confer economic benefits for certain policy choices by moving their operations and aspects of their supply chains to wherever conditions are most favorable. Just the *possibility* of this may be sufficient to shape public policy as states compete with each other for the economic benefits global corporations may confer, given the global markets, industries, and intersectoral links they control. In the process states initially become "competition states" whose key policy objectives are "the promotion of free enterprise, innovation and profitability in both the private and public sectors" (Cerny 2000, 302; see also Cerny 2010). Over time, as states pervasively behave in such a manner, global corporations are "no longer dependent clients of their home states, and the new global partnerships between states and corporations are more likely to be manifest in collaborations in transnational networks and sharing in regulation and economic governance" (Wilks 2013, 166).

Global corporations are not so much lithe, economic entities that must entrepreneurially respond to global competitive market forces as they are in a position to make and control the markets in which they operate. Therefore, a Marxist account that stresses the control of the means of production exercised by powerful transnational capital would seem more accurate than a liberal one that emphasizes market forces, as they are in a strong position before they bargain for what they want, given their control over their sectors and the economic fortunes of even the most powerful states. Their resulting structural power enhances their instrumental power because they may count on their size, dominance, and indispensability to national and global economies to enhance their leverage. To put it in Culpepper's terms (2011), they need to rely less on the "noisy" power that characterizes instrumental arguing, cajoling, influencing, and maybe even threatening. In addition to attracting more critical attention, such "displays" tend to suggest that an argument needs to be made that may be lost if not well prosecuted. For this reason, corporations would much rather rely on their structural power. However, both these first two faces of power are enhanced when they possess discursive power.

Discursive Power

Discursive power focuses on the power of ideas, and is therefore the hardest to observe. It is also potentially the most important because it relates to the creation of one actor's interests in another's. As Lukes (1974, 23) explains, "A may exercise power over B by getting him to do what he does not want to do, but he also exercises power over him by influencing, shaping or determining his very wants." This goes beyond buying access and being influential with the right contacts, or being in a structurally powerful position to determine outcomes, to the *right* to get them. As Elbra (2014) puts it, "Interests do not need to be pursued if they can be created," and essentially through the creation of "truths" global corporations can promote the "projection of a particular set of interests as the general interest" (Levy and Newell 2002, 87; see also Clapp and Fuchs 2009). This enhances both their structural and instrumental power, as it allows them to claim their interests are synonymous with the interests of states and their citizens.

Discursive power therefore underpins perceptions of legitimacy. It creates "a generalised perception or assumption that the actions of an entity are desirable, proper, or appropriate within some socially constructed system" (Suchman 1995, 574). The creation and control of dominant discourses does not necessarily mean the power wielded by global corporations is *intrinsically* legitimate, though. Legitimacy is a complex concept, encompassing inputs to the policy process, the process itself, and the outcomes it produces. Qualitatively, it encompasses pragmatic, moral, and cognitive dimensions. Pragmatic legitimacy involves actors abiding by an accepted standard because of the benefits conferred on them in so doing (i.e., out of self-interest); moral legitimacy involves a belief that actions taken are "right" and therefore that it is appropriate to behave in accordance with the standards underpinning them; and cognitive legitimacy involves the norms advocated being so widely accepted they effectively become institutionalized as taken for granted (Cashore et al. 2004; see also Cashore 2002; Bernstein and Cashore 2007). Cognitive legitimacy is the highest or, more accurately, the most deeply institutionally embedded form of legitimacy because it involves accepted "rules of the game" among actors to the extent that arrangements that favor certain actors and certain outcomes are no longer questioned. If institutions are "a set of rules, formal or informal, that actors generally follow, whether for normative, cognitive, or material reasons" (Hall and Soskice 2001b, 9), then they become what may be thought of as standard operating procedures. They are accepted as "part of the sociological and organizational landscape" (Aldrich 1999, 230). As per Finnemore and Sikkink's (1998) model of the norm lifecycle shown earlier in Figure 2.1, elites drawn from both the public and private sectors come to abide by them as a matter of course, and do so because they rely more on consent than on coercion in order to maintain their control. In the process, they "manufacture" consent on the basis of "common sense" (Patnaik 1988) to produce what Galbraith (1958) termed "the conventional wisdom."

Whether or not this is the case, and the extent to which it occurs, is almost impossible to measure because it involves observing the cognitive functions of the actors involved—i.e., getting "inside their heads." Yet this is exactly why discursive power is so important, because "power is at its most effective when least observable" (Lukes 2005, 64). Even so, it may be inferred from the discourse surrounding action. Constructivists like Blyth (2002a) have traced the way in which the widespread "truth" that neoliberal globalization was inevitable, if not universally desirable, emerged over the course of the 1970s to become institutionally embedded in most states after the 1980s. The idea that the market, and by implication market actors, either should be or inevitably must be in charge came to be widely accepted as a "fact" even as it was widely criticized, and embedded in the policy processes of states and the international organizations to which they belong (e.g., see Cahill 2014; Thatcher 2007). To question this, let alone refute it, came to be seen not just as critical or radical, but wrong. As Chang (2008, 21) observes, there is an "official history of globalization" that promotes a "fable" about the inevitability and benefits of globally free markets and therefore free market actors. Evidence for why this is true or not may be found, but what matters politically is the belief in it by those in positions of power, and with the power to act on their beliefs. To put it another way, "if policy-makers *believe* in globalisation, then this is likely to shape their approach *whether or not globalisation actually exists*. In other words, neoliberal *ideas* are creating neoliberal policies" (Marsh 2009, 688). More cynically, or realistically, it may be more accurate to say it is not just a matter of them actually believing in it, but constructing this belief in others in order to serve their material interests.

This includes global corporations, which are able to hide their power behind a discourse of market forces. Through the rise of the phenomenon of CSR, increasingly they have also sought to establish a belief that they can be trusted as not just motivated by economic imperatives, but servants of the public good. Their aim is to be perceived as acting virtuously as an end in itself within and between the states and the societies in which they operate. This may seem odd if one agrees with the comedian and social commentator David Mitchell that corporations are simply "robots" of which we should not expect too much because "they don't feel emotions, so we shouldn't feel emotions about them" (Mitchell 2014, 79). Nevertheless we do, and therefore they increasingly seek to portray themselves as agents of societal responsibility rather than just profitability. They may even do so in reality if one accepts that the two goals are linked, so that corporate reputation comes to be seen as an intangible asset that produces material rewards (e.g., see Gotsi and Wilson 2001). If it is the case that global corporations recognize their reputations are "valuable commodities" (O'Callaghan 2007, 114), then the ability of social groups and societal pressure to promote or undermine corporate reputation can function as a self-regulatory mechanism that constrains socially negative aspects of corporate behavior while promoting socially desirable outcomes.

In addition to acting as a self-regulatory mechanism, proactively enhancing reputation through CSR allows global corporations to argue there is a reduced need for government regulation. The "iron law of responsibility" says that those who do not use power in ways that society considers responsible will tend to lose it (Lawrence et al. 2005, 47; originally Davis and Blomstrom 1966), although it might be more accurate to say that they will have to fall back on structural and instrumental forms of power rather than being able to claim their "right" to be in charge. This has led international business scholars to claim the "business integrity thesis" has emerged as a new paradigm in global business, leading firms to "proactively build reputational capital for strategic advantage" (Jackson 2004, 3). According to this thesis, while investors and other stakeholders are interested in profitable businesses, they also wish to see firms mitigate risks by adhering to socially accepted norms around environmental management, social responsibility, and good conduct. Firms perceived to be "doing the right thing," or to be "trustworthy," are capable of leveraging these reputations to avoid the imposition of unwanted regulation, or to receive the regulatory and financial support they desire on the basis that they may argue they are good corporate citizens who can be trusted to serve the public good.

Like structural power, discursive power is probably most visible in times of crisis. If a crisis produces a critical juncture that undermines the legitimacy of corporate interests, then not just policy but paradigmatic change is possible, and legitimacy may not just be lost but transferred to other actors (e.g., see P. A. Hall 1993). For example, the GFC led to the neoliberal ideology of free markets being questioned and criticized much as communism was during the Cold War. In its immediate aftermath Australia's former Prime Minister, Kevin Rudd, called for the world to embrace "social capitalism" (Rudd 2009), and in so doing he echoed calls from other world leaders for a move away from neoliberal to more social democratic forms of the state. For example, France's former President Nicolas Sarkozy danced on the grave of neoliberal capitalism, proclaiming "le laissez-faire, c'est fini," while Chinese Vice Premier Wang Qishan more diplomatically cogitated on the idea that "the teachers now have some problems" (Altman 2009, 11). At the G20's meeting in the immediate aftermath of the 2008 near-meltdown of the global financial system, former British Prime Minister Gordon Brown "unveiled plans to plough more than $1 trillion into the world economy," casting this as the prelude to a "a new world order" in global cooperation to manage economic affairs (Winnett et al. 2009). Even the World Bank declared that "there's no question the Washington Consensus is dead" (Cooper and Savage 2008). By implication, the risk for the big banks dominating global finance was that they would have to resort to instrumental and structural forms of power, having lost discursive legitimacy. This is actually what Johal et al. (2015) suggest the City of London's banks had to fall back on: threats and implied rewards via direct lobbying, and their underpinning of their state's economy, as well as the global economy, as a way of getting the regulations they desired. This put them in a weakened position, as it suggested they must overtly and publicly "fight" the prospect of increased state intervention and regulatory oversight rather than be seen to justifiably claim it as self-evident that this was unnecessary.

Power that is believed to be exercised responsibly comes to be institutionalized as "normal," or at the very least "tolerable" (Wilks 2013,

177), because it is seen as legitimate. It endures and institutionally re-embeds itself rather than having to be continually asserted. Discursive power that leads to legitimacy therefore reinforces instrumental and structural power by institutionalizing widely accepted norms of behavior on the basis of it. If global corporations primarily rely on threats and rewards, or on making demands based on their economic dominance, then the continuity of, and commitment to, their agendas and interests is always threatened. If support for them is given grudgingly, then this suggests potential for their agendas and interests to be controlled by others.

Conclusion

Global corporations control their industries and the markets for their products and services. This is a key reason why they are best conceived as political rather than market actors in the pursuit of their economic interests. However, it does not simply follow that this means they get whatever they want. The political power they wield is not just a matter of them being "big." Although this is the most basic form of their power, and the source of it, in this chapter an understanding of the manner in which perceptions of their identities and strategies, and how these are discursively constructed, explain their political power was the end point of a discussion of the multi-faceted nature of it. The key point is that the reason why ideas, and the discourse that constructs and legitimizes them, are important is not because they explain everything. The three faces of power discussed in this chapter should be seen as mutually reinforcing rather than existing discretely. As such, global corporations' power is a function of them exercising leverage given the material wealth they possess, whether instrumentally or structurally, with this enhanced by discursively constructing themselves as legitimately entitled to wield it.

Generally speaking, "whoever sets the terms of discourse will almost always determine the outcome" (Lowi 2001, 131), and if global corporations can achieve such discursive legitimacy they can make widely accepted claims which are not easily "dismissed by a skeptical and cynical public" (Tienhaara 2014, 167). Discursive power, and the legitimacy to which it potentially gives rise, is the political "prize" global corporations seek because it facilitates the creation of a world in the image of their interests. If power is "the production, in and through social relations, of effects that shape the capacities of actors to determine their own circumstances and fate" (Barnett and Duvall 2005, 3), then this is surely the most crucial aspect of it. As such, while the potential of global corporations to influence governments through lobbying, and, because of their size and economic dominance, they cannot be ignored, if we want to understand how global corporations establish the *right* to do this, then ultimately we need to examine the extent to which they can create their interests in others—i.e., a belief that what serves them also serves the public interest not just nationally, but globally. If the central question for all political scholars is "who governs," and in the context of the debates surrounding globalization how this happens in relation to states, then the political power of global corporations is not just a question of whether they have political influence. It is obvious that they do. But the extent to which they do so, and how they do so, is also related to the question of whether they are seen as possessing the discursive legitimacy to set agendas and maybe even govern in their own right.

This means that any of the waves of conceptualizing globalization and the major IPE traditions may potentially be applicable. These tend to focus on states and/versus markets, but what was shown was that there are also implications for the relationship between states and/versus global corporations. The role states play is traditionally seen as governing on behalf of their citizens, but depending on the political power global corporations wield relationally with them, states may instead give preference to the interests of these global corporations. Whether or not this is desirable depends on support for private actors performing public roles for profit (a liberal versus Marxist perspective) and whether or not it serves the national interest (a nationalist perspective). To the extent that a preference for one of these perspectives dominates, or indeed a hybrid form of them (e.g., a liberal agenda to serve nationalist goals), depends on the normative support for such a state of affairs, and perhaps also on the particular issue in question. Thus, a focus on the role of ideas, as suggested by the constructivist challenge to the main IPE traditions, is useful for understanding the ideational support for one perspective versus another and how this becomes institutionalized over time as self-evident. In this respect, relational entanglement between states and global corporations always applies, and as such a transformationalist approach to globalization is the most tractable starting point for analysis, given that politically the focus is on the way in which states that are territorially constrained share the power they possess as a result of their sovereignty with corporations that are said increasingly to not be so. The extent to which this is the case must also be addressed, and this is the subject of the next chapter.

3 GEOGRAPHICAL CONCENTRATION

Chapter 2 addressed the disembodied debate around the political power of global corporations that often shrouds their power in market terms. It located global corporations in the main IPE traditions and conceptualizations of globalization, and demonstrated that where they "reside" is a matter of the political power they wield instrumentally, structurally, and discursively. As noted in Chapter 1, much of the debate is also rather de-territorialized, and it may be noted that IPE is now often more fashionably known as "global" political economy. This is because globalization entails economic power relations less defined by national territorial boundaries than they used to be, and more by global interconnectedness. Although corporations have always been relationally entangled with states in exercising their power, because national jurisdictions are territorially defined while the global economy is increasing less so, it is often claimed that global corporations are breaking free from their previous links with states. This implies global corporations should increasingly become political actors in their own right, as it follows that relations within and between states no longer matter as much as relations within the global *system*.

The agenda to produce this outcome has its genesis at the close of World War II, when liberalism was embedded in the global economic system through the development of the Bretton Woods Institutions and the General Agreement on Tariffs and Trade, which in 1995 became the WTO. As the European and North East Asian powers recovered or developed trade and investment relations between them, North America and other developed and developing states became increasingly liberalized. Through acceptance of what Wade (2010) calls the "globalization consensus," as a matter of policy they surrendered sovereignty over their economies. This is why global corporations came to control and determine financial, investment, and trade flows rather than the governments of nations. They did so first as a matter of policy choice, and later as a matter of inevitability, given that even by 1971 the liquid assets of the top 100 US MNCs exceeded the combined reserves of the largest industrialized states. The structural power this afforded them, combined with the conventional wisdom that a world of liberally interconnected free markets was desirable before it became inevitable, meant that they and private financial institutions could control the destinies of nations (e.g., see Panic 1995, 51).

The result is that, rather than global market forces undermining states, it could be contended that global corporations came to be in a position to do so. As noted in Chapter 2, neo-Marxists like Sklair (2001; see also Robinson and Harris 2000) declare the emergence of a transnational capitalist class: a ruling elite that controls the global economy with global corporations as the key organizational basis for doing so. As opposed to the neoliberal ideal of a world of free markets, they see global corporations as the vehicles through which the capitalist class maintains its power, while state bureaucracies and international organizations provide the regulatory architecture that enables them. The Marxist critique is particularly useful for highlighting the problematic nature of conceiving global corporations as possessing nationalities, as opposed to a class-based study of the structural basis of capitalist relations of production. But whether it is a matter of the neoliberal project to actively dismantle states and the boundaries between them to put market forces in charge, or the increased structural power of the transnational capitalist class that results from doing so, from a nationalist perspective the state is undermined as a political actor. Therefore, speaking of the nationality of global corporations seems increasingly redundant.

Those who find the Marxist perspective too dismal may nevertheless also be skeptical of the liberal pronouncements on the basis that "the globalizers have it exactly backwards" because "integration is the result, not the cause, of economic and social development" (Rodrik 2001, 59). As discussed in Chapter 2, such thinking resonates with the nationalist view that successful states must possess the capacity to harness the political power of *their* global corporations in the national interest. If so, global corporations are not so much supplanters of state power as global agents of it. This is exactly the approach Fields (2012) suggests that states such as Japan, South Korea, and Taiwan took in their development. His analysis, along with other more nationalist renderings of global corporate power, stresses the ways in which states can strategically develop their national economies by supporting their global corporations, which may be thought of as "national champions" (Hayward 1995; see also Helleiner and Pickel 2005). In the past, this often involved pursuing a quite overtly interventionist industry policy, but in a more economically globalized world it may involve liberal to neoliberal policies for powerful industrialized, and even some industrializing, states. This is because such policies permit their global corporations to "colonize" other states' industrial bases. In the process they also conquer and control global markets. Superficially, economically powerful states appear to sacrifice their sovereignty by embracing market forces through a free trade and investment agenda, but in reality they are empowering their global corporations to act on their behalf. In a related vein, Cerny (2000, 5) suggests that in a globalized world "the state still has a major national yet paradoxical role to play—to expose the domestic to the transnational in order to ensure that citizens keep up with the multiple pressures and demands of that increasingly interpenetrated political, economic and social ecosystem."

In other words, global corporations also remain national corporations in a more economically globalized world. How else could one explain why around 600 US corporate and industry representatives were permitted access by the Office of the US Trade Representative (USTR) to drafts of the Trans-Pacific Partnership (TPP) agreement during negotiations, while anyone else interested in the contents of these drafts relied on leaked copies (Palmberg 2012)? Unless the reason the USTR provided such access was to proactively undermine US sovereignty, it seems to logically follow that corporate interests were served in the belief that this would also serve the US national interest. And of course they do. At the time the US was driving the TPP negotiations, the USTR declared that "the rules of the road are up for grabs in Asia" and that the US must "write those rules" (Office of the United States Trade Representative 2016). But more accurately, the US together with its major global corporations was negotiating the TPP. Therefore, the 2017 decision by the incoming Trump administration to subsequently not ratify the agreement surely depended not just on the mood of the American electorate, nor simply on the ideological leanings of President Trump himself, but whether or not national and corporate interests were believed to be mutually served by it.

The result is that as there is a tension between the globalist versus skeptical conceptualizations of globalization, so there is a tension between whether a more traditionally nationalist conception of global corporations' influence still applies, or whether global corporations should be seen as political actors in their own right. The tension between the two perspectives is in fact "one of the classic fault lines in the study of international business power" according to Wilks (2013, 155), who poses the question: "Is the influence of multinationals simply an extension of the power of their home states (as state-centric comparativists would have it), or have global corporations, global markets and an international society taken on an autonomous and relatively stable existence?" He declares himself in the latter camp, but I have previously declared myself more in the former (e.g., see Mikler 2009, 2011), agreeing with authors like Dicken (2015, 132, echoing earlier arguments made by authors such as Hampden-Turner and Trompenaars 1993; Boyer 1996; and Pauly and Reich 1997) that corporations "are 'produced' through an intricate process of embedding in which the cognitive, cultural, social, political and economic characteristics of the national home base play a dominant part." This embedding is normative and institutional, and the subject of Chapter 4. In this chapter the aim is to establish the *prima facie* evidence for seeing corporations as national as well as global actors. In other words, to demonstrate that, as claimed in Chapter 2, a more mainstream transformationalist understanding of the concept of globalization permits the possibility that the reality is somewhere in between.

In the first section, data on the headquarters and transnationality of the world's major global corporations are presented to demonstrate that, far from a global diffusion of their operations, only ten states account for the majority of them, with the US alone accounting for nearly half of them. It is also primarily in their sales and location of their productive assets, rather than in employment, that they are transnational, and this is particularly the case for their senior management. To consider the extent to which this may be changing, the second section considers global investment patterns measured by data on mergers and acquisitions (M&As) and FDI stocks and flows. What these demonstrate is that there has been a process of territorial consolidation and concentration as global corporations have primarily invested in each other's home territories. In both sections it is also shown that while new global corporations from emerging market economies are taking their place on the world stage, these are primarily from China. To the extent that they are now represented in the rankings of corporations of other nationalities, this is a reflection of a global reorientation in patterns of national and regional economic power, rather than the destruction of these patterns.

The central claims made are therefore that global corporations are less transnational than is often asserted, and that their political power remains mutually entangled with the states in which they are headquartered even as they invest and operate beyond them. In fact, the conclusion reached is that there is reason to believe that states' power is expressed through their global corporations. Global corporations' economic power mirrors that of their home states' and regions' economic power, rather than being an alternative to it. Rather than being agents that globally diffuse economic power, global corporations are emissaries of their home states in reorienting and reflecting it.

National as well as Global Political Actors

Very few corporations are truly global in terms of either their location or interests. While corporations are increasingly multinational, it is more problematic to say they are global in the sense that they operate and have interests in so many places they may be thought of as essentially placeless. As noted in Chapter 1, the size and territorial reach of global corporations means they rival all but the most economically powerful states. Yet it is also the case that it is in these states that they are based. Table 3.1 demonstrates that 84 percent of the FT Global 500 corporations are headquartered in just ten states, with these largely located in the triad of North America, the EU, and East Asia. The US alone accounts for nearly half of their headquarters. The same geographical concentration of corporations' headquarters is evident in other rankings. The FT Global 500 ranks corporations on the basis of their stock market capitalization, while the Fortune Global 500 ranks them on the basis of their annual revenues, and the Forbes Global 2000 does so on the basis of a composite index of their sales, profits, assets, and market value. Whatever the basis for measuring their size and market dominance, the results are strikingly similar. The top ten headquarters for the Fortune Global 500 corporations also account for 84 percent of them, while the top ten countries where the Forbes Global 2000 corporations are based account for 73 percent. They are also largely the same states that are the headquarters for those listed on the FT Global 500, with US corporations overwhelmingly dominant (Fortune 2015a; Forbes Global 2000 2015).[1]

Table 3.1 also demonstrates that the composition of the FT Global 500 corporations' headquarters has changed in the last ten years with the rise of those from China and India. This is likewise the case for

Table 3.1: Top Ten Headquarters of FT Global 500 Corporations

2006		2015	
US	195	US	208
Japan	60	China[a]	55
UK	34	Japan	35
France	30	UK	27
Canada	22	France	24
Germany	19	Canada	19
Italy	11	Germany	18
Switzerland	11	India	13
Saudi Arabia	9	Switzerland	11
South Korea	9	Sweden	10
TOTAL	400 (80%)	TOTAL	420 (84%)

Source: *Financial Times* (2016). The ranking is on the basis of their stock market capitalization.
[a] The FT Global 500 lists China and Hong Kong separately, but they have been combined here.

those in the Forbes Global 2000 and Fortune Global 500. However, the rise of Indian and Chinese corporations appears to have occurred at the expense of those from Japan (with the number of corporations in the list halved), South Korea and Saudi Arabia (both of whose corporations no longer make the top ten), and some European corporations. This is not to say that the corporations from these states are now irrelevant, nor necessarily smaller in size. However, there has been a shift in the geographical center of global corporate power over the past decade that reflects shifts in the economic significance of the states from which they hail. In this respect, it is notable that US corporations have retained their dominance, and in fact have slightly increased it by now accounting for 42 percent of the headquarters of the FT Global 500 corporations, by comparison to 39 percent in 2006. Those from China have rapidly climbed the list of the world's largest corporations to take second place behind the US, accounting for 11 percent. As China now has the world's second-largest economy after the US, so too are its corporations second on the list as the headquarters of the world's largest corporations (World Bank 2016).

The data suggest the structural power possessed by global corporations is related to, and it seems reasonable to say is a reflection of, their geographical concentration in economically powerful states. This concentration may also underpin their instrumental and discursive power vis-à-vis their home states' governments. The extent to which this is the case depends on how nationally focused they remain. As noted in Chapter 1, one measure of this is UNCTAD's TNI, which calculates corporations' transnationality as the arithmetic mean of three ratios: foreign assets to total assets; foreign sales to total sales; and foreign employment to total employment. Table 3.2 presents the average TNI for the world's 100 most transnational corporations, as well as ratios of foreign to total assets, sales, and employment, respectively. What is immediately noticeable is that the states with the most transnational corporations are almost identical to the ones on lists of the world's largest corporations, and again primarily from the triad of North America (especially the US), the EU (more accurately Western Europe), and East Asia. In the case of East Asia, as China has emerged as a global economic power, its corporations have made the list of those that are the most transnational, as well as the largest, along with Japan.

Table 3.2: Nationality and Transnationality of the World's Top 100 Nonfinancial Corporations, 2013

	Average TNI (%)[b]	Average Assets (%)[b]	Average Sales (%)[b]	Average Employment (%)[b]
US (23)	51	52	52	48
UK (16)	71	78	68	67
France (11)	62	57	69	61
Germany (10)	63	55	75	58
Japan (10)	61	65	61	55
Switzerland (5)	80	80	80	79
Italy (3)	70	70	74	67
Spain (3)	64	69	60	62
China (3)	20	21	30	9
Sweden (2)	77	69	86	75
Others (14)[a]	69	61	81	65
AVERAGE ALL	60	59	65	57

Source: UNCTAD (2014a). The ranking is on the basis of their foreign assets.
[a] One each from Australia, Austria, Belgium, Brazil, Canada, Denmark, Hong Kong, Israel, South Korea, Luxembourg, Malaysia, the Netherlands, Norway, and Taiwan.
[b] These calculations treat the top 100 corporations, and then those from each country, as a group, so that their transnationality is calculated based on the sum of their assets, sales, and employment.

Transnationality also appears related to national factors pertaining to corporations' headquarters. While on average the most transnational corporations have a TNI of 60 percent, those with the highest TNIs are based in states with the smallest domestic markets, such as Switzerland and Sweden. By comparison, the US has among the least transnational corporations, and China's corporations' average TNI is lower still. In addition to the size of China's domestic economy, Chinese corporations' lower transnationality may also reflect their state's more recent emergence as a global power, along with the large (even controlling) role played by the Chinese state in their emergence. This is discussed in Chapter 4, where the institutional basis for capitalist relations of production in corporations' home states is considered. For now it suffices to say that the Chinese government's role and economic policy choices are reflected in the transnationality of China's global corporations. The same may be said to be the case in other states. For example, the high transnationality of the UK's global corporations is probably a reflection of its particularly strong embrace of a neoliberal market approach to corporate governance since the 1980s. Therefore, factors like domestic market size, stages of development, and national policy choices all potentially have an influence on, and therefore are reflected in the extent of, corporate transnationality.

As such, there is a danger in not seeing the national "trees" for the global "forest." In this respect, there is a body of scholarship demonstrating that a very significant proportion of the Fortune Global 500 corporations are more accurately bi-national or regional rather than global in their operations and interests (e.g., see Rugman and Girod 2003; Rugman and Collinson 2004; Rugman 2005, 2007). On the basis of their sales in particular, the vast majority of global corporations are not as transnational as a simple ratio of foreign to total sales makes them appear. Rugman and Verbeke (2009) demonstrate that *only nine* of the top 500 global corporations have sales in so many regions of the world that they may be regarded as truly global, while 320 of them still derive 80 percent of their sales from their home region. Of the others for which they have data, 25 are more accurately defined as bi-national or bi-regional on the basis of their sales. The same may often be said of where their productive assets are located. For example, Voss (2013) notes that corporations headquartered in Taiwan and Hong Kong have very high TNIs simply because they locate factories in mainland China but nowhere else. They may therefore be seen as regionally Chinese, or perhaps East Asian corporations, rather than global.

Similar observations may be made for global financial corporations like the world's major banks, which are included in the FT Global 500, Forbes Global 500, and Fortune Global 2000 lists but not in UNCTAD's TNI calculations. This is because their transnationality cannot be measured in the same way as nonfinancial corporations, as they do not have productive assets like factories, nor do they make sales. Instead, they have geographically spread subsidiaries conducting investment operations that generate revenues. Although the top fifty most geographically spread global financial corporations have 12,352 foreign affiliates in 33 states on average, suggesting that their operations are very widely dispersed, it is nevertheless the case that a third of them are based in either the US or the UK (UNCTAD 2013d). These two states are also the centers of global finance. Fichtner (2016) demonstrates that both on the basis of assets controlled and bilateral financial activity in the form of portfolio investment and banks' foreign claims, the US is at the center of the global financial system, while the UK represents a second major center closely connected to the US. In turn, nearly all other major financial centers, including the next five largest of Japan, Germany, France, the Netherlands, and Luxembourg, have their largest bilateral financial relations with either the US or the UK. Putting it simply, all financial roads lead to either Wall Street or the City of London to the extent that "the international banking network is not flat, but hierarchical with the US and the UK as the only global hubs" (Fichtner 2016, 17; see also Oatley et al. 2013). Therefore, although finance is one of the most globalized aspects of the world economy, and indeed a key driver of the economic interconnectedness that characterizes globalization, it is also the case that it is fundamentally Anglo-American.

The TNI data therefore overstate corporate transnationality, and the example of finance illustrates why even corporations that are highly globally networked in their operations may be so due to the importance of their geographical hubs. Another feature that may be noted from Table 3.2 is that, while average TNIs range from 51 to 80 percent, it is either sales or assets that are the main drivers of corporations' transnationality. That the most transnational corporations' workforces are the least transnational aspect of their operations is a point that deserves greater attention than it normally receives. While sales indicate where corporate material interests lie, and assets indicate where productive capacity resides, the places where global corporations wield their political power surely depend on the location of their people.[2] Furthermore, what the TNI data do not reveal are the nationalities of their senior strategic decision makers, and in this respect several studies have demonstrated remarkably little national diversity in the composition of corporate boards. On the one hand, there is evidence of increasing diversity in board members' nationalities, so that according to Staples (2007) three-quarters of the 80 largest global corporations had at least one non-national board member in 2005 by comparison to around a third in 1993 (i.e., those of a nationality different from the corporation's headquarters). On the other hand, he also finds that no more than 25 percent of the board members of these companies comprise non-nationals, and that for only 10 percent of them were the majority of board members non-nationals. Furthermore, he finds the main way that boards become more globalized is through M&As, not because of their global sales and production interests. He concludes that "like a wide but shallow lake, board globalization does not yet reach very deep" (Staples 2007, 317). Van Veen and Marsman's (2008; see also van Veen and Elbertsen 2008) study of Europe's 363 largest corporations and their 2,229 board members reveals similar profiles. Only 15 percent are of a different nationality from their corporation's country of origin, again largely due to M&As. Of them, British and Americans are represented to such an extent that "besides the USA and the UK, there are no countries with large contingents of top managers working abroad" (van Veen and Marsman 2008, 193). If the world's major global corporations actually come from just a handful of states, and either the location of their headquarters or M&As determines the nationality of their board members, then rather than a "transnational capitalist class" (Sklair 2001) that owes allegiance to no state and no territory, the reality is a *national capitalist class* drawn from the elites of a few of the world's largest and most economically powerful states.

Similar trends are evident for global corporations from emerging market economies. Table 3.3 lists the top ten headquarters for the FT Emerging 500 corporations, and shows that the national concentration evident in the established corporations' headquarters is structurally duplicated in those from the emerging economies. Eighty-nine percent of them are based in just ten states, with China accounting for around 40 percent of them. Therefore, rather than a trend toward the increasing diffusion of power in the global system, instead what is exhibited is a reorientation of global economic power to global corporations from an alternative handful of states, with China rather than the US in a dominant position to almost exactly the same degree. The same patterns are also evident in their transnationality, shown in Table 3.4. Although on average they are less transnational in their

Table 3.3: Top Ten Headquarters of FT Emerging 500 Corporations, 2015

China[a]	202
India	51
Taiwan	29
Brazil	24
Mexico	20
Saudi Arabia	19
South Africa	19
Malaysia	18
Russia	17
Thailand	15
TOTAL	443 (89%)

Source: *Financial Times* (2016)
[a] The FT Global 500 lists China and Hong Kong separately, but they have been combined here.

Table 3.4: Nationality and Transnationality of the World's Top 100 Nonfinancial Corporations from Developing Countries, 2013

	Average TNI[b] (%)	Average Assets (%)[b]	Average Sales (%)[b]	Average Employment (%)[b]
Hong Kong, China (18)	73	73	85	75
China (12)	13	13	19	8
Taiwan (10)	66	57	72	69
Singapore (9)	72	59	69	87
South Africa (8)	60	69	61	50
India (7)	43	49	57	22
Brazil (5)	30	18	39	34
Russia (4)	30	12	67	9
Malaysia (4)	51	40	75	37
Mexico (4)	51	56	60	51
United Arab Emirates (3)	43	49	47	33
Turkey (2)	37	55	16	40
Others (14)[a]	39	23	60	33
AVERAGE ALL	37	27	44	39

Source: UNCTAD (2014b). The ranking is on the basis of their foreign assets.
[a] One each from Algeria, Argentina, Egypt, Kuwait, the Philippines, Qatar, Saudi Arabia, and Venezuela. South Korea is also included in the list, with six corporations in the top 100, but these are excluded from the table because it seems odd to class South Korea as a developing country given its size and stage of development.
[b] This treats the top 100 corporations, and then those from each country, as a group, so that their transnationality is calculated based on the sum of their assets, sales, and employment.

operations than the global corporations from industrialized states, no doubt reflecting their earlier stage of global economic emergence, again those from states with smaller domestic markets such as Singapore and Taiwan have the highest TNIs, while those from states like China, India, and Russia have the lowest TNIs. However, while the transnationality of corporations from the established triad of the US, Europe, and Japan is driven more by sales and assets than employment, this is not as clearly the case for those from emerging market economies. In fact, those from Hong Kong, Taiwan, Singapore, Brazil, and Turkey are substantially transnational in their employment as well as assets and sales. These may be contrasted with Chinese and Russian corporations which are much more transnational in their sales and assets than employment. This suggests they, like those of an older vintage, have retained greater control in national rather than foreign hands.

The picture painted by the above data is of global corporations that are geographically headquartered in ten established states and ten emerging ones, with dominance of the former by those from the US and of the latter by those from China. Geographical concentration is evident for both nonfinancial and financial global corporations. Rather than a global economy with global market forces and corporations whose power is a function of their de-territorialization, instead it is a reflection of the economic power of their home states.

National and Regional Rather Than Global Investment

Whether or not this is likely to change over time is indicated by global trends in ownership and control and investment patterns. As an indication of these trends, the data on M&As, FDI stocks, and FDI flows suggest the extent to which there is a breakdown or reorientation in the established nationalities of global corporations. The data show that rather than greater global diffusion, there is actually evidence of increasing national and regional consolidation of the territorial basis for global corporate power over time, so that as global corporations become more multinational they are also becoming more nationally and regionally focused.

Mergers and Acquisitions

The M&A data demonstrate a long-term trend toward greater concentration in the national and regional hubs that are home to the world's major global corporations. From 1990 to 2013, 81 percent of the US$8.1 trillion in M&A purchases were carried out by corporations from developed states, with those of the US and Europe alone accounting for 67 percent of the total. The top two states from which the purchases came were the US (17 percent) and the UK (14 percent) (UNCTAD 2014c). It is also the case that over the same period of time, 84 percent of M&A sales were carried out by corporations from developed states—i.e., a similar percentage to M&A purchases—again with those from the US and Europe accounting for the vast majority at 73 percent of the total, and with the top two states being the US (25 percent) and UK (16 percent) (UNCTAD 2014d). As such, the corporations from the world's economically dominant states have been buying each other, further concentrating not just power in the industries they dominate but also the geographical basis for doing so. It is no coincidence that because those of British and US nationality are key drivers of M&As, these are the same two states whose nationals tend to be most globally mobile in populating the boards of corporations of nationalities other than their own. As noted above, this is to be expected if corporate board transnationality is largely driven by M&As rather than corporate interests and operations.

Therefore, the M&A data demonstrate that it is not the case that global corporations are coming to resemble vast global webs where nationality is increasingly irrelevant as they merge and take each other over. Quite the opposite. This is not to say that they do not potentially rival weaker states beyond the ones that are their home bases. Given that their economic interests transcend national boundaries, coupled with their size and economic dominance through affiliates and supply chains, they may also challenge even the more powerful states where they are headquartered. Nevertheless, on the basis of their ownership and control they potentially form an integral part in the economic and political power these states possess in the global economy, effectively being a vehicle by which they can increase their virtual territorial footprint and political influence over other states. The extent to which this actually is the function they perform depends not on a lack of opportunity, but turns on whether these states possess the political will and institutional capacity to work with their corporations to achieve this end.

Foreign Direct Investment Stocks

It also turns on the extent to which global corporations have spread their assets beyond their home states. As noted above, the TNI data give only a rough indication of this because they do not indicate the geographical spread of global corporations' investments. FDI stocks do, and like M&As they indicate that the states where the world's major global corporations are based are also primarily where they have invested.[3] Although FDI stocks grew more than tenfold from just over US$2 trillion in 1990 to US$26 trillion in 2013 (UNCTAD 2014e, 2014f), Table 3.5 demonstrates the following:

(1) The majority of both inward and outward FDI stocks are accounted for by a handful of states in North America, Europe, East Asia, and Australia. Within Europe, the UK, Germany, and France dominate FDI stocks, as they do the headquarters of the largest European corporations.

(2) Changes since the 1990s reflect the rise of China, Russia, and Brazil as both sources of and destinations for FDI. For example, China has challenged Hong Kong as the location in Asia for inward FDI since the handover of the territory in 1997, and both have increased their importance as sources of outward FDI stocks. Similarly, Brazil and Russia are now both sources of and destinations for FDI, the latter since the opening of its economy after the fall of the Soviet Union.

(3) US and European states' outward FDI stocks tend to be greater than their inward FDI stocks.[4] Relatedly, the major European corporations' headquarters of the UK, France, and Germany are the largest for outward FDI stocks. Therefore, the data indicate that when US and European corporations invest abroad, if they are not investing in each other's territories they tend to be sources of FDI rather than destinations for it. If not each other's home territories, the destinations for their outward investment tend to be Asia or Latin America, particularly states like China/Hong Kong, Singapore, Brazil, Mexico, and Australia.

(4) It is remarkable that while Indian corporations have grown to the extent that they are now ranked among the world's largest, India as both a source of and location for FDI remains relatively insignificant. In this sense (i.e., based on investment patterns), Indian corporations tend to not be global corporations.

(5) There is the curious case of the British Virgin Islands as a source of and destination for FDI. This reflects its status as an offshore financial center, sometimes less charitably referred to as a tax haven because it offers its territory as a low-tax

Table 3.5: FDI Stocks

	Inward FDI Stocks			Outward FDI Stocks		
	1990 (%)	2000 (%)	2013 (%)	1990 (%)	2000 (%)	2013 (%)
Developed	75	76	63	93	89	79
North America	31	40	22	39	37	27
US	26	37	19	35	34	24
Canada	5	3	3	4	3	3
Europe	39	33	37	42	47	46
UK	10	6	6	11	12	7
Germany	5	4	3	7	7	7
France	5	5	4	5	12	6
Belgium and Luxembourg	3	3	4	2	2	5
Netherlands	3	3	3	5	4	4
Switzerland	2	1	3	3	3	5
Italy	3	2	2	3	2	2
Spain	3	2	3	1	2	2
Ireland	2	2	2	1	<1	2
Sweden	<1	1	2	2	2	2
Other Developed	5	2	4	2	1	2
Australia	4	2	2	2	1	2
Asia	16	16	20	13	12	17
Japan	<1	1	<1	10	4	4
Hong Kong	10	7	6	<1	5	5
China	1	3	4	<1	<1	2
Singapore	2	2	3	<1	1	2
India	<1	<1	1	<1	<1	<1
Latin America/ Caribbean	5	7	10	3	2	5
Brazil	2	2	3	2	1	1
British Virgin Islands	0	1	2	0	<1	2
Mexico	1	1	2	<1	<1	1
Africa	3	2	3	1	<1	<1
Transition Economies[a]	0	1	4	0	<1	2
Russia	0	<1	2	0	<1	2

Sources: UNCTAD (2014e, 2014f). All data rounded to the nearest whole percent.
[a] These are the states that were formerly part of Yugoslavia and the Soviet Union.

jurisdiction for the registration of offshore companies, as well as the investment of offshore funds (e.g., see Sharman 2006). The data therefore reflect the financial services it offers rather than the nationality of the corporations behind the FDI figures.

Even with the increasing importance of the BRICs, the states where the largest and most transnational corporations are based still dominate both inward and outward FDI stocks. This, together with the geographical concentration of ownership and control, and consolidation of this via M&As, suggests global corporations use their headquarters as a base from which to dominate their regions, while seeking to control others.

Foreign Direct Investment Flows

This is likely to be an ongoing trend based on FDI flows. These indicate the likely shifts in FDI stocks over time.[5] Growing from around US$200 billion per annum in the early 1990s to between US$1–2 trillion per annum since 2000, their size would seem to demonstrate the increasing transnationality of corporate investment (UNCTAD 2014g, 2014h). However, they also demonstrate shifts in the importance of states from which FDI is sourced and those that are its destination. In this respect, Table 3.6 indicates the following:

(1) Since 2000, FDI is not flowing between developed states to the extent that it was. Asia has become much more important as both a source of and destination for FDI, as has Latin America. This is a point made by others who see the rise of the BRICs as meaning the geography of the global economy is no longer as triadically dominated by North America, Europe, and Japan (e.g., see Goldstein 2007).

(2) However, although the US has declined as a destination for inward FDI, its importance as a source of outward FDI has *doubled*.

(3) This is not the case for Europe, where the region's inward and outward FDI flows have fallen quite dramatically since 2000. This is true across the states that were previously the major drivers of the flows—i.e., states like the UK, Germany, and France.

(4) For Asia, Japan remains an important source of outward FDI, while China and Hong Kong have grown to be more important sources of and destinations for FDI.

Table 3.6: FDI Flows

	Inward FDI Flows			Outward FDI Flows		
	1990 (%)	2000 (%)	2013 (%)	1990 (%)	2000 (%)	2013 (%)
Developed	83	81	39	95	88	61
North America	27	27	17	15	15	27
US	23	22	13	13	12	24
Canada	4	5	4	2	4	3
Europe	50	52	17	58	70	23
UK	15	9	3	8	19	1
Germany	1	14	2	10	5	4
France	8	3	<1	15	14	<-1[b]
Belgium and Luxembourg	4	6	2	0	0	<-1[b]
Netherlands	5	5	2	6	6	3
Switzerland	3	1	<-1[b]	3	4	4
Italy	3	1	1	3	1	2
Spain	6	3	3	1	5	2
Ireland	<1	2	2	<1	<1	2
Sweden	1	2	1	6	3	3
Other Developed	5	2	4	1	1	1
Australia	4	1	3	<1	<1	1
Asia	10	12	29	26	10	33
Japan	1	1	<1	21	3	10
Hong Kong	2	3	9	1	6	7
China	2	5	5	<1	<1	7
Singapore	3	1	4	1	1	2
India	<1	<1	2	0	<1	<1
Latin America/Caribbean	4	7	20	<-1[b]	4	8
Brazil	1	2	4	<1	<1	<-1[b]
British Virgin Islands	0	1	6	-1[b]	3	5
Mexico	1	1	3	<1	0	1
Chile	<1	<1	1	0	<1	1
Africa	1	<1	4	<1	<1	1
Transition Economies[a]	0	<1	7	0	<1	7
Russia	0	<1	6	0	<1	7

Sources: UNCTAD (2014g, 2014h). All data rounded to the nearest whole percent.
[a] These are the states that were formerly part of Yugoslavia and the Soviet Union.
[b] A negative FDI inflow indicates that divestment by corporations in a country is greater than investment. The converse is the case for a negative FDI outflow.

(5) Latin American states like Brazil, Mexico, and Chile have grown in importance as destinations for FDI, but not sources of it. The exception to this rule is again the British Virgin Islands due to its growing importance as a center for offshore financial services for other states' corporations. According to Colin Riegels (2014), the Global Head of Banking and Finance at the British Virgin Islands law firm Harney's, and whose father was one of the authors of the state's International Business Company Act, these have primarily been based in the US and Hong Kong.

(6) As with FDI stocks, the opening of Russia means that it is more important as both a source of and destination for FDI.

What is demonstrated by the data is the increasing and enduring importance of US and Japanese corporations in driving outward FDI, the relative decline of European corporations in doing so, and the rise of Russia and China as sources of and destinations for FDI. Brazil and other Latin American states are increasing their importance as recipients of FDI flows, but not as sources of it. To the extent that European corporations have a less dominant role in investing in other states, the importance of those from China and Russia have increased. Other states, such as India and those of Latin America and Africa, are increasingly recipients of FDI from corporations based in these states.

Investment Patterns as a Reflection of National Economic Power

The geographical investment patterns revealed by the data raise the point that some states are relatively more penetrated by FDI from other states or, to be more accurate, they are penetrated by these states' corporations. This is a reflection of their relative economic size and power. Table 3.7 shows that those industrialized states with the highest FDI stocks tend to have smaller domestic economies. The four industrialized states with outward FDI stocks as a percentage of GDP higher than 100 percent are the Netherlands, Switzerland, Ireland, and Luxembourg. By comparison, the UK, France, Germany, the US, and Japan have outward FDI stocks as a percentage of GDP of 23 to 74 percent. The same is true for inward FDI stocks as a percentage of GDP. The three industrialized states with inward FDI stocks as a percentage of GDP greater than 100 percent are Switzerland, Ireland, and Luxembourg, while the UK, France, Germany, the US, and Japan

Table 3.7: FDI Stocks as a Percentage of GDP in Industrialized States, 2013

Inward FDI Stocks (%)		Outward FDI Stocks (%)	
>100 %		>100 %	
Luxembourg	234	Luxembourg	301
Ireland	173	Ireland	231
Switzerland	115	Switzerland	194
		The Netherlands	134
Largest Economies		Largest Economies	
UK	63	UK	74
France	38	France	57
Germany	29	Germany	45
US	19	US	32
Japan	3	Japan	23

Source: OECD (2014b, 19)

have inward FDI stocks as a percentage GDP of between 3 to 63 percent.

That the smallest industrialized states are relatively more penetrated by FDI than larger ones is borne out in measurements of states' TNIs. The analog of a corporation's TNI, a state's TNI measures the degree to which its economy is internationalized, based on the average of four indicators: FDI flows as a percentage of fixed capital formation; FDI inward stocks as a percentage of GDP; foreign affiliate value added as a percentage of GDP; and employment by foreign affiliates as a percentage of total employment. As with their global corporations, it is the smallest states that tend to have high TNIs. The highest are Belgium, Singapore, and Luxembourg with TNIs of 66, 65, and 65, respectively (UNCTAD 2008). Likewise, because they have very small domestic markets, the global corporations emanating from them also have very high TNIs. By comparison, Japan, the US, and Germany have TNIs of just 2, 7, and 11, respectively (UNCTAD 2008). Therefore, the TNI of corporations reflects the TNI of the states from which they hail.

Even so, and tellingly from the point of view of political power, all these economically powerful industrialized states have lower levels of inward FDI stocks as a percentage of GDP than outward FDI stocks. Regardless of their market size, economically powerful states' global corporations are relatively more investors in other states than other states' global corporations invest in them. No wonder that of the US$7.2 trillion in profits made by corporations globally, around two-thirds are captured by those from developed states, with North American and Western European corporations accounting for over half the global profit pool (26 and 25 percent, respectively), followed by China (15 percent). This share of profits on the basis of corporate nationality is projected to largely remain the case for the next ten years, with the falls in the share of profits flowing to North American and European corporations (1 and 4 percent falls, respectively) flowing to Chinese corporations (a 7 percent increase) as the role they and their state play in the global economy increases (Dobbs et al. 2015). The result is that the national shares of global corporations' profits reflect their nationalities, their ownership and control, and their patterns of investment.

Conclusion

The considerable amount of data presented in this chapter demonstrates that it is not so much a matter of opinion, or ideology, that the world's most transnational corporations are more national and regional than global. Their ownership and control, as well as investment, employment, and sales profiles, demonstrate this. If corporate power were becoming increasingly globally diffuse, so that it no longer made as much sense to talk of the nationality of global corporations as to see their power as exercised transnationally, then we should expect to see an increasing multitude of nationalities represented in the various lists of the largest global corporations. The FDI data should also reflect a move away from the handful of states and regions that have characterized stocks and flows in the past to encompass the entire global economy. This is not the case. There are no more than ten states that are the headquarters of the largest global corporations. These represent the existing economic centers of the world. The same geographical concentration is evident among key emerging market economies. It is between these states that they primarily invest, further entrenching power in the handful of states and the regions they dominate. The US particularly dominates the established industrialized states as both the headquarters of the world's major corporations and as the source of investment by them in other states and regions. China's corporations are emerging to challenge them, just as the Chinese state is rising to rival the US. To the extent that other economically weaker states are involved, such as those of Latin America, they are more destinations for corporate investment rather than sources of it.

The structural power of global corporations is therefore reflected in the structural power possessed by their home states and regions. It is in these national and regional contexts, and from them, that they exercise their power in all its "faces." In particular, the world's most transnational global corporations are least transnational in their employment. To the extent that their national identities are being eroded, this is largely driven by M&As with/by corporations from other major industrialized states. In this respect, just as European (particularly British) and US corporations tend to invest in each other's territories, so they tend to acquire or merge with each other. Relatedly, rather than being seen as increasingly transnational, they are more accurately increasingly bi-national and regional in their investment and material interests. Again, this is a reflection of the economic power of their home states: large economically powerful states tend to be less transnational, just as the corporations that hail from them are and vice versa. The data further suggest that the national and regional structural patterns of economic power produced are becoming more deeply embedded over time, rather than diminishing.

These observations lend support to a Marxist interpretation of globalization and the role of global corporations in facilitating it. Rather than an interconnected world of placeless markets, the data illustrate as per Wallerstein's World Systems Theory a divided world of core and periphery states, with corporations as the agents of global capitalist relations of production that concentrate wealth and power in the hands of the few states in which they are headquartered (e.g., see Wallerstein 1984, 2004). However, as suggested in the introduction to this chapter, it also indicates that a nationalist interpretation may apply given that rather than disembodied notions of market actors rivaling states, the reality is a world characterized by power in the hands of several hundred global corporations from a handful of states. If the underlying power interests between states endure, then surely they may find expression through their corporations' operations and investment patterns. Corporations are increasingly global, states by definition cannot be; however, they can work with and use their corporations as agents of what previously would have been regarded as colonization. The modern nation state may no longer overtly conquer others' lands and resources, but their corporations certainly do conquer other states' economies and industrial bases. If it is the case that global corporations remain based in a handful of states, that these are the most economically powerful ones, and that they remain interested in their power relations vis-à-vis other states, then it is important to recognize that these states have an interest in, and benefit from, their corporations succeeding beyond their borders.

Mann (2004) makes the point that it would be a mistake to imagine that globalization means great power rivalries are now irrelevant. If they persist and continue to underpin the international order, then the political power of global corporations and their home states could be viewed as two sides of the same coin. At the very least, there are limits to how much the relationship between corporations and states may be de-territorialized, and therefore speaking of the nationality of global corporations is not a contradiction in terms, but reflects the co-constitution of their identity and power. Contrary to Strange's (1996) declaration—that global economic interconnectedness means that what some states have lost others have not gained due to a global diffusion of economic power—it seems more accurate to say power between states is mediated by their global corporations. As they wax and wane, they structurally redistribute their home states' power on the international stage. How they do so is a question of their power relations with their home states, as well as those in which they invest. Of course, material interests drive these relations, but, as per the discussion in Chapter 2, global corporations' discursive power enhances the economic and territorially defined structural power they possess and the instrumental exercise of it. Given that the national and regional contexts from which global corporations operate remain important for understanding the sources of the power they wield, this raises the question of the norms and the institutions pertaining in these contexts that shape their motivations and strategic behavior. These are the subject of the following chapter.

4 NATIONAL INSTITUTIONAL EMBEDDEDNESS

Global corporations derive their political power and exercise it across multiple dimensions. As noted in Chapter 2, their power is expressed through their instrumental lobbying activities and connections with policy makers, as well as their structural underpinning of production and the economic wealth to which it gives rise, but their ability to shape discursively what is regarded as self-evident is their ultimate goal. This is because global corporations are most powerful when they establish their *right* to achieve their desired outcomes, to be in a position where they may claim their interests are synonymous with those of states and their citizens. To create such discursive legitimacy builds norms that endure by becoming institutionalized. There are many definitions of what institutions are, but they may basically be defined as sets of formal or informal rules followed by political actors because they become taken for granted. They are "sets of regularized practices with a rule-like quality in the sense that the actors expect the practices to be observed; and which, in some, but not all, cases are supported by formal sanctions" (Hall and Thelen 2009, 9). Institutions therefore underpin the construction of what are regarded as legitimate political systems.

If the discourse creates the norms which create the institutions that underpin political systems, then the question is: which political systems? As Chapter 3 demonstrated, global corporations are based in a small number of economically powerful states, and primarily invest and operate in and between these same states. It would be wrong to characterize relations between these states as akin to a closed system. Nevertheless, the data show corporations from them have tended to become global by investing in each other's territories, thereby further entrenching their geographical as well as market concentration. To the extent that this is not the case, the data also suggest economically powerful states' global corporations effectively "colonize" weaker states' markets and by implication their industrial bases, rather more than corporations from these states do the converse. Therefore, to a significant degree global corporations remain national and regional in their interests and orientations, even as they become more global in their operations. They still employ their instrumental power in their home states, but more importantly it is in *and from* them that they derive their structural power, and it is in and from their national institutional contexts that global corporations construct their discursive legitimacy.

This being the case, it is important to acknowledge that the states where global corporations are headquartered, and from which they invest in others, are institutionally constructed in different ways. The purpose of this chapter is to examine the institutional diversity of capitalist relations of production in the states from which global corporations hail, and where they have mostly invested: the US, EU, and East Asia. Relatedly, the role played by global corporations promoting convergence on a particular form of capitalism, versus the maintenance of capitalist institutional diversity between states, is considered—i.e., the role they play in politically transforming or embedding national institutions. In the first section, the institutional embedding of global corporations in the industrialized states where global corporations are primarily based is considered. It is not an oxymoron to speak of global corporations' nationalities because, as Jones (2006, 22) notes, and as demonstrated in Chapter 3, despite pronouncements of the stateless corporation operating in global markets, the reality is that a corporation's nationality is rarely ambiguous, and that "it usually has a major influence on corporate strategy and seems to be growing in political importance." As such, the comparative capitalism literature, especially Hall and Soskice's (2001a) firm-centered Varieties of Capitalism (VOC) approach, is used to illustrate why global corporations potentially perceive their interests and relations with other actors in differing ways depending on their nationalities.

The second section turns to the impact of globalization on the evolution of states' national capitalist systems. The VOC approach will be defended in the process, and it is important to state that this will be the case given that its relevance has been much attacked (e.g., see Hancké 2009 for a summary of the debates around it). Many scholars feel the approach is too blunt a comparative instrument in characterizing states as tending to be more liberal versus more coordinated. Others normatively stress the desirability of one form of capitalism versus another, or prefer to focus on the exploitative evils of all forms of capitalism. However, one of the most damning criticisms is that it is too static, and in failing to account for historical institutional evolution it ignores the tendency for globalization to produce convergence on a liberal to neoliberal form of capitalism. It seems out of date in a world characterized by global economic connectedness and all that this implies as stressed by the globalists, especially those of a strong liberal or Marxist persuasion. The pressure for convergence on a liberal market institutional basis for corporate-state relations is contrasted with data and empirical studies that lend support to arguments that national institutional diversity persists. In light of this, the case is made for why institutional variations endure because global corporations and their states together establish different "rules of the game ... that structure political, economic and social interaction" (North 1990, 97). They do this at the national level, but if one accepts that global corporations remain mutually entangled with states, then as they go regional and global they also potentially "export" their national institutional preferences along with their operations.

In the third section, the emergence of new global corporations from the BRICs is considered for the manner in which their relationship with their states potentially mirrors, as well as differs from, those already established.[1] In all cases, what is suggested is that non-market relations tend to dominate their strategies, and that the economic emergence of their home states is very clearly linked, indeed institutionally entangled, with their emergence on the world stage. As they are more explicitly controlled by their home states, they are also more explicitly servants of their home states' economic interests than is the case for the more established global corporations. China in particular is focused on in this context, given the growing predominance of its global corporations in the various lists of the world's largest companies. What is demonstrated is that in the case of China it is the state's *leadership*, as opposed to coordination, of its global corporations that is germane to understanding the political power they wield.

The conclusion reached is that there have been pressures for convergence on a liberal form of capitalism globally, and global corporations may be seen as agents of this political agenda. Even so, diversity persists in the institutional basis for the relationship that global corporations of different nationalities have with their home states. The evidence also suggests that as global corporations from the BRICs come to play a more dominant role in the global economy, they and their states are likely to converge on a more coordinated, rather than liberal, form of capitalism. Therefore, the future may be one in which states play a relatively more dominant role than market forces in coordinating economic activity, and in which global corporations are more clearly their emissaries acting in their home states' national interests.

Global Corporations' Institutional Embedding in Industrialized States

Globalization has been characterized as "what states make of it" (Clark 1999, 55). However, based on the discussion in the previous two chapters it is more accurate to say that globalization is what a handful of powerful states and their global corporations make of it. The relationship between them is important for understanding the political basis, and bases, from which they mutually derive their power. Therefore, the differing ways in which their entanglement becomes institutionalized over time are, and remain, important. In this regard, while the neoliberalizing tendencies of globalization have been stressed by those who focus on the homogeneity of the structural relations underpinning capitalism (e.g., Marxists), or the inescapable and desirable imperatives of it (e.g., liberals), others have focused on the manner in which the institutional interpretation and expression of capitalism varies between states. Despite a liberalizing agenda underpinning the ideology of globalization, and the increasingly liberal global trade and investment order it has produced, it does not follow that capitalism as practiced within national boundaries resembles a liberal, let alone neoliberal, "institutional monoculture" (Watson 2003, 227). A considerable literature therefore examines the distinct national institutional complementarities that have become embedded in the course of industrialized states' development, as a product of their different histories and policy choices.

For example, contemporary Japanese capitalism has its roots in the Meiji Restoration of the nineteenth century. The industrial conglomerates that this spawned, along with the drive for education and skills development, industrialization, and the competitive drive for market share, were then further re-interpreted through the lens of the country's post–World War II defeat. Similarly, the Prussian state's desire to unite Germany, the impact of Nazism, and the imperatives of postwar reconstruction helped to shape its variety of capitalism, including the cartelization of industry, the representation of unions on company boards, the role of banks in financing growth, and an incremental, inclusive, consensus approach to decision making. By comparison, the establishment of the stock market as the prime factor in a company's perceived worth was established in the US as early as the 1920s when the separation of management from ownership of major publicly listed corporations was entrenched (e.g., see Hollingsworth 1997; Dore et al. 1999). The distinct capitalisms these states developed as a result of differing historical developmental trajectories have become deeply institutionally embedded to endure over time.

While each state represents a distinct case, there are categories into which states may be placed for comparative analysis. Authors such as Esping-Andersen (1990, 18–19; see also Goodin et al. 1999) focus on varieties of welfare states—i.e., the different ways "state responsibility for securing some basic modicum of welfare for its citizens" is expressed. They identify three categories: liberal, corporatist, and social democratic. Liberal states provide social assistance on the basis of means testing, with modest transfers and social insurance programs that are largely designed to cater to those members of society on low incomes. Therefore, market relations predominate and are supported by the state. Corporatist states focus less on markets and market efficiency as a means of providing welfare, instead acting to uphold more traditional class relations underpinned by such institutions as organized religion and family, with rights assigned and underpinned by the state on the basis of class and social status. For social democracies, an agenda of equality and high social standards is stressed, with services and benefits guaranteed to all members of society by the state. The archetypical examples of states from each category are the Anglo Saxon states led by the US (liberal);[2] Western European states such as Austria, France, Germany, and Italy (corporatist); and Scandinavian countries (social democratic). This is an admittedly brief outline of the three welfare state types, but they have been used to consider the role of the state versus/underpinning/modifying the market and, by implication, the activities of corporations.

Other authors have focused on national business systems defined in terms of corporate governance, collaboration, and employment relations. These produce differing "systems of economic coordination and control" (Whitley 1999, 34), which are resistant to change. Even in the face of greater global economic interconnectedness, they endure to the point that Pauly and Reich (1997, 3; see also Doremus et al. 1999) find that "the institutional legacies of distinctive national histories continue significantly to shape the core operations of multinational firms." Similar groupings of states are evident as for the varieties of welfare states. For example, focusing on Europe, Schmidt (2002) identifies three "ideal" types of capitalism: market, managed, and state capitalism. Market capitalism, which may be thought of as liberal capitalism, corresponds to the market-driven relations underpinning the economies of the US and UK such that there is an "arm's length" relationship between the state and business. Less market-driven states such as Germany, the Netherlands, and Sweden exhibit more non-market managed relations. Rather than competition between firms, relations based on negotiation and consensus that produce coordination between the state and firms are stressed, and often enshrined by law. State capitalism as practiced by France and Italy involves a yet more interventionist state that goes beyond coordinating economic affairs to organizing them, including directing firms in what amounts to state control of the economy, albeit still in an overall capitalist setting. In the case of France, this has produced what is widely termed its *dirigiste* model of capitalism. Again, this is a brief explanation of the categories, and again the point is that there are nationally distinct institutional alternatives to the manner in which capitalism may be practiced.

However, firms are not central in these analyses of the states and categories to which they are seen as belonging. Out of the comparative capitalism literature, and in order to address this important difference in analytical focus, came Hall and Soskice's (2001a) VOC approach. Even its critics have hailed their *Varieties of Capitalism: The Institutional Foundations of Comparative Advantage* as the "emblematic citation" of comparative capitalism studies (Crouch 2005, 442), to the point of being "hegemonic" in the field of comparative political economy (Howell 2003, 103). Blyth (2003, 215) labels it "canonical." At the time it was published it represented a bold attempt to synthesize the key insights of the wealth of related literature, with the aim of achieving three key, interlocking goals: first, to locate firms centrally in the study of states' capitalism; second, to establish a framework for analysis that explicitly recognizes the persistence of diversity in global capitalism, rather than convergence on a single inevitable, or even "ideal," model; and third, to use this framework to "open up new research agendas on an unusually broad set of topics, ranging from issues of innovation, vocational training, and corporate strategy to those associated with legal systems, the development of social policy, and the stance nations take in international negotiations" (Hall and Soskice 2001b, 2). With these goals in mind, the VOC approach categorizes capitalist states as tending toward liberal market economies (LMEs) versus coordinated market economies (CMEs) to consider the relationship that corporations as the "crucial actors in a capitalist economy" have with the states in whose institutions they are embedded (Hall and Soskice 2001b, 6). In essence, LMEs favor economic coordination via market competition, whereas CMEs exhibit greater non-market cooperative relationships in coordinating economic activities, with the state playing a greater role in this. This is true in respect of industrial relations, corporate governance, vocational training and education, inter-firm relations, and the management of employees. I have argued previously (Mikler 2009, 2014) that one may also think of the differences in terms of corporations' roles in financial, product, and labor markets. Table 4.1 summarizes these, along with the management objectives and corporate state-relations resulting from them.

Financial Markets

Reliance on stock markets and the interests of shareholders is a (or rather *the*) major focus of LME-based corporations. This is why the US is often seen as both the exemplar of the LME category and of "stock market capitalism" (Dore 2000b). Its corporations, along with others from states such as the UK, Canada, and Australia, rely on equity finance to the extent that stock market capitalization is of a magnitude two to three times greater by comparison to CMEs such as Germany and Japan (Hall and Soskice 2001b, 18–19). In practice, the result is not just a focus on shareholder returns, the share price, and short-term profitability because of a normative preference for such indicators. It is because LME-based corporations' access to finance is dependent on shareholders' approval, with this contingent on assessments of publicly available financial data and financial returns in the form of dividends. Furthermore, shareholdings are volatile as they are often held by portfolio investors who seek the highest short-term returns, rather than stable institutional investors. Corporations must likewise adopt short-term, shareholder-focused strategies or risk being starved of investment capital (Vitols 2001). Failure to pay dividends reflecting their profitability can rapidly lead to negative sentiment which, at the extremes, may even lead to ownership changing hands if shareholders dump their stock. LME-based corporations are therefore "dependent on the whims and strategies of stockholders" (Hollingsworth 1997, 293).

In contrast, CME-based corporations' greater reliance on debt finance means they can embrace a longer-term perspective. Their major banks and other debt financers have a stake in company fortunes at a more strategic level. Being more "immune" to stock market fluctuations, they can focus on strategic goals other than short-term profit maximization. Unlike their LME-based counterparts, they may

Table 4.1: LMEs versus CMEs

	LMEs: US, UK, Australia, Canada, New Zealand, and Ireland	CMEs: Austria, Belgium, Denmark, Finland, Iceland, Germany, Japan, Norway, South Korea[a], Sweden, Switzerland, and the Netherlands
Financial markets	• Company finance, largely via equity finance • Focus on shareholder value and the share price • Short-term focus on profits	• Industrial finance, largely via debt finance • Focus on long-term company prosperity
Product markets	• Strong inter-company competition • Production and market strategies that seek to exploit easily transferred assets	• Production and market strategies that seek to exploit the advantages of nontransferable or specific assets • Cooperation in technology and standard-setting across companies
Labor markets	• Deregulated labor markets • General education	• Cooperative industrial relations • High levels of vocational and firm-specific training
Management Objectives	• Management concerned with hostile takeovers and market metrics	• Management concerned with responsibility to bankers, committed shareholders, peers, and juniors within the firm
Relationship with the state	• Arm's length • Lobbying, conflict, deregulation	• Cooperative/coordinated or state-guided • Consensus, negotiation, co-regulation

Sources: Hall and Soskice (2001a) and Jackson and Deeg (2008), also drawing on Dore (2000a and 2000b); Vitols (2001); Pauly and Reich (1997); Doremus et al. (1999); and Hampden-Turner and Trompenaars (1993)

[a] Although South Korea was not included in Hall and Soskice's (2001b) original typology, many authors consider it a CME (e.g., Hall and Gingerich 2009), and high levels of economic strategic coordination by the Korean state suggest it should be (e.g., see Kim 2013; Thurbon 2016).

strategically plan over a longer time frame with their stable and more committed investors on other goals like increased market share or technological innovation for environmental sustainability, which may bear fruit in the form of profits in the longer term. This is why CME-based corporations have been seen as embodying "stakeholder capitalism" rather than stockholder capitalism (e.g., see Dore 2000a; Jacoby 2005).

Product Markets

The differences in strategic time frame and focus produced by the differences in financial markets are mirrored in the functioning of product markets. Market imperatives motivate LME-based corporations more than those headquartered in CMEs. They tend to drive corporate strategies for the former, as opposed to reflecting them for the latter, because CME-based corporations have more latitude to create products for which there is no clear immediate demand in the short term, but for which there may be in the longer term (e.g., see Mikler 2009). This produces a preference for a less interventionist state in the former, as "free" markets are held to be of paramount importance because of the efficient outcomes they produce and the immediate material rewards that result. These are required to satisfy shareholders' needs for value in their investments. Markets (or, perhaps more accurately a market *mentality*, given that global corporations are more controllers and makers of their markets rather than competitors in them) play a dominant role in organizing economic activity and determining corporate production strategies in LMEs. Therefore, when the state does intervene in an LME setting, governments "should find it more feasible to implement market-incentive policies that do not put extensive demands on firms to form relational contracts with others, but rely on markets to coordinate their activities" (Hall and Soskice 2001b, 49). Putting it another way, there is discursive legitimacy on the part of corporations that claim the market should "work things out" rather than the state playing a strategic role in what the outcomes should be, and there is institutional support for the expression of this preference.

Markets play less of a strategic organizing role in CMEs. It is not that market forces are irrelevant, but they are not the driving force they are accepted to be in LMEs. Instead, communitarian obligations to the state and society, and higher levels of trust and coordination between firms rather than competition, are more the norm. There tend to be institutional arrangements, both informal and formal in nature, that facilitate cooperation rather than competition. In addition to market success, there is the notion of firms possessing a social contract with society, of them naturally playing a public as well as a private role. The difference is between the firm serving society in CMEs, versus and the firm serving itself in LMEs with this seen as implicitly synonymous with the good of society. By way of illustration, Wilks (1990, 138) notes in the case of Germany that government support for industry's interests is reflected in private entrepreneurs seeing themselves as embodying principles of "good citizenship," with public obligations as important as "the private concerns of selfish individuals." Thus, German private enterprise sees itself as serving societal interests as well as amassing private wealth. In the case of Japan, the authority of the state is reflected in a broader desire to act for the greater good on the part of business. The result is that "the fear of letting down the side, of breaking with consensus, of not meeting expected standards provides the main psychological drive for generating what must be the most impressive political and social power in Asia" (Pye and Pye 1985, quoted in Wilks 1990, 141).

Labor Markets

Given their shareholder/market focus, LME-based corporations tend to be best characterized by their status as legal entities, places where one works for the moment, where hiring and firing workers occurs in response to changed market (i.e., profitability) conditions, and where management has the power to do this and is expected to do so. There is also a large gap between managers and workers' rewards that reflects the power dynamics of top management and the board exerting control over the firm. The relations this produces between management and employees tend to be adversarial, given that shorter job tenures and the casualization of the workforce are the kinds of outcomes produced as corporations pressure the state for labor market deregulation in embracing economic gains and minimizing losses. By comparison, management-labor cooperation and collaboration are more the norm for CME-based corporations from Germany and Japan. As Dore (2000b, 106) puts it, "They remain economies in which the stock market plays a much less central role, and the state a larger one; in which the financial sector is less dominant; and manufacturing industry correspondingly more important; in which engineers tend to have the edge over accountants; and the doctrine of the supremacy of shareholder value is still a much weaker element in determining company goals."

In the case of Germany, this leads to a "structural bias towards consensus decision making" (Hall and Soskice 2001b, 24) that reflects a greater stakeholder basis for capitalist relations of production more generally. Long-term, cooperative product development and productivity growth are emphasized, to the extent that cooperation and consensus building are legislated (Dore 2000a, 182). The German Codetermination Act of 1976 mandates that all companies of more than 2,000 employees must have supervisory boards with employee as well as shareholder representation on them. The result is that 48 percent of the seats on the supervisory boards of the 100 largest German industrial corporations are held by union or employee representatives (Pauly and Reich 1997, 12). All companies with more than five members must also have a Works Council through which managers are reminded on a daily basis about group morale and opinion on productivity and specific issues in the workplace.

For German corporations "it is not so much convention as law ... which governs the owner/manager/worker relationship" (Streeck 1997; see also Fioretos 2001), but for Japanese corporations it is more a matter of culture. There is still almost no external market for executives in Japan, or at least it is a very small one and is largely the preserve of foreign firms operating there. The norm is "internal labor markets characterized by long-term/lifelong employment" (Walter and Zhang 2012b, 17) so that Japanese CEOs tend to be appointed from within their firms. In contrast to the US LME model where firms hire and fire employees in the face of economic pressures that threaten the share price, at least in the sense of who determines its destiny nobody really owns a Japanese firm but the firm itself. By way of illustration, Dore (1997, 20) notes that a US company chairman is likely to address a meeting of shareholders by talking about "your firm," whereas a Japanese company chairman will talk about "our firm." Traditionally, workers and management share a relationship, which he sees as akin to that of "a soldier's sense of regimental loyalty," with a firm's top management closer to the status of "elders" than "agents of shareholder principals" (Dore 2000b, 107). In economic downturns, the "sense of responsibility for managing difficult processes of restructuring within tight traditional constraints is palpable" (Pauly and Reich 1997, 11; see also Dore 2000a, 24–26), with the shedding of labor a last rather than first resort.

Management Objectives

Firms' different perspectives on the role of the state and markets produces implications for key management objectives. In LMEs, corporate leaders focus on making profits and delivering these to shareholders via dividends in the short term. In CMEs, they have greater concern for the long-term prosperity of the firm, and their reputation within it. It would of course be wrong to caricature the leaders of LME-based firms as being solely driven by profit and shareholder value maximization, yet it has been observed that it is their key motivator to the extent that it is their "dominant touchstone objective" (Dore 2000b, 103), to the point that the share price has become "an obsession" (Jacoby 2005, 2). And the differing motivations produced by German and Japanese capitalism in particular, by way of contrast to that of the US, have been borne out in many studies. For example, in their survey of 15,000 managers from European, American, and Asian companies, Hampden-Turner and Trompenaars (1993, 32) found that 74 percent of US managers saw a company as a system designed to perform functions and tasks efficiently, versus 41 and 29 percent of German and Japanese managers. Similarly, while 40 percent of US managers saw the prime goal of a company as making profits, only 24 and 8 percent of German and Japanese managers agreed with this. Instead, they stressed the wellbeing of a wide range of stakeholders whose needs and concerns must be attended to for corporate success in the longer term.

The crucial inference that may be drawn from this for management objectives is that even as LME-based corporations profess concern for employees, customers, suppliers, the environmental impact of their firm's activities, and in general CSR (on which more is said in Chapter 5), it is less likely this will be at the expense of profitability and their companies' share prices. By contrast, the quality of a corporation's activity is emphasized more in CME-based corporations. Profits are the *means* of generating further activity rather than an end in themselves. CME-based managers can be focused on making an excellent product via a customer/stakeholder focus, and enduring over the longer term, rather than primarily achieving short-term profits to satisfy shareholders. The difference is between a stakeholder focus to do with more intangible notions such as service, quality, and timeliness, versus a market focus to do with profits and margins. Putting it simply, the divide is between value in production (CMEs) versus value in the market (LMEs).

Relationship with the State

As avowed supporters of the LME model, Micklethwait and Wooldridge (2003, 182) claim that "drawing up long lists of when companies have acted responsibly (and when they have not) risks missing the bigger point," which they see as being that "we are all richer as a result." In other words, the market and its rewards, mediated by corporations that are "free" from state-imposed social responsibilities, or at least given a high degree of freedom to determine what these are, produce the best results for society. This is why Hampden-Turner and Trompenaars (1993, 213) observe that US managers tend to believe that "if they are profitable, then everything else must be all right," whereas "for Germans, value must be deeply imbedded in products of solidity and worth [because] they do not like it when money and its enjoyment becomes separated from worthwhile artifacts."

More generally, a picture emerges of what politically motivates LME- versus CME-based corporations. In LMEs, the separation of the state from business, with a relationship between the two that is more adversarial than cooperative, reflects a belief in free markets with state intervention only in cases of market failure, and then more to regulate rather than create or shape markets. Markets are seen as natural coordinators of economic activity, and this translates into a belief that corporate freedoms in markets should be the default position rather than state control, guidance, or direction. Short-term financial results are the aim, given a focus on more immediate market rewards, with the imperative of paying dividends to shareholders on the basis of the resulting profits and maintaining the share price. By contrast, CMEs are characterized by closer state-business relations for coordinating economic activity. Greater prominence is given to relational rather than competitive factors in product, financial, and labor markets. The result is a longer-term perspective, but also a more coordinated, consensus-driven relationship with the state based on ongoing negotiation, rather than an arm's length relationship characterized by lobbying and conflict with the aim of market deregulation.

Globalization and the Evolution of National Capitalist Systems

The above discussion is of course more by way of a conceptual map than a congruent reputation of reality. Even so, it illustrates the point that what is regarded as legitimately the focus and aim of corporations can vary according to their nationality. This is because the state of affairs which becomes socially taken for granted, and is discursively explained and re-explained as normatively "right" to the point that it becomes institutionalized to endure over time, varies. More technically, it is not just that there is a logic of consequentialism (the outcomes of taking certain courses of action) that drives actors on the basis of material interests. It is also that ideas and social behavior (i.e., norms) based on a logic of appropriateness underpin beliefs that there are appropriate ways to act not necessarily contingent on the outcome of such behavior (March and Olsen 1989, 1998). Therefore, institutional preferences can endure even when they no longer serve a particular purpose, nor necessarily achieve certain outcomes, but because they become taken for granted. Although it may be possible to generalize that all corporations, global or otherwise, desire profits, increased market share and other indicators of financial performance, nevertheless what is regarded as the appropriate manner to achieve these ends can vary. The question is the extent to which they endure, and in regard to the VOC approach this has bearing on the salience of an analytical focus on states in an era of globalization characterized by corporations less territorially defined in their operations.

Institutional Continuity

Hall and Soskice (2001b, 2 and 6) desired "to bring firms back into the center of the analysis of comparative capitalism," in recognition that they are "the crucial actors in a capitalist economy." Doing so was seen as long overdue by authors such as Blyth (2002b), Coates (2002), and Marzinotto (2002).[3] However, what is striking about so much of the discussion in, and criticism surrounding, their emblematic approach is that the state remains inevitably central to their analytical framework. The VOC approach categorizes states as a way of analyzing firms, on the basis that "in any national economy, firms will gravitate towards the mode of coordination for which there is institutional support" (Hall and Soskice 2001b, 8–9). If corporations are initially creations of, and embedded in, their home states' institutions, it logically follows that as they become more global in their interests and operations they become disembedded. This should undermine the coherence of the VOC approach's categories, and indeed the whole rationale for a comparative national focus. Furthermore, the market imperatives of a global economy driven by market actors responding to market forces that are no longer territorially bound should produce convergence on the LME model, hence the debates about the desirability of supposedly inevitable neoliberal globalization as a simulacrum of this model.

However, because they are more makers of market forces rather than responders to them, and more nationally or regionally than globally focused, it is not obvious that corporations should intrinsically prefer one set of national institutional arrangements over another. If the VOC approach "take[s] the nation state seriously as a locus of economic regulation" (Howell 2003, 110), it follows that so too must the global corporations that are based in them, and invest and operate from them. This being the case, there is evidence that national institutions, once embedded, tend to endure despite global interconnectedness. There is no particular reason why they should not, because neither liberal nor non-liberal capitalist states appear to suffer adverse material economic or social outcomes, and nor do their corporations. Quite the contrary, according to Goodin et al. (1999, 260) who conclude on the basis of their analysis that "far from it being a matter of 'horses for courses,'" the social democratic welfare regime is "the best of all possible worlds" in terms of both economic and social outcomes. But whatever one's normative preferences, both the LME and CME categories, as well as options on the spectrum between them, should remain stable and viable alternatives for economic success, and there is no reason why one or the other should necessarily predominate *unless there is conscious political action to make this so*—e.g., Washington Consensus–style policies imposed on economically weak EU member states as a condition of financial assistance since the GFC, or WTO agreements that force nonliberal capitalist states to dismantle national industry protection.

The role played by global corporations in this regard depends on whether or not they seek to wield their power to sustain the economic model in which they were originally institutionally embedded. It stands to reason that they should be motivated to do so. Over time "firms will gravitate towards the mode of coordination for which there is institutional support" (Hall and Soskice 2001b, 8–9), and having gravitated will be most suited to operating in a manner commensurate with their national institutions. If they are accustomed to market freedoms and an arm's length relationship with the state that characterizes the LME model, they will seek to maintain it and bring pressure to bear on other states to adopt it as they go global. Corporations accustomed to the support and greater state coordination that characterizes the non-market relations of the CME model will likewise seek opportunities for similar relations wherever they operate (e.g., see Cartwright 2011; Geppert and Dörrenbächer 2011). Seen in this light, the preponderance of US-based firms among lists of the world's largest global corporations, and their historical as well as increasing dominance of international trade and investment flows, is one reason why neoliberalism is seen as "the model" for global capitalism. It might also be argued that LME-based corporations are more likely to attempt to impose their form of capitalism globally as "best practice" given that they face pressure from their shareholders to deliver value wherever they operate. By comparison, those from CMEs may be more inclined to share their decision making with a range of other stakeholders including the governments of states in which they operate. Being accustomed to a more relational form of capitalism with their home states, theirs by definition is not a global but an inter- and intra-national model.

In theory, global corporations possess the ability and flexibility to absorb and gain new knowledge in any national context in which they operate (e.g., Kogut 2005; echoing Levitt 1983). They can change and adapt according to their circumstances to "translate the relationship of globalization and regionalization into an organizational challenge" (Heidenreich 2012, 557). However, if the reality is that global corporations "are 'produced' through an intricate process of embedding in which the cognitive, cultural, social, political and economic characteristics of the national home base play a dominant part" (Dicken 2010, 122), then in addition to being accustomed to a certain way of operating there are substantial costs in shifting to alternative organizational forms, or adopting multiple forms for coordinating their activities as they operate in multiple jurisdictions. Because they are "produced" by their home states' VOC, where possible they choose not to do so (Whitley 2009). Critics of globalization may find Wolf's (2004, 191) statement, that "multinational corporations would not dare operate plants in very different ways in different countries," challenging, to say the least, because there is surely no need to provide the abundant evidence that they use their global supply chains to offshore lower-paid manufacturing and "dirtier" operations to developing states. Yet, in institutional terms, the statement rings true because, in addition to being global, corporations remain very much nationally and regionally embedded, especially at their management levels. If "the national embeddedness of companies contributes to the reduction of uncertainties and to the solution of organizational coordination problems," then there is little incentive for global corporations to spend time and resources to "fix" what they may not regard as "broken" (Heidenreich 2012, 567).

Despite having global strategies, corporations therefore display a range of national and regional identities, rather than a singular global identity. Studies such as Kahancová (2007) demonstrate the existence of corporate organizational inertia, as routines that have supported growth and legitimacy in global corporations' home states tend to be retained where possible when they operate in others. Rather than some disembodied, transnational form of capitalism being spread by corporations, because they are adapted to particular and differentiated national business systems they may be seen as effectively "exporting" these to other states, particularly those states with highly internationalized economies. Indeed, their ability to do so may be critical to sustaining competitiveness in institutional contexts with which they are initially unfamiliar (e.g., see Kelly and Amburgey 1991; Miller and Chen 1994; Xia et al. 2009). It is not just that they potentially colonize other states' markets, as suggested in Chapter 3, but that they also seek to colonize other states' institutions. This means that the states in which they operate find themselves having to adjust to the practices of global corporations more than these corporations feel the necessity to adapt to their new national circumstances. The result is that states with economies highly penetrated by corporations of other nationalities are likely to find themselves pressured to conform to modes of behavior which these corporations are familiar with "at home." Therefore, while it may be claimed that because of globalization national variations must break down, it is equally possible to argue that globalization has permitted an institutional battle on the global stage that once took place within national borders, with global corporations as its main protagonists.

Institutional Change

This brings us back again to the entanglement of states and their global corporations. If a handful of states and their corporations respond *together* to the challenges they face, then the different ways in which they are institutionally enabled or constrained in their responses matters for understanding their power relations. States and their corporations are not blank canvases on which policy choices for addressing economic challenges are drawn. Instead, these choices are substantially institutionally determined. It may be the case that in the process of their formation, institutional preferences may be "in" actors who seek to create these in their national polities. But over time, actors find themselves "in" their institutions. It may seem tautological to speak of an institutional approach to institutional change, which is effectively the argument of Mahoney and Thelen (2010; see also Olsen 2009), yet institutional change is path dependent not because a certain set of institutions is necessarily inevitable or "better" (though it may be so, depending on the normative preferences of whoever weighs up the different systems) but because these institutions bound and shape change once in place. Rather than being easily adopted or discarded "institutional innovations ... follow well-worn paths rather than branching out in entirely different directions" (Weiss 1998, 24; see also Berger 1996; Boyer 1996; Hall 1999).

Path-dependent change along established institutional trajectories is more likely, and indeed easier, than radical shifts to alternative modes of capitalist relations. A key reason for this is that economies which are more liberal or coordinated in one sense tend to be more so in others, with the institutional complementarities established mutually reinforcing (e.g., see Amable 2000). This is the rationale for why states can be considered not just as discrete cases, but as wholly formed LME versus CME categories. Because "one set of institutions is said to be complementary to another when its presence raises the returns available from another," their mutual reinforcement means "efforts to reform one sphere of the political economy may yield negative economic results if unaccompanied by parallel reforms in other spheres" (Hall and Gingerich 2009, 450–451). It also implies that switching from one complementary set of institutions to another is not easily achieved. Such change requires economy-wide policy reforms, and entails the redistribution of material rewards and the reorientation of political advantages that produce them (e.g., see Weiss 2003). As they are not neutral mechanisms for coordinating economic activity, those groups benefitting from them will resist change. Therefore, it is also the case that "institutions are complementary when their joint presence favors the protection of the interests that define the groups" (Amable and Palombarini 2009, 34), and, being so, those groups will seek to retain the institutional complementarities.

Even so, because they are the product of history, norms and institutions can and do change. As Dore et al. (1999) note, it would be naive to believe that a certain state will possess the same institutional configuration forever. To do so risks institutional determinism by which it may seem that "an alternative exists only if one is prepared to move to a different country" (Howell 2003, n. 14; see also Coates 2002; Hay 2005). While "self-reinforcing institutional 'complimentarities' [sic]" (Blyth 2002b, 238) underpin institutional inertia, there are dangers in taking an approach that effectively "flattens history" and ignores "the moments of crisis and conflict that are a central part of comparative political economy" (Howell 2003, 112). Equally, it is simplistic to proclaim one institutional form as inevitable because of neoliberal globalization. Yet this is what has been claimed by those who see the world as having gone through a "second Great Transformation of the state" leading to the "permanent dismantling of collective capacity to resist liberalisation or bind it into and reconcile it with a nonliberal institutional context" (Streeck 2001, 38; echoed in Blyth 2002a).

Definitive evidence for institutional change/convergence versus continuity/diversity is difficult to find, because it does not just depend on what may be observed quantitatively, but on the nature of the relationship between the state and corporations—i.e., what is normatively constructed as legitimate. However, several studies have confirmed that the institutional complementarities of LMEs versus CMEs are mutually self-reinforcing. These include that of Hall and Gingerich (2009), who demonstrate that while there has been a global tendency to liberalization since the 1980s as predicted by those stressing liberal convergence, the degree of liberalization varies to the extent that it is more rapid in LMEs than in CMEs, thereby producing greater divergence between the states in each category. A "slide" toward more liberal capitalism is evident, but the institutional gap between states in each category has widened, suggesting that it is politically easier for LMEs to become more liberal than it is for CMEs, and that the institutional complementarities that have served states and interest groups within them well in the past tend to be reinforced in the face of international challenges rather than abandoned. The result is "a politics of institutional stability" rather than flux (Hall and Thelen 2009, 12).

A range of studies focusing on Germany and Japan specifically has likewise shown that their CME capitalisms have been resistant to the pressures for institutional change said to be produced by globalization (e.g., Iversen and Pontusson 2000; Hall and Soskice 2003; Hall 2007; Aoki et al. 2007; Streeck 2009). A decade after the end of the Cold War, Vogel (2001) declared the result was that non-liberal capitalist states were "stalled on the road to the liberal market model" while in essence the LMEs had their foot on the liberal accelerator. Later, in the immediate aftermath of the GFC it was suggested that the LME model of capitalism that characterizes states like the US and the UK might similarly be dismantled in favor of more CME-like forms (e.g., see Kaletsky 2010). Yet despite the severity of the impact of the GFC and its seemingly chronically ongoing nature, Kang and Moon (2012, 96) find that in these states "shareholder-value-driven corporate governance has not been sufficiently discredited to warrant a path-shifting change."

Straightforward conclusions as to the liberalizing preferences, let alone political force, of global corporations and their home states are also problematic. In an attempt to reach some, Table 4.2 presents OECD indices on the extent to which the major LMEs and

Table 4.2: State Intervention/Control in Corporate Affairs in Industrialized States

	1998	2003	2008	2013
Strictness of Employment Protection Legislation: Individual and Collective Dismissals[a]				
LMEs				
US	0.26	0.26	0.26	0.26
UK	1.10	1.26	1.26	1.10
Average all LMEs	1.06	1.14	1.07	1.12
CMEs				
Germany	2.68	2.68	2.68	2.68
Japan	1.70	1.70	1.37	1.37
Average all CMEs	2.30	2.25	2.18	2.18
Product Market Regulation[b]				
LMEs				
US	1.50	1.30	1.11	–
UK	1.32	1.10	1.21	1.08
Average all LMEs	1.63	1.37	1.32	1.30
CMEs				
Germany	2.23	1.80	1.41	1.29
Japan	2.11	1.37	1.43	1.41
Average all CMEs	2.17	1.66	1.47	1.40
State Control of Business Enterprises[c]				
LMEs				
US	1.62	1.43	1.50	–
UK	1.68	1.15	1.63	1.57
Average all LMEs	1.98	1.72	1.84	1.93
CMEs				
Germany	2.57	2.15	1.99	1.86
Japan	1.87	1.66	1.90	1.85
Average all CMEs	2.67	2.14	2.10	2.05
Barriers to Entrepreneurship[c]				
LMEs				
US	1.97	1.64	1.23	–
UK	1.96	1.82	1.74	1.49
Average all LMEs	2.02	1.72	1.51	1.54
CMEs				
Germany	2.95	2.41	1.90	1.66
Japan	3.22	1.69	1.65	1.67
Average all CMEs	2.68	2.08	1.76	1.61

Table 4.2: *Continued*

	1998	2003	2008	2013
Barriers to Trade and Investment[c]				
LMEs				
US	0.91	0.85	0.60	–
UK	0.32	0.32	0.25	0.20
Average all LMEs	0.88	0.69	0.59	0.44
CMEs				
Germany	1.16	0.84	0.34	0.36
Japan	1.24	0.75	0.74	0.71
Average all CMEs	0.91	0.65	0.52	0.49

Sources: OECD (2016h), OECD (2016i)

[a] This index presents "indicators of the strictness of regulation on dismissals and the use of temporary contracts." Higher scores denote stricter protection (OECD 2016h).
[b] These are "a comprehensive and internationally-comparable set of indicators that measure the degree to which policies promote or inhibit competition in areas of the product market where competition is viable. They measure the economy-wide regulatory and market environments in OECD countries in (or around) 1998, 2003, 2008 and 2013, and in another set of non-OECD countries in 2013" (OECD 2016i). Higher scores denote higher levels of regulation.
[c] A subset of the product market regulation index.

CMEs regulate corporate affairs in respect of employment protection and product market regulation, two measures of the extent to which the state versus the market coordinates economic activity. Little convergence in respect of employment protection is evident, so that despite a slight trend to deregulating employment protection in the CMEs, labor markets remain far more coordinated in them than in LMEs. However, the UK increased its employment protection over 2003 and 2008, while LMEs on average have higher levels of employment protection than they did in the late 1990s. For product market regulation there are clearer signs of convergence between CMEs and LMEs, and for a tendency of the former to liberalize over time. In fact, the data suggest that, contrary to studies indicating LMEs can liberalize more easily and rapidly than CMEs, as Koske et al. (2015, 32) note, "countries with the strictest regulations have implemented the biggest reforms." Yet, again there are dangers in drawing simple conclusions, because while liberalization of product market regulation is evident for CMEs across the board, and particularly in respect of barriers to entrepreneurship, convergence has also been produced by LMEs *increasing* their control of business enterprises since 2003 (i.e., re-regulating business), as well as barriers to entrepreneurship since 2008.[4] The clearest case of liberalization is in respect of the removal of barriers to trade and investment, but this is more likely to be due to international agreements—whether at the bilateral, regional, or global level—than political pressures or policy choices taken by states individually. Overall, what can be concluded is that there is evidence that the CME model is under attack, but not completely and not universally. And there is even evidence of LMEs re-regulating and potentially evolving toward the CME model in some respects.

Emerging Market Economies

If neither the established industrialized states nor the corporations from them must converge on the LME model, this seems even more the case for the newly emerging market economies of the BRICs. Prior to the rise of China and the other emerging market economies of the BRICs, the states that "mattered" most were the US and those comprised by the EU. As such, a global economy centered around the transatlantic with an emerging East Asia produced the geographically triadic relations referred to in much of the literature (e.g., see Hamilton and Quinlan 2005; Andersen et al. 2008). It also means that states like China are "white space(s) on the map of the VOC debate" because the VOC approach "was developed exclusively in the context of 'advanced capitalist nations'" (Peck and Zhang 2013, 2–3). The BRICs vary institutionally, as states within the LME and CME categories do, but nevertheless they share similarities in their corporate-state relations. As Goldstein (2013a, 2007) notes, in the process of their development the BRICs' global corporations were either state-owned or -controlled. In the cases of China and Russia, in the early 1990s state ownership was the case for all production, while 44 percent of the turnover of Brazil's largest firms was accounted for by the state (Siffert and Souza e Silva 1999). If it was not the state that was in control, then the main private shareholders for Indian and Brazilian corporations were often families. Their management was comprised of "first-generation self-made moguls" (Goldstein 2013b, 57) with engineering degrees rather than business qualifications, who had close links with the state as well as their families. Relatedly, there was a very low degree of internationalization in their operations, so that they were almost exclusively national before they became global corporations. This is why in 1990 *none* of them appeared in UNCTAD's rankings of the most transnational corporations.

The results can be seen in the structures and relations exhibited by the BRICs' corporations today. National firms dominate the lists of their major corporations, still often family if not government controlled. In the case of China, nearly all its new global corporations remain state-owned enterprises. For private Chinese global corporations such as Haier, Huawei, and Lenovo, "Managers and workers own the company's shares under the supervision of the local government" (McGregor 2010, 202). In fact, Liu and Sun (2005, 48) find that "the state is in the ultimate and absolute control of 81.6 percent of all publicly quoted companies via two control patterns: (1) government direct control of 9 percent of the quoted companies, and (2) government indirect control of 72.6 percent of the listed companies via stock pyramids." As such, corporate ownership remains highly concentrated, with the state being the largest shareholder in the country's major listed corporations. Less than 1 percent of A-listed companies on the Chinese stock market are widely held (Bianco 2010; Amit et al. 2010). As a result, Breslin (2012, 32; see also Beeson 2009) finds that there is "a symbiotic relationship (at the very least) between state elites and many of the economic elites; they have effectively co-opted each other into an alliance that, for the time being, mutually reinforces each other's power and influence (not to mention personal fortunes)." For this reason, Walter and Zhang (2012b) label the Chinese variety of capitalism as "state-led." In a similar vein, Nölke (2010a, 2012) labels China a "state-permeated market economy."

This is not to say that China's liberalization of its markets is an unimportant feature of its emergence as a growing global economic power, but clearly the relationship the state has with its corporations is important for understanding both their and their state's economic and political emergence. The Chinese case is emblematic of the state-led capitalism said to be underpinning the global corporations emerging from the BRICs (Anon 2012), similar to the manner in which states like the US and UK are seen as the archetypal LMEs, and Germany and Japan the archetypal CMEs. Although simplistically applying such categories risks abstracting too much from the reality of variance between states, as well as sub-national differences at the provincial and city levels within them, even so it is possible to say that "the close relationship between private Chinese multinationals and the Chinese state is a typical example of the emergence of state-permeated capitalism in large emerging economies such as Brazil, China or India" (Nölke 2014, 89). A variety of formal and informal cooperative relationships between state authorities and corporations means the BRICs embody versions of state capitalism that are neither based on the mercantilist protectionism of the nineteenth century, nor the economic nationalism of the post–World War II East Asian developmental states, but which embrace a global orientation with control of the corporations that are the mechanisms for it. The exact form of capitalism these states and their new global corporations will come to resemble is hard to predict because their institutions are in the process of formation and the existing typologies are not easily applied. What can be said is that there are clear signs the LME model is not the one they have adopted at present.

This has implications not just for China but for the global economy. As Beeson (2009; see also Halper 2010; Peck and Zhang 2013) notes, China's state-led capitalism means that the neoliberal orthodoxy of the Washington Consensus is being replaced with a more pragmatic "Beijing Consensus" that accepts greater state control. For the other BRICs, the view that they must tend toward the LME category because "the relationships of trust that are so central to the CME way of organizing an economy are hard to build and easy to destroy" (Goodin 2003, 211) is similarly under attack. While it follows that the trust necessary for coordination may take centuries to develop, but the economic dividends paid by the competitive self-interest underpinning the LME model can pay dividends now, China's rise clearly demonstrates that it is not just the economic dividends from the competitive self-interest underpinning liberal economic relations that are driving its economic success. It, and other states with the necessary institutional capacity to coordinate and drive economic development, seems likely to continue doing so. There are reasons to think that their institutions will evolve path-dependently, as has been the case for industrialized states. Table 4.3 presents the same OECD employment protection and product market regulation indices for the BRICs as for the established industrialized states shown in Table 4.2. It shows that their employment protection is higher than that for the established CMEs and not converging on the LME level. Although for product market regulation and the elements that comprise it there is evidence of liberalization, it is very gradual and again from a much higher level of regulation than either the established CMEs or LMEs. This is even the case for barriers to trade and investment. In some cases state intervention and control have increased, such as for India in respect of state control of business enterprises, and Brazil for barriers to entrepreneurship and barriers to trade and investment. This stands to reason if one accepts that established global corporations have what amounts to either an oligopolistic or monopolistic hold on their industries, and that therefore states have a role to play in facilitating the emergence of their newer, rival global corporations to level the playing field if not tip it in their favor.

Table 4.3: State Intervention/Control in Corporate Affairs in the BRICs versus Industrialized States

	2008[a]	2013
Strictness of Employment Protection Legislation: Individual and Collective Dismissals[a]		
Brazil	1.43	1.53
Russia	3.06	3.06
India	3.29	3.29
China	3.26	3.26
Average BRICs	2.76	2.78
Average all LMEs[b]	1.07	1.12
Average all CMEs[b]	2.18	2.18
Product Market Regulation		
Brazil	2.54	2.54
Russia	2.69	2.22
India	3.40	3.10
China	3.17	2.86
Average BRICs	2.95	2.68
Average all LMEs[b]	1.32	1.30
Average all CMEs[b]	1.47	1.40
State Control of Business Enterprises		
Brazil	2.65	2.51
Russia	3.84	3.41
India	3.73	4.02
China	4.08	3.57
Average BRICs	3.58	3.38
Average all LMEs[b]	1.84	1.93
Average all CMEs[b]	2.10	2.05
Barriers to Entrepreneurship		
Brazil	2.80	2.88
Russia	2.28	1.54
India	4.12	3.61
China	3.16	3.13
Average BRICs	3.09	2.79
Average all LMEs[b]	1.51	1.54
Average all CMEs[b]	1.76	1.61
Barriers to Trade and Investment		
Brazil	2.17	2.24
Russia	1.94	1.71
India	2.35	1.67
China	2.27	1.89

Continued

Table 4.3: *Continued*

	2008[a]	2013
Average BRICs	2.18	1.87
Average all LMEs[b]	0.59	0.44
Average all CMEs[b]	0.52	0.49

Sources: OECD (2016h), OECD (2016i)
[a] Data not available for BRICs prior to 2008.
[b] From Table 4.2.

Ozawa (2014, 36) suggests in respect of China that "the role of government is meant to be enduring, pervasive, and motivated primarily for political purposes." China's state-led capitalism means that management motivations are driven less by market and shareholder imperatives, and much more by the goals of the state and the national interest. Goldstein (2013a, 167) goes so far as to say that "in the west ... many consider Chinese corporate strategies as part of a wider plot to control the world economy." Whether or not this is the aim, though from a national interest point of view there is every reason why a state with the potential for this should embrace the opportunity, the increasing political power of China expressed through the rise of its global corporations suggests that in future scholars could be debating the potential for, and extent of, convergence on the Chinese state capitalism model. Already, its variety of capitalism is reflected in similarities to be found in the other BRICs, and as the center of the world economy shifts more to the East Asian sphere it is worth noting that *none* of the emerging and industrialized states of this region is classifiable as an LME (Walter and Zhang 2012b). Fligstein and Zhang (2011) predict that if China does not retain its state-led version of capitalism, it is most likely to tend toward the CME category over time. They even envisage the potential embedding of institutions similar to the French *dirigiste* model. This may seem odd at first glance, yet others such as Tiberghien (2007) have previously noted that other East Asian states like South Korea share many institutional similarities with France for the manner in which the state and state elites direct, as well as coordinate, economic activity. What will ultimately eventuate is hard to predict, but if China's institutional evolution is emblematic of that of the other BRICs, their capitalism is at least as likely to remain characterized by close and overtly mutually supportive corporate-state relations, and non-market forms of economic coordination in general, as it is to tend toward liberalization.

Conclusion

It is easy to reach the conclusion that because they can operate globally, global corporations are global political actors. But there are limitations to viewing global corporations purely through a global capitalism lens. Just as it is not inevitable that neoliberalism must be the default position for the global economy, but is more accurately something of an ideological crusade, equally it is not obvious that neoliberalism must be embraced by all states. To the extent that it is, this requires purposive political actors, including global corporations, to construct such an outcome. Harrod (2006, 34) stresses that "the international or global power of the corporation is more a function of the power it has achieved within powerful headquarter states." Therefore, "to focus on the study of the global activities of the corporation means to study the point of entry rather than the source of its power and activity." Capitalism is global and global corporations are the actors that help make it so, but the sources of their power are the home bases from which they wield it.

In painting relatively broad brushstrokes of national institutional variations in capitalism there is the risk of "a kind of rough, tough macho-theory that concentrates on the big picture and ignores detail" in simplistically applying categories such as those of LME, CME, or "state-led" capitalism (Crouch 2005, 452; see also Amable 2003; Molina and Rhodes 2007). Nonetheless such categories are useful. As Pontusson (2005, 17) puts it, "We should not think of typologies as being right or wrong. Rather, we should think of them as heuristic devices—ways of organizing information—that may be more or less useful." They give us a way of understanding the political basis for interests and power that global corporations wield, or at least a starting point for so doing. While management autonomy to act on the basis of market demands and shareholder preferences is preferred in LMEs (hence the focus on competition, short-term financial returns, etc.), in CMEs there is a greater focus on cooperative relationships with stakeholders more broadly defined. The role of the state in LMEs is more in assuring management autonomy to set corporate strategy on the basis of market signals. Therefore, the state tends to act as a market regulator by comparison to CMEs where it acts more as a market shaper, working with corporations and industry associations to further national objectives, and helping to strategically coordinate economic activities. Rather than an arm's length relationship between the state and corporations, in CMEs it is more the case that they operate hand-in-glove. While LME-based corporations desire deregulation and hands-off *laissez faire* market operations, CME-based corporations operate more on the basis of consensus-oriented negotiation and cooperation with the state. While business "cooperation" with government has as its goal the capture of regulatory agencies, or reducing their capacity to intervene in markets, in CMEs it is more readily accepted that the state's role is that of an agenda setter, coordinating firms or informally suggesting strategies. Rather than what may be characterized as a more lobbying-conflict model between the state and corporations in LMEs, in CMEs corporations operate within a collaborative consensus environment through which business and government develop regulations, agree on targets to be met, and establish priorities and goals to be achieved in the national interest.

Institutions do not define outcomes. They do not define products or processes. They do not predict the relative success or failure of corporations' performance. A global corporation headquartered in an LME may be as successful as one from a CME or one of the emerging state-led BRICs. As such, variations in capitalist relations of production do not have explanatory power on their own. However, they do affect the strategic adjustment paths taken by corporations as they go global, just as they affect the nature and implementation of the policy options of states. This is because institutions, once deeply embedded, produce power-distribution and -advantages effects, so that they are not neutral coordinating mechanisms but underpin the differing interests and power relations of purposive actors in differing national contexts. Just as it would be wrong to rush to assume there is an inevitable global form of the corporation, so there is the danger of assuming the only model possible for the institutional context in which global corporations are embedded must be a liberal one. Just as it is overly simplistic to see the LME and CME categories as congruent representations of reality, in the sense that they are the only alternatives rather than the end points of a spectrum of possibilities, so it must be recognized that in reality there are many ways to coordinate economic governance. Indeed, Hall and Soskice (2003, 245) agree that they "do not think that economies in the 'middle ground' ... must move inexorably towards the poles represented by a 'pure' CME or LME."

It is also simplistic to see the BRICs as inevitably converging on an established category. The newer Chinese global corporations, and others from the BRICs, are in the process of developing their capabilities and emerging on the world stage. As they do so, they must reconcile their material interests with the demands of their states. As Wank (1998) and more recently Chen et al. (2009) note in respect of China in particular, relationships with party officials and political considerations override market and shareholder imperatives. As such, while it may be accurate to characterize the Chinese institutional environment as in a state of emerging flux and transition, it is also the case that national development is the overriding priority. Chinese corporations at this stage of the capitalist development of the Chinese state are therefore very much state-led and state-controlled. If global corporations "are basically the creatures of structural changes at home" (Ozawa 2014, 51), then the geographical patterns of their operations are a way of expressing these changes beyond the borders of their home states. This may be easier to forget for the global corporations from states that currently dominate the global economy, but it is certainly clear for those from the BRICs as they emerge to challenge the incumbents.

5 PRIVATE AUTHORITY AND THE POTENTIAL FOR PRIVATE GOVERNANCE

As demonstrated in the previous chapters, global corporations' political power flows from their market control and geographical concentration. In Chapter 4 it was argued that their institutional embedding in their home states is also the basis for the power they wield abroad. These factors—market control, geographical concentration, and institutional embedding—are also the source of their private authority, which global corporations have an interest in enhancing. This is because while their lobbying and connections with policy makers mean they are in a good position to argue their case, and their structural power means they possess the ability to organize things "in" and "out" of politics, even so "structures do not come with an instruction sheet" (Blyth 2003b). The instructions must be written by purposive political actors, and they then become embedded and endure over time as accepted institutional preferences. This involves not just influencing debates, but framing and constructing them around what is appropriate by discursively creating "truths," and thence claims of political legitimacy.

One could certainly contend, as for instance Marxists do, that the structural power of global corporations puts them in a strong position to get what they desire without asking for it, or to successfully lobby in their interests if they do need to ask. But institutions are not just a function of material wealth and leverage, nor are they just about efficiently delivering outcomes. They are created and supported by "rules of thumb" about what is regarded as normatively right. When what is constructed as right changes, so follows the institutions. By implication so does the ease or difficulty of corporations' ability to achieve their desired outcomes. This is the "game" that global corporations engage in, as they seek to convince governments and their citizens that they have a legitimate right to the authority they possess.[1] They increasingly claim not just that states should govern in their private interests, on the basis that this equates to national interests and supports society at large, but that they may be relied on to govern in their own right through private governance initiatives. In so doing, they claim that their goals are social as well economic.

With such claims in mind, this chapter first considers the private authority that global corporations possess. A definition of private authority is problematic, and reaching one verges on an exercise in semantics about the nature of the concept of "authority" in general as well as specifically private terms. But as the contributions in Cutler et al. (1999a) make clear, it involves firms being "increasingly engaged in authoritative decision-making that was previously the prerogative of sovereign states" (Cutler et al. 1999c, 16). At the core of a capacity to engage in such decision making must be accepted claims of the right to do so. That is to say, like states, global corporations must be regarded as possessing the legitimacy necessary to make rules that have an obligatory quality to them. They must be seen as not just achieving desired ends on the basis of strategic calculations, but as engaging in governance that is normatively appropriate (e.g., see Bernstein and Cashore 2007). The manner in which they employ their private authority involves a spectrum from informal norms and practices to more formal mechanisms for governance that ultimately include private regimes, such as the ISO. These are outlined and discussed to demonstrate how corporate involvement in global governance both rivals, and complements, traditional state regulation.

However, this is not a book about governance so much as it is about political power—i.e., one of the fundamental building blocks, along with organization, that comes *before* governance. As such, while it is important to identify the possible governance arrangements resulting from global corporations employing their private authority, in the second section the focus is more on the rationales for these. There are basically two, and they are the same as those underlying the concept of CSR: strengthening brand value to serve the material interests of shareholders, and preventing unwanted regulatory intervention.[2] The central point made is that while beneficial outcomes for society may be produced, nevertheless the democratic legitimacy of these outcomes is always problematic. This is because for the outcomes to serve both the interests of global corporations and the public at large one would have to believe that their interests are usually synonymous, and this seems highly unlikely in both a material and normative sense.

It therefore produces a conundrum for states and their societies. Given the political power they undoubtedly possess, it is surely desirable that global corporations be socially responsible. However, their actions do not always equate with the pronouncements they make. This may seem an intuitively straightforward observation, but it presents challenges not just for states and their societies. It presents challenges for global corporations themselves. While they seek to discursively construct their legitimacy, and in so doing increase their private authority and political power, they risk losing it if they do not live up to the socially enlightened motivations they profess. Putting it simply, they can lose discursive legitimacy as well as gain it. The third section therefore contrasts public confidence in corporations with the views of global corporations' board members as to what constitutes an "admired" company. The former's relatively low confidence in corporations by comparison to governments and NGOs is contrasted with the latter's greater focus on financial performance and material interests. The case of global tax avoidance is used to illustrate the disconnect between their social and material motivations, and the reason why the existence of this disconnect does not just damage global corporations' brand values and community standing, but also opens the way for them to surrender the political initiative to national and international regulators.

The conclusion reached is that in seeking to establish their legitimacy as socially responsible self-regulators and private governors, the goal of global corporations is to maintain and increase their political power. This may serve the public interest. However, primarily the aim of global corporations is not to share the power that flows from their private authority with states, but to challenge and, if possible, replace the power states possess through their sovereignty. The discursive legitimacy they seek to construct should be seen critically in this light.

Forms of Private Authority

As the transformationalist wave was building in conceptualizing globalization, a growing literature on private authority in world affairs also emerged. Rather than stressing the inevitability of neoliberalism and global market forces, those contributing to this literature considered the manner in which private actors like global corporations govern via forming relationships with states, societies, and each other (e.g., Cutler et al. 1999a; Haufler 2001; Hall and Biersteker 2002a; Cutler 2003; Sell 2003). Just as states reach agreements to share sovereignty for governance beyond their borders, and construct international regimes to achieve the ends they desire (e.g., see Ruggie 1992, 1998), so too global corporations employ private authority to achieve theirs. In order to do this they "construct a rich variety of institutional arrangements that structure their behavior" (Cutler et al. 1999b, 333), which also serve to enhance their political power in relation to states and their societies. Cutler (2002, 28–29) identifies six potential ways in which they can do this, covering a spectrum from informal industry norms and practices that result in influence, to more formal forms of authority that may be translated into private governance including private international regimes.

Informal Industry Norms and Practices

As a result of tacit understandings and repeated practices within and between firms, corporations promote informal industry norms and practices. As these norms and practices become regularized they often become formalized. For example, most of the British commercial code was initially developed by merchants who desired standards and rules by which to conduct commerce (Haufler 2006). Similarly, European laws surrounding marine industry insurance were originally the standards and codes of practice the industry had adopted for itself (Porter 1993; Haufler 1997). But given the market concentration that characterizes the operations of global corporations, it is also important to stress those informal norms and practices that arise as a result of their global market dominance not just within, but between states. These are not mandated by regulations, nor necessarily reflected in particular states' laws, but global corporations are in a position to standardize goods and services to the extent that over time such standardization comes to have the force of authority.

An emblematic example is Microsoft's operating system, which runs on 80 to 90 percent of desktop personal computers worldwide (Statista 2016; see also Haufler 2006, 91). In addition, there is overwhelming familiarity with its suite of programs, particularly those bundled in Microsoft Office, which is regarded as practically essential on all computers. This gives Microsoft private authority in the sense that the use of either its operating system or its programs is taken for granted. There is no official standard that requires this, no agreement between software providers, and certainly no formal laws regulating that it should be the case. Therefore, it may be hard to sustain the argument that Microsoft "governs" other than in respect of its own operations. However, its market dominance means it possesses the structural power to control consumers' preferences. This control goes beyond simple economic notions of monopolistic market power. It affects the format in which prose is written (i.e., on Microsoft Word), the way in which data is analyzed and the results reported (i.e., with Microsoft Excel), the nature and structure of public presentations (i.e., using Microsoft Powerpoint), and other aspects of everyday communication and information provision. It also shapes the type and format of the products and services offered by other corporations, which take for granted that the platform it offers for them must inescapably be part of their business plans.

Coordination Services Firms

Coordination services firms exist whose *raison d'être* is the promotion, sanctioning, and regularization of the behavior and practices of other firms. As Amoore (2006) sees it, they engage in concerted efforts to make states in their "image," with this also the image they promote for other global corporations. As such, they are global corporations that embody and enact the informal industry norms and practices that are accepted by global corporations and industry associations, and in so doing they potentially govern other corporations and the governments of nations. It might even be said that ultimately this means that they regulate the operation of the global economy.

A good example is the function performed by the three major credit rating agencies: Standard and Poor's, Moody's, and Fitch Ratings. As with the market and geographical concentration of global corporations generally, these three firms are US-based (in the case of Fitch Ratings, dual US–UK based) and are responsible for 95 percent of all credit ratings issued worldwide (CFR.org staff 2015; US Securities and Exchange Commission 2012). They make what verge on being official pronouncements of the creditworthiness of both corporations and governments. Therefore, they act as "reputational intermediaries" (Gourevitch and Shinn 2005, 114). So do professional services firms in accountancy, law, and management consulting. Of these, the "Big Four" (as they are colloquially known) are PwC, Deloitte, KPMG, and EY. Together they audit 99 percent of the corporations on the FTSE 100 Index, and offer a variety of advisory and business consulting services to the world's largest global corporations—e.g., PwC provides services to 422 of those listed in the Fortune Global 500 (PwC 2016; Christodoulou 2011). As with credit rating agencies, not only do they dominate the global market for their services, but their headquarters are geographically concentrated in the US and Europe, in the latter case primarily the UK. From there, they operate vast networks of firms owned and managed independently, but sharing a common brand and offering standardized services.

In coordinating these networks from their headquarters in the US and the UK, they do not neutrally or simply technically ensure accounting best practice, nor operate from a global perspective about the economy, so much as they promote accounting and financial management standards that are specifically compatible with the Anglo-Saxon (i.e., LME) form of capitalism (e.g., see Nölke 2010b). While they operate according to the laws in the countries where they offer their services, nevertheless their networks are not vehicles for promoting alternative forms of corporate order, such as those which characterize Islamic finance or East Asian state-coordinated forms of capitalism. As they justify global corporations' actions and interests "in an ideological debate about how the corporate system enhances public benefits and the public interest" (Wilks 2013, 79), the function they serve is not just quasi-regulatory. They are agents of constructing and enhancing the legitimacy and discursive power of global corporations worldwide in a liberal institutional context.

Production Alliances and Subcontractor Relationships

Global corporations, individually and collectively, govern the industries they control through their production alliances, subcontractor relationships, and other complementary activities. They do not just exist as unitary entities, but as networks of operations, and, as noted in Chapter 2, this is why intra-firm trade dominates trade statistics. For example, while the production of computer components could be seen as globally fragmented between many states, it is also controlled by global corporations that oversee the assembly and sale of the final product. These are not so much manufacturers in their own right as they are coordinators of diverse networks of manufacturing, sales, and distribution processes (Ernst 2004). Indeed, all global corporations sit atop extensive global supply chains. For example, Nike employs more than 800,000 workers in a global network of 600 factories. It does not own *any* of these, but strategically controls them as a matter of corporate policy from its corporate headquarters in the US, which is also where it conducts its research and development (Dicken 2015, 160).

The nature of global corporations' networks vary. They may be hierarchical (through vertical integration within a firm with governance of subsidiaries and affiliates based on the headquarters' managerial control); captive (via engagement of small suppliers that are dependent on larger buyers); relational (resulting from complex interactions between buyers and sellers creating mutual dependence); modular (producing to a customer's specifications); or market-based (through repeated transactions between parties) (Dicken 2015). Whatever organizational form they take, however they are controlled or coordinated, and whether they are more nationally, regionally, or globally focused, are strategic decisions made by global corporations in addition to the nature of the goods and services they provide. Whether their production networks are stable or dynamic are also decisions over which they have discretion. This puts them in a position of power to extract the most favorable conditions from their workforces, such as demanding flexible labor arrangements with less unionization, and higher rates of part-time and temporary contractual work not just in one state, but across the states and regions in which they operate (e.g., see Kalleberg 2009).

They are in a particularly strong position to negotiate with governments to exercise leverage over the economic benefits of their investment choices when first deciding whether or not to invest in a country. In the international business literature, this gives rise to what is known as the "obsolescing bargain model" (e.g., see Bakir 2015; Eden et al. 2005; Ramamurti 2001; originally Vernon 1971), named as such because a state is in a weaker position to extract demands from a global corporation before it has made the decision to invest in its territory than once it has decided to do so and its operations are relatively less mobile. As such, its power to dictate the terms of bargaining with the state obsolesce once it has made the decision to invest. But it is not just economic threats and rewards that global corporations potentially offer as a result of their structural and instrumental power. Discursively, with the growth of debates around CSR, they have moved to develop codes of conduct to govern their supply chains that enforce standards and practices in areas beyond production systems (e.g., see Ougaard 2006). In other words, they are not just governing their supply chains and global networks in an operational but in a qualitative sense. Their motivations for this are discussed further below.

Cartels

Cartels involve agreements between corporations to control production (e.g., by limiting output), segment markets, fix prices, or control technologies. Such behavior was widespread before World War II but because it is collusive, and by implication anti-competitive, it has since been regarded as undesirable. Therefore, most states now have regulations prohibiting cartels (Porter 1999). However, as corporations have become more global in their operations, employing these regulations is not as straightforward as it once was. States now must attempt to apply their anti-cartel regulations to corporations whose operations cross their borders.

The problematic nature of this is illustrated by the case of Visa and MasterCard. Collectively owned by banks, they control the vast majority of payments for retail transactions globally, but were prosecuted under US anti-trust legislation. They were charged with using their market dominance and control of the technology and systems for retail payments to fix interchange fees (i.e., the fee paid between banks for transactions using credit cards) at artificially high rates. Visa and MasterCard attempted to settle the case in 2012 by paying retailers over US$6.05 billion in compensation as well as a US$1.2 billion temporary reduction in fees. However, this record settlement was appealed and in 2016 overturned by the US Court of Appeals on the basis of being "unreasonable and inadequate." Having commenced in 2005, the dispute remains unresolved (Sidel 2016; Abrams 2016; see also Levitin 2007). If Visa and MasterCard control interchange fees in other states, and if they do so in a similar manner to that alleged in the US, it potentially remains an unresolved issue in multiple jurisdictions. The debate rages on as to the nature of the problem, as well as whether it is a problem, with differing approaches to it taken in different states—e.g., in the case of the EU, interchange fees have been capped under Regulation EU 2015/751 of the European Parliament (Official Journal of the European Union 2015).

It is not just a matter of the wheels of justice turning slowly, and inter-jurisdictionally, but of the hidden extensity of cartel-like arrangements. If the reality is global markets characterized by control rather than competition, it is surely natural for global corporations to tend to collude rather than compete for outcomes in their mutual interest. Preventing them from doing so is often only achieved with the help of those involved. For example, in 2011 the US corporations Procter and Gamble and Unilever were found guilty of fixing the price of laundry powder detergents in eight European countries over 2002–2005. Under EU anti-trust regulations they were ordered to pay fines of €315.2 million in 2011 (Tait and Wilson 2011). The reason why Procter and Gamble and Unilever were fined, and the amount they paid, had at least as much to do with a breakdown of the cartel arrangement as good policing by regulators. In 2008 the German company Henkel, which had been part of the cartel, reported the arrangements in order to secure immunity from fines. Ultimately, the case was prosecuted over 2008–2011 on the basis of the other corporations' cooperation and admissions of guilt. Both were given a 10 percent reduction in fines imposed for agreeing to settle the case with the European Commission, in addition to prior 50 percent (Procter and Gamble) and 25 percent (Unilever) reductions for agreeing to cooperate in the investigation (European Commission 2011; Corfield 2013).

The case illustrates that limiting the anti-competitive behavior that characterizes cartels may require the cooperation of the very corporations that have the incentive and ability to create them. This is probably why the advice of law firm Clayton Utz to corporations is to be "first in" (like Henkel) to inform on the operations of other firms if a cartel is suspected, and to be as cooperative as possible with regulators if another cartel member informs first (like Procter and Gamble and Unilever) (Corrigan and Modrak 2010, 17). Their advice is contained in a compendium of advice from forty-two law firms on *Cartel Regulation: Getting the Fine Down in 42 Jurisdictions Worldwide*. The implication of the publication's title, as with the advice from law firms contained therein, is that minimizing penalties when cartels are discovered should be corporations' aim rather than avoiding cartel arrangements in the first place.

Industry Associations

Industry associations coordinate and formally represent the interests of their members, many of which also govern their members' activities. Increasingly, the most important ones operate globally, like the corporations whose interests they represent. They wield their political power in all dimensions (i.e., geographically as well as conceptually) and as such may be seen as the precursors to private international regimes. Some embody aspects of these as well.

The International Chamber of Commerce (ICC), as one of the most established examples, illustrates the point. Since its foundation in 1919 "to represent business everywhere" (ICC 2016a), it has been "a steadfast rallying point for those who believe ... that strengthening commercial ties among nations is not only good for business but good for global living standards and good for peace" (ICC 2016b). As such, it exists to promote not just its members' interests, but to discursively construct these as synonymous with the interests of states and global society. Its governing body, the World Council, "is the equivalent of the general assembly of a major intergovernmental organization. In this case, however, the delegates are business executives and not government officials" (ICC 2016c). Beyond being a "rallying point" for global corporations, it exists to work with and influence governments and the international organizations to which they belong. In addition, it acts in a similar manner to the WTO's Dispute Settlement Body via the ICC International Court of Arbitration. This resolves business disputes worldwide on the basis that the parties to the Rules of Arbitration choose to follow and be bound by its decisions (ICC 2016d). Therefore, the ICC both advocates for and shapes the global agenda for business, and is also a governing body in its own right that makes decisions imposed on its members.

The ICC is primarily economically oriented, but increasingly there are many global industry associations that are explicitly focused on issues beyond those normally associated with business interests. Notable among these are those promoting and coordinating CSR initiatives, particularly environmental sustainability. The World Business Council for Sustainable Development (WBCSD) is a good example. Founded in 1995 as a CEO-led organization, its membership comprises the world's most powerful global corporations, as well as a global network of over 65 national and regional business councils involving thousands of business leaders (WBCSD 2016). Since its inception, its central aim has been to "participate in policy development to create a framework that allows conditions for business to make an effective contribution to sustainable human progress" (WBCSD 2002, 13). It aims to set the global agenda for corporate environmental sustainability, being the global voice of industry in international organizations such as the United Nations and World Bank, and participating in multilateral negotiations such as those of the United Nations Framework Convention on Climate Change that produce rules for the world (WBCSD 2016). In so doing, it links environmental sustainability with traditional business goals to frame solving environmental problems in economic terms, as opposed to addressing social or scientific imperatives. Ultimately, Kolleck (2013, 142–143) sees it as explicitly pursuing "a strategy of increasing discursive power" so that in representing its members' interests it may "talk and act like a *Praeceptor Mundi* (global teacher)."

Private International Regimes

Private international regimes are the highest form of private governance arising from private authority. Defined as "an integrated complex of formal and informal institutions that (are) a source of governance for an economic issue area as a whole" (Cutler et al. 1999c, 13), they represent the most formal arrangements by which global corporations translate their authority into governance. They are the potential governance end point to which private authority may give rise.

Standard-setting organizations are the most notable among these, such as the International Accounting Standards Board. Comprising 143 industry bodies from 104 countries, it develops and promotes globally accepted accounting standards (Camfferman and Zeff 2007, 496). In the process, it basically functions like a state regulator. Other standards bodies do so as well, but in most cases it is more accurate to say that they serve this function *with* governments rather than instead of them. For example, the Internet Corporation for Assigned Names and Numbers (ICANN) was established by the US to privatize the management and assignment of internet names and addresses, yet with the US government still having oversight responsibilities, and a Governmental Advisory Committee drawn from 111 states (Weil 1998; ICANN 2016; ICANN GAC 2016). Standard-setting organizations like these focus on particular industries, technologies, and issues, but beyond these the ISO is as comprehensive in its coverage as it is global. In ensuring standards that are universally applied across all manufacturing industries, it also facilitates global trade and investment and therefore plays a central role in the formal economic organization of a globalized world. As such, it is worth discussing in more depth.

Individual corporations cannot be members of the ISO, but the 163 national standards associations to which they and their industry associations belong are (ISO 2016a). For example, the US is represented by the American National Standards Institute, which represents the interests of 125,000 companies. Its membership comprises a broad range of businesses and industry associations, as well as standard-setting and conformity assessment bodies, trade associations, labor unions, professional societies, consumer groups, academia, and government organizations (ISO 2016b). It is funded through the "sale" of its standards to its member national associations, which in turn charge a fee to the firms complying with them. Once a standard becomes globally dominant, there is little incentive for firms to adopt alternative standards, effectively ensuring that rival standards and standard-setting organizations are financially penalized, and therefore in a weaker position. Given the composition of the ISO's membership, the result is a quasi-public or public–private international regime.

As there are national and regional aspects to the dissemination of the ISO's standards via its membership, so too are there political implications of this in its operations and whose interests it represents. Büthe and Mattli (2011) demonstrate that over time the EU has effectively taken the lead in international standard-setting. Their award-winning study[3] shows the reason why this is the case by employing institutional complementarity theory—i.e., the extent to which domestic and international institutions confer a strategic advantage on the stakeholders "by amplifying their voices in the international standardization process" (Büthe and Mattli 2011, 49). They demonstrate that there is greater institutional complementarity between European standard-setting and the ISO than is the case for the US. In what would seem to be a reflection of the different varieties of capitalism exhibited by European states versus the US, as discussed in Chapter 4, the US is characterized by competition and overlap between standard-setting bodies while the EU system is more hierarchical and highly coordinated. They find that the latter is more suited to a globally economically integrated world.[4]

The national and regional aspects of standard-setting reflect a history of differing nationally specific standards being used as a means of protecting national industries. This is because even when states do not explicitly use standards as nontariff barriers, differing product standards can increase the cost of foreign goods equal to a tariff rate of 2 to 10 percent (Chen et al. 2006). With the emergence of the ISO, states embraced the opportunity to employ such measures extraterritorially to not just impose the standards that protect their corporations at home, but to project them beyond their borders. Therefore, international standards have not just come to act as "a lubricant for global trade" (Heires 2008, 357) on either the basis of market forces or scientific/technical expertise. They have become extensions of the power of economically dominant states. While either the US or EU system may have served their respective territorial jurisdictions well in the past, global corporations based in the EU are in a position to "possess better information about international standardization initiatives and pursue their interests more effectively" (Büthe and Mattli 2011, 160). This may change as global economic power shifts. Negotiations in the ISO's technical committee responsible for bicycle production standards illustrate the point. All ISO members agreed on the standard, with the exception of those from China and India. As their corporations are responsible for 90 percent of global bicycle production, to pass it without their support would have meant it was "predestined to fail, for it would undermine organizational authority and legitimacy" (Koppell 2010, 225). The result was that the standard was sent back for review.

If national standards bodies work with their global corporations and governments to effect favorable ISO standards, and these "become de facto requirements for doing business around the world" (Haufler

2000, 128), then they become a way of ensuring that some states' standards are globally imposed on others. As a reflection of the institutional entanglement of powerful governments and global corporations, the result is the entrenchment and potential enhancement of the political power of both. Global corporations, with the backing of their states, are in a position to require "their partners and subcontractors along supply chains to be certified to ISO standards" with compliance "a condition for access to global markets" (Heires 2008, 358). In addition to regulatory competition between industrialized states expressed through the standards adhered to by their global corporations, the implication is that weaker developing states are reduced to being "regulation takers rather than regulation makers" because they and their corporations have fewer resources and weaker national member organizations (Louis and Ruwet 2016, 8). Another implication is the exclusion of civil society as all states' citizens have less say in the standards imposed through the ISO and its dominant national standards association members.

On the other hand, the ISO is increasing the scope of its activities beyond technical production standards, to standards in management (ISO9000 series), the environment (ISO14000 series), and social responsibility (ISO26000 series). These make global corporations responsible for a wider range of issues beyond adhering to technical specifications, and their development has been driven by global corporations seeking to reduce the potential proliferation of multiple national standards in these areas (Clapp 1998). As the scope of the standards increases, and at the behest of global corporations themselves, this may address the question of developing states and civil society being comparatively "voiceless." The privatization and globalization in governance this produces may mean global corporations willingly become agents of the changes necessary to address their collective concerns. The extent to which their willingness produces beneficial results depends not just on the standards themselves, but on their rationale for private governance.

The Rationale for Private Governance

The examples presented above demonstrate how private authority may be translated into private governance. The two are mutually reinforcing: the greater the private authority, the greater the potential for private governance, which in turn enhances private authority. Over time, this feedback loop produces an acceptance that self-regulation "represents an increasingly viable alternative to the market and the state" (Porter and Ronit 2006, 41). It is not the purpose of this book to delve deeply into the mechanisms of public, private, and multi-stakeholder governance. Other studies do a fine job of this, such as Bell and Hindmoor (2009), who stress the enduring centrality of the state, and Cashore (2002) and Cashore et al. (2004), who examine the increasing role played by non-state actors (see also Mikler 2008; O'Callaghan and Vivoda 2013). Here the focus is on the political power that lies behind the governance of which global corporations are capable and their motivations for engaging in it—in other words, how global corporations discursively construct their legitimacy to be perceived as effective self-regulators, and whether this stands to reason in the light of the rationale they would have to do so. This raises the question of whose interests global corporations serve. It seems overly optimistic to think the answer to this is the global public interest. There are two reasons for this, neither of which is pejorative so much as simply standing to reason.

First, a global corporation that prioritizes broader social concerns like environmental sustainability over financial performance puts itself at risk. Unless a business case can be found for, or at least reconciled with, such a focus, by definition it must be choosing lower profitability. The risks are fairly obvious for publicly listed global corporations whose shareholders' interests must be served by law, and not just in the states where they are based but wherever they operate. As they are legally obliged to act in their shareholders' interests, publicly listed global corporations which prioritize issues that reduce or risk shareholder returns put not just their profitability but their existence at risk. They may face legal action for abrogating their responsibility to maximize profits and dividends,[5] and ultimately open themselves to hostile takeover bids as their share price falls. Before this happens, they may be starved of capital as investors become less enthusiastic about their prospects. Such risks are most acute for LME-based corporations which, as discussed in Chapter 4, are not just predominantly reliant on equity rather than debt finance, but on short-term portfolio rather than stable institutional investors (e.g., see Lazonick and O'Sullivan 2004; Culpepper 2011; and, in respect of environmental considerations, Mikler and Harrison 2013). But in general, it might be regarded as impossible for the interest of society at large to be served by publicly listed corporations at *any* level, whether this be national, regional, or global, unless shareholder or consumer activism leads to demands they focus on measures of performance other than, and in preference to, financial returns. Consumers must demand higher-priced goods and services, and shareholders riskier or lower returns, because the result is better social and environmental outcomes.

Second, if global corporations do respond to social concerns arising from their operations, those expressed by their consumers and shareholders are often inadequate. Sadly, there is little evidence that their concerns produce the impacts on firms' financial performance necessary to sting them into action. The well-documented exploitative practices in Apple's global supply chain are a case in point. The scandals over recent years surrounding employment conditions in Chinese factories manufacturing its products have received the greatest publicity, particularly those of Foxconn Technology, which manufactures its iPhones. Its employees were reported to be living in cramped, unhygienic dormitories, and suffering from sleep deprivation as a result of working up to 100 hours per month in overtime for very low pay (Tam 2010; Adams 2012). Several employees have committed suicide, allegedly because of these appalling conditions. In 2010, thirteen workers died from seventeen attempts between January and November, after which the company installed safety nets at some of its dormitories to prevent more deaths. The bad publicity resulted in "ritual burnings" of pictures of iPhones in Hong Kong demonstrations, and a university study of the abusive practices endured by workers at twelve Foxconn factories that characterized them as "labor camps" (Myers 2013, 11). Apple's CEO Tim Cook visited China in person in the aftermath of the allegations, independent observers were admitted to the factories, audits were conducted, and demands made by Apple that working conditions be improved in light of its own investigations (Schmidpeter and Stehr 2015). Even so, as Adams (2012) noted at the time, "Apple is such a hugely popular company and the buzz around the new iPhone is so great, reports of continued worker abuse will not dampen the public's enthusiasm for Apple products or affect the company stock price." Far from suffering negative impacts, the data show that in the years following revelations of the suicides Apple was the world's most profitable mobile phone manufacturer (Myers 2013, 3). More allegations of exploitative practices emerged five years later in 2015, including that other Chinese manufacturers of its products employed workers on the basis of "bonded servitude" by forcing them to surrender ID cards and forfeit a month's wages in return for employment. The ongoing discovery of such problems was defended by Apple's Chief Operating Officer, Jeff Williams, in its *2015 Progress Report* as evidence that the company's processes were working rather than failing (Anon 2015). No doubt Apple hopes the general public agrees.

The exploitation of workers in Apple's global supply chain is not an isolated example of the negative social and environmental impacts of global corporations. Vogel (2010, 478) points out that campaigns aimed at US and European firms such as Nike, Home Depot, Shell, Ikea, C&A, Gap, Tiffany and Co., Nestlé, Starbucks, Hennes & Mauritz, Rio Tinto, Freeport Mining, and Citibank have made them "public symbols of 'corporate irresponsibility.'" Nevertheless, Apple's response to the allegations—condemnation by its CEO, ongoing reporting, and the concern it expresses for allegations as opposed to dismissing them—demonstrates that global corporations are motivated to ensure their reputations are not tarnished by their actions. As Dauvergne (2016) shows, they can and do respond to campaigns by wealthy consumers and shareholders whose social activism has resulted in real changes in global corporations' supply chains and the products they produce, such as more fuel-efficient automobiles and less wasteful packaging. They hardly welcome negative publicity, and there are examples of them responding to reputational threats.

For example, O'Callaghan (2016) analyzes Royal Dutch Shell's "ethical transformation" from an oil company with a reputation for wreaking social and environmental damage to one that embraces responsible business practices. He identifies 1995 as the company's *anus horibilis* and its turning point. Among other scandals in the same year, Shell was attacked for its plans to tow and sink its Brent Spar oil storage facility in the North Sea.[6] This was a huge structure, moored to the seabed by six anchors, 137 meters tall, weighing 14,500 tonnes and with a storage capacity for 300,000 barrels of oil (Royal Dutch Shell 2008). O'Callaghan (2016, 109) characterizes the ire it attracted from NGOs like Greenpeace, politicians, and the public at large as "like a runaway train." The result was the following statement released by the company on 20 June 1995:

> Shell UK aborted the operation because the Shell position as a major European enterprise has become untenable. The Spar had gained a symbolic significance out of all proportion to its environmental impact. In consequence, Shell companies were faced with increasingly intense public criticism, mostly in Continental Northern Europe. Many politicians and ministers were openly hostile and several called for consumer boycotts. There was violence against Shell service stations, accompanied by threats to Shell staff. (O'Rourke and Collins 2008, 95)

Ultimately, Brent Spar was recycled as a ferry terminal in Norway, but the impact on the company's reputation haunted it for a decade afterward. This is despite it being a founding member of the WBCSD, and accepting international agreements on human rights and greenhouse gas emission reductions to combat climate change. It is also despite it increasing the transparency of its operations, including releasing detailed environmental and social performance data which indicate that the negative impacts of its operations have been greatly reduced—e.g., a two-thirds drop in employee and contractor fatalities, a reduction in the need for armed security personnel, and improvements in waste emissions.

The case of Shell's Brent Spar platform therefore illustrates the point that possessing a good reputation is more desirable than the time-consuming advocacy and lobbying necessary for it to be continually asserted. No doubt Apple feels the same way. If global corporations' interests are seen as synonymous with the public good, then they are in a much more politically powerful position. To be clear, this is not an argument about whether or not global corporations are moral, although their actions may be assessed for the extent to which the outcomes they produce are. It is about them acting to maintain and enhance their private authority via increasing perceptions of their legitimacy. It is about them maintaining their discursive power, rather than surrendering their right to set the agenda. These are the motivations behind the global embrace of CSR programs which emerged in the 1990s. There is still no clear definition of CSR, and from a democratic, as opposed to discursive, legitimacy perspective it is reasonable to question whether corporations should have social responsibilities at all, rather than the elected governments of nations who represent their citizens (Crane 2008, 4; see also the contributions in Crane et al. 2009). However, if it is accepted that they do, then beyond traditional notions of philanthropy and charity, and beyond a more cynical definition of it as "crisis scandal response" (Vogel 2010, 478), CSR suggests an active concern for stakeholders very broadly defined, not just customers and shareholders. It involves a willingness to embrace responsibility for diverse concerns including environmental sustainability, labor standards, human rights, disclosure of information, effective corporate governance, public safety, privacy protection, and consumer protection. In other words, to mitigate the negative consequences of *all* business activities on an ongoing basis to prevent, rather than respond to, reputational crises, and in so doing to self-regulate in the public interest.

If the reality lives up to the promise, or if it is at least perceived that it does, CSR programs that enhance corporate reputation may be used as leverage to avoid government regulation. They may also enhance profitability. Margolis and Walsh's (2001) review of the international business literature finds that 68 percent of studies identify a positive correlation between socially responsible firms and profitability, while just 15 percent find a negative correlation. More pragmatically, Vogel (2005, 17) argues that although "there is no evidence that behaving more virtuously makes firms more profitable ... conversely the fact that CSR does not make firms *less* profitable means that it is possible for a firm to commit resources to CSR without becoming less competitive." They may also reduce costs and increase access to human and investment capital. This is essentially the argument of Mark Royal, Senior Principal of Hay Group, the consulting firm which undertakes the surveys and analysis to produce the list of the Fortune Global 500's World's Most Admired Companies:

> We know the reputation of a company has an impact on the ability of the company to attract and retain talent. People are anxious to get in the door and take advantage of the opportunity that a successful company such as a most admired company can provide. They may be even willing to accept lower salary offers in terms of base pay than might be available elsewhere. It's a real tangible benefit. There are also real benefits in terms of stock price that come from being a most admired company. (Fortune 2015b)

The desire of top graduates to work for socially responsible corporations with good reputations means these corporations do not have to be as proactive in attracting them, and can employ them at a discount and retain them, while satisfying the interests of shareholders.

CSR is also unconstrained by national borders. The enhanced discursive power corporate reputation confers potentially convinces governments and the societies they represent to not just accept but to *promote* private regulation, and to enable corporations to do so globally. As authors like Zadek (2007) and Kolleck (2013) note, global corporations that embrace CSR may do so because of changing attitudes, investor expectations, and public pressures, but they also seek to proactively shape these. Therefore, the political (as opposed to coordinating or administrative) aim of global corporations in exercising private authority and engaging in private governance is to create widely held norms that give rise to potentially global institutions—i.e., to globally increase their discursive power to claim the right to be legitimate self-governors. Rather than a confrontational form of politics in which they overtly seek to serve their material interests, or use their structural power to get what they want, discursive power helps to build a sense of "partnership," cooperation and coordination for self- or co-regulation among "stakeholders" (e.g., see Utting 2002).[7]

This is commensurate with the transformationalist wave in conceptualizing globalization, with its notions not of states being overwhelmed by global corporations, nor corporations merely serving national interests, but of the two sharing power to institutionally embed new forms of governance (e.g., see Elbra 2016). If global corporations can widely disseminate norms of socially responsible business behavior then they are potentially agents of real positive effects, in fact a "race to the top" rather than to the bottom (Vogel 1995; see also Leonard 1988; Cashore et al. 2004; Vogel 2005). The end result may be that private authority comes to resemble not just "market authority" but also "moral authority" (Hall and Biersteker 2002b, 7). If there is a perceived connection between the two, they gain discursive legitimacy: the right to wield power, reframing themselves not as purely profit-seeking entities but "corporate citizens" that serve society (Wright and Rwabizambuga 2006). However, if the reality is somewhat different so that there is a perceived disconnect, they may also lose it.

The Promise versus the Reality

To possess power is not to possess authority, because authority requires political actors to be perceived as legitimate by those whom they affect or govern in exercising it. As Hall and Biersteker (2002c, 204) observe, "As long as there is consent and social recognition, an actor—even a private actor—can be accorded the rights, the legitimacy, and the responsibilities of an authority." Do global corporations possess legitimacy sufficient to exercise their private authority as self-governors? This is a hard question to answer because it is so intangible. "Levels" of discursive power and the legitimacy they "produce" are very hard to measure. Yet we know discursive power exists and that it grants political actors legitimacy. For example, Nye (2004a, 2004b) stresses the importance of soft power for states. Soft power is basically another name for discursive power, and states with high levels of it are able to be co-opting and mutually supporting in creating and shaping institutions, to effectively make rules for the world. They do not need to resort to being coercive or punitive, and therefore avoid using harder structural or instrumental forms of power, such as economic punishments or payments, or the use of military force. Likewise, through their discursive power as opposed to their structural dominance of their industries or relationships with policy makers, global corporations seek to promote their interests as synonymous with those of states and their citizens, and operating globally to be granted license to act in the interests of *all* states and their citizens. This is why authors like Elbra (2014, 247) stress that private governance emerges "in the shadow of state power, and before societal audiences" (Elbra 2014, 247).

The notion that private authority and the potential for private governance to which it gives rise is regarded as legitimate because it achieves the consent of states and their citizens is related to arguments about state-corporate entanglement. In fact, van Ham (2002, 2008) shows that it is possible to approach state soft power from a corporate perspective. He suggests that because the world's major corporations aim to enhance their reputations to promote their brands, states realize that this can reflect on, and enhance, their soft power. This is because "brands are not only seen as the engines of business, but also of politics" as they deliver "a competitive economic *and* political edge" (van Ham 2002, 253). Just as states are proactively concerned with increasing their legitimacy and soft power in global affairs, so are corporations by deriving the legitimacy that flows from institutionalizing their perspectives and interests in others. Therefore, both corporations and states deliberately and proactively work together to "deliver a message about their value and values to the widest possible audience" (van Ham 2002, 251). They understand that their power is greatest when they can "inspire rather than control" (van Ham 2002, 255), or as Nye (2004a, x) puts it, they know the value of having "the ability to get what you want through attraction rather than coercion or payments." Therefore, while the worlds of corporate public relations and international relations may seem quite separate, there is actually considerable overlap in terms of the language, practices, and goals employed by states and corporations in increasing their brand and soft power globally.

The World's Most Admired Companies

Table 5.1 illustrates the links between these worlds. It presents the top ten states in which the Fortune Global 500 corporations are headquartered, and compares them with the headquarters of the Fortune 500 World's Most Admired Companies and ranking of states with the highest levels of soft power in the Soft Power 30.[8] The top ten states for global corporations' headquarters, which account for 84 percent of those on the Fortune Global 500 list, are also the top ten states for soft power, with the exceptions of China and South Korea. In the case of China, despite it embarking on a "soft power blitz" over the course

Table 5.1: Global Corporations' Headquarters, World's Most Admired Companies, and Soft Power, 2015

	Fortune Global 500	Fortune 500 Top 50 World's Most Admired Companies	States' Soft Power Index (Rank)
US	128	40	73.68 (3)
China	98	–	40.85 (30)
Japan	54	1	66.86 (8)
France	31	–	73.64 (4)
UK	29	1	75.61 (1)
Germany	28	2	73.89 (2)
South Korea	17	1	54.32 (20)
Netherlands	13	–	65.21 (10)
Switzerland	12	1	67.52 (7)
Canada	11	–	71.71 (5)

Source: Fortune (2015a), Fortune (2015c), Portland Communications (2015).

of the past decade, including establishing a global network of Confucius Institutes and an extensive global portfolio of aid and development projects, it is the lowest-ranked state in the Soft Power 30. This is due to the country's poor record in areas such as human rights and freedom of expression (McClory 2015, 27–28). What is most noticeable, however, is that among the top fifty most admired companies, forty are based in the US, while five of the remaining ten are from the states that dominate both rankings for corporate headquarters and soft power, even if none is Chinese. As such, there seems a strong relationship between national economic power, soft power, and company reputation, with the US in a dominant position.

Table 5.2 focuses on the reasons why corporations are on the Fortune 500 World's Most Admired Companies list. The list is compiled annually by *Fortune Magazine* and is based on questionnaires provided to corporate representatives (Melo and Garrido-Morgado 2012). The survey takes place in two rounds. Respondents from 668 firms across twenty-nine countries are first asked to rank their industry peers across the nine attributes, one of which is community responsibility. Second, the industry leaders who responded to the first round of surveys (4,104 in total in 2015) are asked to select their ten most admired corporations overall. This produces the list of the top fifty most admired. A ranking for each firm is therefore produced on the basis of the nine criteria, as well as an overall ranking for the top fifty.

Table 5.2: Fortune 500 World's Most Admired Companies Ranked by Key Attributes, 2015

	Community Responsibility	Management Quality	Quality of Products/Services Offered	Innovativeness	Value as a Long-Term Investment	Soundness of Financial Position	Ability to Attract, Develop, and Retain Talent	Wise Use of Corporate Assets	Effectiveness in Conducting a Global Business
Most Admired									
1. Apple (US)	—[a]	—	4	1	7	3	5	9	3
2. Google (US)	—	6	5	2	3	1	2	—	5
3. Berkshire Hathaway (US)	—	—	—	—	10	—	—	—	—
4. Amazon (US)	—	—	3	4	—	—	10	—	—
5. Starbucks (US)	—	9	—	8	—	—	—	—	—
Top Ranking for Community Responsibility									
6. Walt Disney (US)	1	1	2	3	1	5	4	1	1
18. Whole Foods Market (US)	2	—	7	—	—	—	—	—	—
33. Nestlé (Switzerland)	3	10	6	—	2	4	7	5	2
36. Unilever (UK/Netherlands)	4	—	—	—	—	—	—	—	—
11. Johnson and Johnson (US)	5	—	—	—	9	—	—	—	—
24. Toyota (Japan)	6	—	—	—	—	—	—	—	8
Deere[c](US)	7	—	—	—	—	—	—	—	—
22. Wells Fargo (US)	8	3	8	—	—	6	—	2	—
US Bancorp[c](US)	9	2	—	—	6	7	8	4	—
NEXTEra Energy[bc](US)	10	—	—	10	—	—	—	—	—
Cisco Systems[bc](US)	10	—	—	—	—	10	—	—	—

Source: Fortune (2015c and 2015d).
[a] A dash signifies that the company was not ranked in the top ten.
[b] Tied.
[c] Not ranked in the top fifty "most admired."

What is striking about the top five most admired companies is that none of them is ranked in the top five for the criteria of community responsibility. In fact, they do not even rank in the top ten. These firms' rankings are derived mostly from other attributes, particularly management quality; quality of products/services offered; innovativeness; and soundness of financial position. In other words, they are admired for focusing on more traditional material drivers of success.

This is not to say that these other attributes and community responsibility are mutually exclusive. Many of the corporations ranked in the top ten for community responsibility also ranked highly for them too. Disney in particular stands out, but this is probably because as a corporation synonymous with global family entertainment, community responsibility is central to its business case, as opposed to supporting it. The same may be said of Whole Foods Market, which has "redefined grocery shopping in the US, becoming a stage for artisanal food companies trying to break into the national market" (Fortune 2015c). Therefore it is not so much a global corporation (although it does also have stores in the UK) as one focused on the promotion of community-based food suppliers "with an unshakeable commitment to sustainable agriculture" as "America's Healthiest Grocery Store" (Whole Foods Market 2016).[9] The only other attribute in which Whole Foods Market is in the top ten is quality of products/services offered, which surely is linked to its focus on community responsibility. Likewise, NEXTEra Energy is a US "leading clean energy company" whose focus is "helping solve [sic] America's energy challenges sustainably and responsibly" (NEXTera Energy 2016). In addition to ranking in the top ten for community responsibility, it is probably not surprising that the only other attribute on which it ranks similarly is innovativeness. Therefore, many of the companies that ranked highest for community responsibility did so because this attribute is central to their business case rather than supportive of it, and there is a sense that they are more locally/nationally rather than globally focused.[10]

Global Corporate Tax Avoidance

The Fortune 500 World's Most Admired Companies list represents the opinion of business insiders from the world's largest, best-known firms. As such, it can be criticized for presenting their views rather than those whose judgment actually confers or undermines the reputations corporations seek (e.g., see Brown and Perry 1994; Fryxell and Wang 1994). But what it reveals that they think matters most has implications for their companies' strategic motivations. The greater importance they accord attributes other than community responsibility suggests CSR is unlikely to be a primary driver for corporations on issues of major global importance. Global corporate tax avoidance is a salient example. It has become a major issue in recent years as companies like Apple, Google, Amazon, and Starbucks, all of which are in the world's top five most admired companies, have faced public criticism for their global corporate taxation structures (e.g., see Callaghan 2015). As they operate across multiple jurisdictions, they have taken advantage of opportunities to reduce or eliminate their taxation obligations by doing business in one national jurisdiction while notionally, and legally, shifting the location where they report their profits. They do not have to shift their actual physical operations, so that the national institutional contexts in which they are embedded and shape their preferences for operations discussed in Chapter 4 may effectively be retained, while for tax purposes they are irrelevant.

For example, in 2011 Google shifted 80 percent of its pre-tax profits from international subsidiaries to Bermuda, where a corporate tax rate of zero applies to the company (Allard 2014). This, and its use of complex tax maneuvers through Ireland and the Netherlands as tax centers due to their low tax rates, means it pays 2.4 percent tax on its non-US revenues (Johnston 2014). Inquiries into Google's taxation strategies were held in the UK in 2012 and 2013. The terms of the 2013 inquiry noted that in order to avoid corporate tax, "Google relies on the deeply unconvincing argument that its sales to UK clients take place in Ireland, despite clear evidence that the vast majority of sales activity takes place in the UK" (UK Public Accounts Committee on Tax Avoidance—Google 2015). Apple has similarly created subsidiaries in countries like Ireland to claim that most of its profits are earned either there or in other jurisdictions. These jurisdictions, in turn, do not regard these profits as taxable. Among the most damning accusations leveled at Apple is that in exploiting the gap between US and Irish tax jurisdictions Apple paid *no* tax on income totaling US$30 billion over 2009–2012 through its Irish subsidiary Apple Operations International, and enjoyed a tax rate of 0.05 percent on income of US$74 billion over the same period through Apple Sales International (US Senate Committee on Homeland Security and Governmental Affairs 2013). In essence, Apple's subsidiaries collect dividends from most of Apple's offshore affiliates and pay little to no tax on these. In fact, they would seem to exist primarily for this purpose. Apple Operations International receives dividends from Apple's offshore affiliates but has no employees and no physical presence. Apple Sales International contracts manufacturers in China to make Apple products that it then sells to Apple Distribution International. It then pays as little as 2 percent tax on its profits, having negotiated this special rate with the Irish government (Anon 2013).

The global annual tax revenue losses resulting from such arrangements are estimated to be US$240 billion (OECD 2015).[11] Commensurate with their dominance of the global economy, the revenue losses to governments from tax avoidance by US-based global corporations alone have been estimated at US$100 billion (Gravelle 2015). That the problem is so large, and global corporations' tax affairs deliberately structured to create it, suggests they are not practicing the responsibility they preach. Since the GFC, as governments have struggled to return their budgets to surplus and in many cases their citizens have endured the resulting austerity measures, it has led to campaigns waged by activists and international NGOs, including the Tax Justice Network, War on Want, Christian Aid, and Oxfam, as well as attracting much critical media coverage. The campaigns have portrayed corporate tax avoidance as a failure of democratic governance, an issue that reflects a growing dissatisfaction with the distribution of power and wealth in society and the failure of global corporations to pay their "fair share" of tax while shifting the burden for so doing to society (e.g., see Oxfam 2016; for a more extended analysis, see Elbra and Mikler 2017).

Statements made in defense of their actions reveal that global corporations' tax arrangements are not just the result of deliberate strategic decisions, but that they are unlikely to voluntarily pay their fair share in response to such campaigns. For example, Google's tax arrangements have been defended by its chairman, Eric Schmidt, in the following terms:

> I am very proud of the structure that we set up. We did it based on the incentives that the governments offered us to operate. ... It's called capitalism. We are proudly capitalistic. I'm not confused about this. (Kumar and Wright 2012).

It takes no great leap of logic to conclude that the intention behind global corporations' CSR commitments is to offset negative perceptions arising from a primary focus on financial performance and shareholder value. This is supported by studies such as Davis et al. (2016), who find companies with the most extensive CSR programs are also those with the most aggressive tax minimization activities. They conclude not only that "the payment of taxes is not viewed as an important socially responsible activity" but also that "CSR and taxes act as substitutes rather than complements" (Davis et al. 2016, 65). In other words, CSR primarily serves the function of "window-dressing."

Community Attitudes

Kolleck (2013, 147) notes that "the discursive power of global companies is ... based on legitimacy and acceptance of business-friendly norms and ideas." In propounding norms associated with CSR and making rules that describe appropriate forms of behavior based on their private authority, they must be seen to abide by them, and if they are seen to fail to do so "they can be sidelined and their credibility and influence may be diminished." They may even come to be seen as essentially psychopathic entities lacking in empathy, altruism, or morality that must be controlled for the public good to be served (e.g., see Bakan 2005). If global corporations' CSR proclamations are widely and increasingly perceived as little more than "spin," this weakens their discursive power and their legitimacy to wield private authority. If they publicly celebrate and promote their strategies, as companies like Google appear to have done in avoiding paying tax, they risk a skeptical public that rejects their right to self-govern. In the case of tax avoidance, and maybe other concerns, the political "space" is opened for national regulation and international agreements to control their behavior to be seen as essential, as opposed to relying on them to do the right thing.

There is evidence that there may be politically fertile grounds for this to occur. Table 5.3 presents responses of those surveyed in the top ten states where global corporations are headquartered, plus the BRICs, to the fifth wave of the World Values Survey. Conducted over 2005–2009 in 58 countries with over 80,000 respondents, it gives an indication of comparative attitudes across the states surveyed.[12] Respondents' confidence in "major companies," "the government," and "charitable and humanitarian organizations" (i.e., NGOs) are presented.[13] Based on their responses we may infer the degree to which global corporations are comparatively viewed as legitimate political actors, and the extent to which their reputation allows them to be regarded as socially responsible self-governors. With the exception of Japanese respondents, who have low levels of confidence across all categories, the percentage of respondents in industrialized states with "a great deal" of confidence in major companies is remarkably small, especially in comparison to charitable and humanitarian organizations. On average, respondents from these states are around twice as confident in charitable and humanitarian organizations compared to

Table 5.3: Confidence in Major Companies, the Government, and Charitable or Humanitarian Organizations

	Major Companies			The Government			Charitable or Humanitarian Organizations		
	Total Confident (%)	A great deal (%)	Quite a lot (%)	Total Confident (%)	A great deal (%)	Quite a lot (%)	Total Confident (%)	A great deal (%)	Quite a lot (%)
Industrialized									
US	25.6	1.8	23.8	36.8	4.8	32	61.5	9.9	51.6
Japan	36.2	1.7	34.5	29.1	1.5	27.6	25.8	1.4	24.4
France	38.8	4.9	33.9	28.9	2.7	26.2	65.8	18	47.8
UK	33.1	3.2	29.9	32.4	4.8	27.6	70.2	18.1	52.1
Germany	25.1	1.7	23.4	22.7	1.5	21.2	59.8	10.7	49.1
South Korea	50.2	3.2	47.0	45.6	2.6	43	71.2	10.9	60.3
Netherlands	30.9	1.2	29.7	26.7	0.8	25.9	46.7	5.2	41.5
Switzerland	38.1	2.6	35.5	65.1	7.4	57.7	64.7	8.4	56.3
Canada	34.8	2.5	32.3	36.7	4.4	32.3	73.4	16.3	57.1
AVERAGE	38.5	2.4	36.1	43.5	3.8	39.7	64.0	10.2	53.8
BRICs									
Brazil	56.8	9.7	47.1	45.9	9.7	36.2	65.6	20.1	45.5
Russia	30.6	3.3	27.3	42.8	5.9	36.9	48.9	12.8	36.1
India	33.6	14.1	19.5	44	18.0	26	30.8	14.2	16.6
China	41.3	6.2	35.1	87.6	37.5	50.1	51.3	13.6	37.7
AVERAGE	40.6	8.3	32.3	55.1	17.8	37.3	49.2	15.2	34.0
ALL	37.9	6.8	31.1	45.3	13.3	32.0	57.9	16.6	41.3

Source: World Values Survey (2015)

major companies. In the case of the US, UK, and Canada the difference is even greater. These are the Anglo-Saxon LMEs, states where there is an institutional acceptance that there should be more of an arm's length relationship between the state and the market, and where liberal ideals of free markets and shareholder value predominate. In the case of the US, it is also where most of the world's major global corporations are headquartered. The greater confidence in government expressed by survey respondents in the BRICs reflects arguments about the heightened role of the state in their economic emergence. Particularly in the case of China, the state capitalism that characterizes the institutional form of its economic relations discussed in Chapter 4 seems reflected in the near universal confidence respondents have in their government, including a sizeable minority with a "great deal" of confidence. But whatever the differences, in all cases either the government or NGOs engender greater feelings of trust than major companies, the former more so in the BRICs, the latter more so in industrialized states. This suggests that despite their declarations of embracing CSR, by their practices and the perception of these they still face major hurdles in establishing the discursive legitimacy necessary to wield their private authority for private governance.

Conclusion

States and corporations have always shared the power they possess as a result of their sovereignty and authority, and therefore public regulations are often a reflection of the state–corporate relations that surround and underpin them. Now this is occurring at a global level. Global corporations' ability to operate in multiple jurisdictions, the knowledge they have of the markets they control, and their expertise in deploying and using their resources across different territories puts them in a powerful position to set as well as influence regulatory agendas at the global level. They also have the incentive to do so, because in preferring (and possessing) market control rather than competition, and seeking to define the rules by which markets operate, they can create global norms and institutions conducive to their interests. The result is that the "exercise of corporate power can shape public policy through its influence on states, but it can also create effects that are quite independent of states, but comparable to public policies in their significance" (Porter and Brown 2013, 107). It follows that they may potentially make rules for the world in their own right, as well as in relation to states. Global corporations are in a position to act in this capacity if states and their societies accept that the practices they adopt are in the broader global interest, and grant them the right to set agendas, whether these be economic, social, or political. The political power they may end up exercising is then not simply a matter of issuing "commands," or of their conditioning the experience of others as a result of their control or underpinning of economic systems. In other words, it is not just a matter of the first two faces of power. Employing their discursive power lends them the legitimacy to convince states and their societies "that not acceding to their demands will be immoral, destructive of the economy, or have some other negative consequence" (Porter and Brown 2013, 99).

However, if global corporations are in a privileged position to make global rules, either in their own right or relationally with states, we should be concerned about their motivations. As the data tend to indicate that their political power, and their exercise of it via their private authority, is driven by their market control and geographical concentration, it would surely also be naive to believe their goals and interests in specific territorial contexts are synonymous with the global public good. There are indications that even those surveyed in the powerful states where they are headquartered are skeptical this is the case. There is anything but an obviously symbiotic relationship between the private interests of global corporations and those of the world's peoples, and if this is asserted then it is likely motivated by those who benefit from it being believed: their board members and shareholders in the powerful (predominantly LME) states where they are based.

6 CONCLUSION: THREE IMPLICATIONS

Global corporations control rather than compete in markets. Their control of their markets is salient to how they express their economic interests, as opposed to having these constrained or dictated by market forces. This is a key reason why they should be viewed, first and foremost, as political actors, and it is important to re-embody them as such to understand their power. It is also important to re-territorialize them as national in their identities and regional in their operations, as opposed to global in their interests. Their home states and regions are the geographical source of their political power, just as their market control is its economic source. Accepting these twin realities, and the analysis in light of them conducted in the preceding chapters, suggests three key implications.

The first implication of conceiving global corporations as political rather than market actors is that the free market, as a concept, is largely defunct for understanding them. This being the case, neoliberalism is also an increasingly problematic theoretical lens through which to view their actions and interests. To the extent that a neoliberal lens is applied, even critically, it serves to hide the political power global corporations possess and seek to wield. In hiding their political power in theoretical abstractions, it could be claimed that the concept of the free market and neoliberal ideology also serves their interests, but the potential for both to continue to be employed as what amounts to a discursive "veil" may be diminishing. With the evidence that markets are neither free nor competitive but controlled by global corporations, it is possible to go further than identifying global corporations as more accurately political than market actors, and declare them *anti-market* actors. They may have been aided in their growth and expansion by free market policies and the neoliberal ideology underpinning them that helped to produce the dominant vision of globalization. But by their nature and their actions, global corporations themselves now give the lie to, and as such threaten the veracity of, this vision.

The second implication is that they are more accurately seen as national or multinational, rather than transnational or global, political actors. If it is time to move on from the rather disembodied debates around free markets and neoliberalism to focus more on the embodiment of economic power in the hands of global corporations, then it is also time to focus more on the places where, and from which, they wield it. These are also the places where responsibility for how it is wielded lies. Rather than a global institutional context, the reality remains that differing national and regional contexts institutionally inform the political power that global corporations possess. These differing institutional contexts are not just contained within state borders, but are now projected and compete on the world stage between states via their global corporations.

The first two implications lead to the third one. Granting global corporations the legitimacy to exercise private authority in support of private governance, either in service of their material interests, or as an extension of the interests of their home states, is unlikely to be synonymous with the interests of the world's peoples. Therefore, the states where global corporations are headquartered bear responsibility for modifying or controlling their political power. The rationale for global governance if powerful states find themselves unable, or unwilling, to govern their global corporations is not that the alternative is a world of neoliberal free markets, but of politically powerful global corporations that call the shots. Allowing them the unfettered freedom to employ their private authority to potentially increase their discursive power only serves to enhance, rather than moderate, the considerable instrumental and structural power they already possess.

The intention stated in Chapter 1 was to engage in some "landscape gardening" of the "oases" of scholarship on global corporate power. Therefore, in drawing out these implications, my intention in this concluding chapter is not to state the "truth" of the political power global corporations possess and employ. This book has not been an exercise in proving or disproving hypotheses, nor in having the final word on what the political power of global corporations actually is. Instead, the aim has been to open up debate about it, and to do so not from a particular ideological standpoint, nor from a point on the political spectrum, but in respect of what the unit of analysis should be: global corporations as political actors in an economically interconnected, but not de-territorialized, world, seeking to construct it in the image of their economic interests.

The Irrelevance of the Free Market

In 1972, Stephen Hymer predicted the global takeover of markets by global corporations from economically powerful states in the following terms:

> Suppose giant multinational corporations (say 300 from the USA and 200 from Europe and Japan) succeed in establishing themselves as the dominant form of international enterprise and come to control a significant share of industry (especially modern industry) in each country. The world economy will resemble more and more the US economy, where each of the large corporations tends to spread over the entire continent, and to penetrate almost every nook and cranny. (Hymer 1972, quoted in Nolan 2007, 69)

Nearly fifty years later, his predictions seem prescient. A world in which 500 corporations account for nearly half the global economy and determine patterns of global trade and investment would not have been surprising to him. Nor are they to the *McKinsey Global Institute* and *The Economist*, both of which conceive the possibility of a near future in which a small number of intersectoral global corporations control the production and distribution of, to all intents and purposes, everything (Dobbs et al. 2015; Anon 2016b).

It is therefore time to pronounce the free market dead, or at least conceptually irrelevant for understanding power relations. Today, globally free markets comprising many players are unusual. Whether by design, inaction, or inability on the part of states is debatable, but there seems little doubt that the classical liberal notion of efficient economic outcomes being produced on the basis of the invisible hand of the free market has been supplanted by the reality of global corporations that control their global production and service networks. It follows that concepts like "competition" and "entrepreneurialism" are also increasingly outmoded. To the extent that competition exists, it is defined more by global corporations than by consumers, who face little choice in the products and services they are offered. Market control is pervasive. It logically follows that so is coordination, and perhaps in many instances collusion. Rather than entrepreneurialism, strategic planning on the part of senior management is the main determining factor in corporate operations, so that global supply chains overseen by vast corporate empires that are household names are the contemporary reality.

To be sure, there may be a great deal of competition in some aspects of states' national economies, with many firms competing to sell their goods and services. Family-owned cafes and restaurants, fashion boutiques, real estate agencies, and the like come to mind. At the global level, there are also some industries that are temporarily characterized by many players and intense competition as new products and services offered by start-up companies emerge, prior to sectoral consolidation as they mature. There is also competition between suppliers to global corporations, or among developers of products and services delivered by the networks they control—e.g., the applications available to users of smartphones on the platforms offered by Apple and Google. And of course, goods and services are produced and exchanged in markets. Things are bought and sold. However, the global economy is not predominantly characterized by small, entrepreneurial firms adrift on, and battling, a roiling sea of market forces. Today, global corporations do not just make the ships on this sea but the sea itself. That the metaphor must be stretched to the point of absurdity highlights the reality of the political power possessed and wielded by global corporations as a result of their control of global economic processes.

Marxists have long predicted this would come to pass. They understand the tendency of capitalism to concentrate economic power rather than disperse it, and as such are not surprised that mega-corporations dominate the global economy. Yet surely their concerns must be converging with those of liberals. The pervasive domination of industries by very few global corporations should be as worrying to those of us who would like to see markets free and competitive as to those who would like to see them eliminated. One does not have to be a Marxist, nor even particularly radical, to observe the growth in inequality evident in the world in which we live, the concentration of economic and political power, and the economic instability produced by "turbo capitalism" (Luttwak 1999), to be concerned. Therefore, it seems reasonable to speculate that if Adam Smith and Karl Marx were alive today they would find much on which to agree. Given they were both focused on the emancipation of populations from those who controlled the means of production in their time (i.e., the state for Smith and the *bourgeoisie* for Marx), we may surmise that their attentions would have been turned to global corporations. Marx would have predicted a systemic failure and revolution to overthrow the transnational capitalist class that uses them as its vehicle for global economic domination.[1] Smith would have preferred competitive markets made up of a multitude of business entities owned by those who ran them, entrepreneurially conducting their affairs on the basis of the market's invisible hand. But while their viewpoints would have differed in terms of the ends they desired, both would have been concerned by global corporations' control of world trade through their global supply chains, their ability to reduce weaker states' self-determination via offering or withholding FDI, and their private authority to shape rather than respond to market forces. It is easy to imagine them disagreeing on the merits of global capitalism for ensuring individual well-being and freedom, while agreeing on the problematic nature of a world in which economic power and processes are held in so few hands.

It is more than a matter of mere intellectual amusement to indulge in such speculation. The data demonstrate that global corporations create and seek to moderate economic conditions in their interests. They decide what is produced, how it is produced, where it is sold, and at what price. They impact on, and make decisions about, labor conditions. They control financial flows. They are central to solving social and environmental problems like climate change while helping to create them in the first place. If they do not make the rules, they influence the making of them in national and international policy-making fora. They are not just powerful market actors because they exercise control over the means of production. They are also not just economic in their focus, though the outcomes they desire are. Their strategic decisions underpin the functioning and economic geography of the world economy. This being the case, believing that neoliberal globalization means societies are either servants of, or served by, markets and market forces in a world in which states are increasingly irrelevant serves as a discursive veil behind which the structural and instrumental power wielded by global corporations in pursuit of their interests may be hidden, while also being enhanced, as discussed in Chapter 2.

That veil may be in the process of being lifted. The election of Donald Trump as President of the US in 2016, following the successful Brexit vote, led Blyth (2016) to announce that "the era of neoliberalism is over (and) the era of neo-nationalism has just begun." It is dangerous to make predictions driven by emotions on the spur of the moment, yet even *The Economist* has suggested "the long pro-business era that began under Ronald Reagan in the 1980s and continued under Bill Clinton in the 1990s is giving way to a much more anti-business mood" (Anon 2016b, 15). More sober analysis by the likes of the IMF has also concluded that neoliberalism has been "oversold" (Ostry et al. 2016), while its Managing Director, Christine Lagarde, has publicly opined that there must be a move toward "inclusive capitalism" as opposed to a focus on capitalism "characterized by excess" (Lagarde 2014). Where this will lead is hard to predict, and in this respect it is important to acknowledge that the ideology underpinning neoliberalism has evolved over time. For example, Davies (2016) sees it as moving through combative, normative, and punitive eras, over which it has challenged, represented, and then defended/imposed its ideology as the status quo. Likewise, Cahill (2014) conceives of neoliberalism as a multifaceted concept, existing ideologically as opposed to in reality, and being embedded (and re-embedded) institutionally in the service of material interests. If one accepts that "theory is always for someone and for some purpose" (Cox 1996, 207), then the reason why neoliberalism has evolved is that it has had to do so in the discursive service of political agendas. It has certainly served those of global corporations, because it has shifted the focus to markets as the pros and cons of a deregulation and privatization agenda were debated, in the process serving to obscure their economically concentrated political power.

It should be overwhelmingly evident that markets are not free, regardless of whether or not one has a preference that they should be. In fact, the period of neoliberal globalization that commenced in the 1980s with the end of the Cold War, and the policies of free trade, deregulation, and privatization that went with it, have not produced the world of free markets and market forces we are so often told we live in, but economic domination by global corporations. It follows that while it may have been the case that global corporations were served and produced by an ideological embrace of neoliberal globalization, it could easily be contended that they themselves now threaten it. They undermine market competition, and therefore they undermine the argument as well as the reality that globalization is neoliberal. Chapter 1 opened with reference to science fiction, and I am not the only author who has drawn the link between global corporate power and the dystopian futures it imagines. Wilks (2013, 2–3) has declared "the corporation with a license to operate has become, in Mary Shelley's image, a Frankenstein's monster, threatening the state that gave it life." It likewise threatens the global free market. If global corporations control markets, and do so both economically and geographically, then in effect they are anti-market actors. It is time to refocus debates from the demise of the state as a result of neoliberal globalization, to include the demise of the free market as a result of their rise.

Multinational, not Global, Corporations

Whether measured on the basis of revenue, stock market capitalization, or a composite index of factors, the world's most powerful global corporations are headquartered in no more than ten states, with one in particular accounting for nearly half of these: the US. Those from emerging market economies likewise hail from ten states while having their headquarters dominated by one: China. As shown in Chapter 3, the data on their production, employment, and sales demonstrate that they are not as transnational as is often said to be the case. To the extent that they are becoming more global in their operations, there are clear geographical patterns evident as a result of their M&As, FDI stocks, and FDI flows between the states where they are headquartered. Power in the global economy remains triadic to a large degree, which is to say it revolves geographically around North America (especially the US), the EU (especially Western Europe), and East Asian states like Japan, South Korea, and more recently China. These states are the places from which global corporations derive their power, in addition to wielding it beyond their borders. The geopolitical patterns of power revealed, as well as produced, by global corporations mirror those of their economically powerful states, and as such they not only reflect these states' power but potentially enhance it. This being the case, a nationalist analysis would seem to resonate, because the states where global corporations are headquartered have an interest in enabling them to do so.

Vernon (1977, 177) saw the potential for this forty years ago when he observed that "the network of the multinational enterprise can become a conduit through which the power of one sovereign state is projected into the territory of another." Where powerful states once built empires by conquering weaker states' territories in order to exert control over their resources and labor, today they facilitate their global corporations to act as their emissaries by promoting and enacting what appear superficially to be liberal policies. Although it could be argued that all states have ceded some of the power they possess as a result of their sovereignty to markets, it could equally be claimed that in so doing economically powerful states have enabled their global corporations to project it beyond their borders, while denying weaker states the opportunity to erect barriers to prevent this (e.g., see Drezner 2007; Braithwaite and Drahos 2000). Therefore, the widely held belief that neoliberal globalization means that markets are in charge also serves the interests of the states where global corporations are headquartered.

It allows both to engage in a "globalization made me do it" narrative.

In reality, global corporations' home states and the regions where they have their operations are a key aspect of their identity, interests, and political power. This is particularly the case for their instrumental power which, as noted in Chapter 2, by its very nature has a more territorially grounded dimension in the manner in which it is exercised. It also has bearing on the structure of the global economy, as underpinned by the geography of the operations of global corporations. The GFC reminded us that powerful states where the world's major global corporations are based will not stand idly by as they collapse, even if those of a liberal ideological persuasion might think they should. Instead, the US and UK bailed out their banks and banking systems, supported their major corporations, and provided rounds of national economic stimuli for their national economies. In the process they shored up the global financial system and stabilized the global economy, but they also shored up their global corporations' dominance of it. Such actions are hard to reconcile with casting corporations as primarily global political actors, rather than national and regional ones. Even if not as evident in more tranquil times, the links between global corporations and their home states endure.

It is similarly worth noting that the G7 states with the largest government expenditures presented in Chapter 1 are the same ones that, prior to the GFC, backed the imposition of Washington Consensus conditionality on less powerful states through the control they exert over the Bretton Woods Institutions (e.g., see Woods 2006). They are also among the states that were instrumental in suggesting the need for a "new world order" in the immediate aftermath of the GFC, but one which ultimately looks very much like that which existed prior to it: an economically interconnected world characterized by free trade and investment. They have not chosen to become smaller and weaker themselves, which is one reason why Chang (2002, 2008) suggests that where possible economically powerful states deliberately "kick away the ladder" to constrain the policy options available to weaker ones, thereby ensuring that their global economic pre-eminence remains unchallenged. In addition to kicking away weaker states' policy options, economically powerful states may extend their infrastructural power beyond their borders through their global corporations, which act as agents of globalizing their power. This is exactly what Starrs (2013) suggests is the case for the US in particular, given its global corporations' dominance of almost every industry sector. Through its global corporations, the US has increased its structural power over the global economy. If the US believes itself economically challenged it is likely to back away from the neoliberal prescriptions it previously embraced and advocated, while the converse might be expected of rising powers such as China. Policies of free markets and, by implication, freedoms for global corporations are promoted by powerful states. Such policies are seen as desirable and accepted as the conventional wisdom as long as they serve their individual or collective national interests.

If market concentration is associated with geographical concentration, it may also produce institutional effects. Rather than being "geocentric" in orientation on the basis of their business interests, to a large degree global corporations remain "ethnocentric" on the basis of their nationality.[2] Given that the US remains the world's most economically powerful state, and is the headquarters of nearly half the world's largest global corporations, this could explain why its model of capitalism approximates the one often said to be inevitable for the world. As noted in Chapter 5, global professional services firms based in the US and the UK also serve to spread and legitimize this model, as much as the US itself does. The rise of the BRICs, and especially China with its form of state capitalism, suggests this could change. Whether or not it does, the point is that in globalizing their economies and working with their global corporations to achieve economic dominance, it is not at all obvious that powerful states sacrifice their national institutional variations, just as it is not obvious that the world is naturally rather than institutionally characterized by neoliberal free markets. While states may work to liberalize the global economy to enable their global corporations if this serves their mutual interests, this does not mean they must adopt a single institutional form at home.

An overly aggregated and general account of globalization can only fail to capture and reflect the institutional specificity of distinct national contexts in which global corporations are based and/or have operations. Furthermore, as global corporations become physically disembedded from their home states when they invest and operate abroad, it does not necessarily follow that they become institutionally disembedded as well. If, as noted in Chapter 4, they tend to maintain the organizational structures that served the institutional context of their home states, then institutionally as well as physically they are potential extensions of their home states' territories. As such, it is not just the case that different varieties of capitalism pertain within states' borders, but that varieties of capitalism compete internationally and that global corporations are one of the mediums for facilitating this. The result is that institutional variations that were once contained within national boundaries are now played out beyond and between them. Unless one is ideologically wedded to one particular political economy perspective, it therefore seems unwise to make claims of some global institutional context where the political power of global corporations is realized, rather than the states and regions where in reality they remain mutually entangled. If such claims are made, they should be seen more as an ideological crusade on the part of those making them, like many of the early globalists, and a reflection of the institutional contest now taking place outside, as well as inside, the borders of economically powerful states.

As Braithwaite (2008) has noted, states and their corporations together shape and benefit from an age of "mega-corporate capitalism." They are mutually politically and institutionally entangled. Because this is the case, in the process of re-territorializing global corporations it is important to abandon the myth not just of the powerless state (Weiss 1998) but of the placeless corporation that in reality is more national or multinational than global.

Balancing Global Corporations' Political Power

Having said this, it is also the case that global corporations do govern themselves and others, in addition to being institutionally embedded in, and extensions of, their home states. For example, as discussed in Chapter 5, they attempt to build discursive claims of social responsibility as a way of increasing their private authority to govern. In theory, CSR and private governance initiatives may produce desirable outcomes. They may do so in reality, too, and this is to be welcomed. However, fundamentally the rationale for CSR is to serve corporate interests, rather than the needs and interests of society. There are some authors who speak of corporate sovereignty (e.g., Barkan 2013), suggesting that the private authority of global corporations is akin to the decision-making ability of states. If this is believed to be the case, and that it is desirable, then they will be in a remarkably strong position to have the freedom to do whatever they like. But the reality is that while states are sovereign over their territories, global corporations are sovereign over their operations only insofar as states, their shareholders, and society (though in most cases more narrowly their consumers) grant them the ability to be so. Therefore, it is difficult to speak of their responsibilities without reference to the other actors whose interests they serve, or whose interests must be balanced against theirs.

Shareholders represent a relatively narrow constituency, and although shareholder activism may modify corporate behavior, it is problematic in the sense that it fails to democratically include the many voices of those affected by global corporations' activities. Consumers represent a broader constituency, but they either face limited choices in the products and services they are offered due to the market control global corporations possess, or they exercise their consciences too inconsistently to be effective in disciplining global corporations. As noted in Chapter 5, the proposed sinking of Shell's Brent Sparr platform led to mass mobilization, whereas the suicides and ongoing exploitation of workers in Apple's supply chain have not. The latter may in fact represent one case in a broader global trend of exploitative and forced labor, the latter of which may be thought of as akin to modern-day slavery. Disturbingly, LeBaron (2014) presents data from the International Labor Organization estimating that at least 21 million people work in conditions of forced labor to earn private business around US$44 billion a year globally, as a result of the subcontracting conditions through which global corporations govern their supply chains. It could be said that forced labor is intrinsic to the business model of many global corporations' supply chains, and further that this is no secret. People are well informed of the bad conditions and low wages of workers in developing countries producing the products they consume, and they know this is why they are cheaper than might be the case if produced domestically. They either do not care enough, or for long enough, for their consciences to provide sufficient motivation for them to consistently act to ameliorate this state of affairs.

This brings us back to state-corporate entanglement. Recognizing that global corporations control often vast networks, yet remain national and multinational rather more than they are global, the question is this: can their powerful home states harness and work with their global corporations to achieve desirable outcomes for their, and maybe other, societies? They should be challenged to do so, because the prospect of self-governing global corporations responding to social concerns expressed through their shareholders or consumers seems very much a second-best alternative. The conventional wisdom is that global problems in which global actors are the main protagonists require global solutions. Yet because global corporations are not as global as is often held to be the case, this may not necessarily be a productive perspective. For example, mitigating climate change is said to require that all states, their societies, and all corporations be involved.

As the problem is so ubiquitous, so must be the solution. Yet, as Giddens (2009) argues, it is largely because climate change is framed in these terms that national solutions in the form of action by the handful of key states and their global corporations are downplayed. If one observes that the US, the EU, Japan, China, and the other states of the BRICs account for nearly two-thirds of all greenhouse gas emissions (IEA 2008), and that these are the same states in which the world's major global corporations are headquartered, then it follows that they not only should but must take the lead in action to reduce emissions. Their dominance of the global economy through their global corporations seems at odds, to say the least, with stressing the necessity of global agreements. Arguments cast in these terms may just ensure that either no agreement is reached or no meaningful outcome achieved. As opposed to minimizing the potential for free riding by having as many parties as possible sign up to international agreements, such arguments may also be seen as designed to get powerful states and their global corporations "off the hook," just like stressing the inevitability of neoliberal globalization discursively shrouds the structural reality of their mutual interests.

The same could be said of the problem of tax avoidance, referred to in Chapter 5. The global corporations that have attracted the greatest public ire for their aggressive tax minimization arrangements—such as Google, Apple, Amazon, and Starbucks—are all US-based. It could be claimed that their overriding focus on financial and economic performance metrics are hallmarks of LME institutional preferences that support shareholder capitalism. It could also be claimed that regardless of this, any corporation will seek to reduce its tax liabilities, given the opportunity to do so. Whether this is related to the national institutional context of their home state or simply a matter of strategic decisions to reduce their tax payments is debatable, but it is certainly the case that these global corporations are taking advantage of the arbitrage opportunities afforded them by states engaged in tax competition. Although a liberal ideological belief in free markets is expressed in defense of their tax minimization strategies by senior corporate office holders, the reality is that free markets have very little to do with these. Market control and corporate-state relations explain far more. In fact, a key reason why progress on an international agreement to combat the problem has proved elusive is the divergent interests of states, not the freedoms of the global market, and in particular the reticence of the US to curtail such activities unless in a position of regulatory control rather than ceding this to multilateral agreements (e.g., see Palan and Wigan 2014). If some states are engaging in tax competition, then they are effectively "stealing" other states' tax revenues and attacking their standards as much as global corporations may be said to be doing so. If stealing is too strong a claim, at the very least it is the case that through their actions some states are enabling global corporations to pay little or no tax, rather than paying it to those who should collect it. As for the corporations themselves, the justifications they offer suggest that, regardless of the CSR literature on the potential for self-regulation to enhance corporate reputation, what matters most to them are traditional metrics of economic performance.

Examples such as these suggest we should question a world in which democratically elected governments are now judged on their ability to attain and retain credit ratings that are determined by private agencies, international standards are largely a matter for industry associations to determine, and CSR is widely claimed by global corporations to be as important as making profits. It is certainly the case that the instrumental and structural power of global corporations has facilitated this, but their discursive power has led them to be perceived as legitimately entitled to perform such functions and make such claims. It is not just their size, nor their ability to influence/control policymaking processes, but their ideological manipulation and conditioning of states and their societies into accepting their desires and ends as not so much private versus public, but as *right*. We cannot uncritically believe that they are. Unless social responsibility is central to their business interests—e.g., the provision of sustainable energy, the sale of organic produce and the like—it is surely the case that there must usually be a tension between the political power they wield in seeking profits and control over economic processes, and the outcomes societies would like to see them deliver in other regards. Therefore, it is desirable that global corporations' private authority should be balanced against the public good, and that this be regarded as a responsibility of the states in which they are headquartered. These states should not promote the liberalization of their global corporations' gains while abrogating a duty to ensure their social responsibilities.

It would also seem reasonable to demand that a different approach be taken to international agreements on trade and investment. If market forces are less important than market control, and if consumer or shareholder action is likely to be insufficient to govern global corporations, then international agreements should not focus on the creation and maintenance of free and competitive markets. This is not because they are undesirable, but because overwhelmingly they do not characterize global corporations' operations. As such, global governance is required not because neoliberal globalization is otherwise inevitable, but because the unfettered dominance of the global economy by global corporations backed by their powerful states is the alternative to it. Therefore, international organizations such as the WTO, IMF, and World Bank should no longer be used as vehicles for liberalizing and deregulating trade and investment. Their roles should be as a counterweight to the political power of global corporations via agreements in such areas as a global rate(s) of taxation, global labor standards, global environmental requirements, and the like. This would ensure that the voices and concerns of weaker states and their societies are heard and acted on, in addition to those of consumers and shareholders in the powerful states where the world's global corporations are headquartered. It would also reflect the reality that markets are not free, and therefore that policies and agreements that maintain the fiction they are free only increase the tendency for political power to be further concentrated in the hands of both global corporations and their home states.

This may seem a naive conclusion to reach, and perhaps a case of wishful thinking, given the use of international organizations by powerful states in pursuit of their interests. Yet it may be in these states' interests that they act proactively to alter international organizations' *raisons d'être*. If legitimacy involves "the capacity of a political system to engender and maintain the belief that existing political institutions are the most appropriate and proper ones for the society" (Lipset 1983, 64), then a failure to act may risk delegitimizing the current global economic order they helped create, just as the nature and actions of global corporations increasingly challenge claims of the inevitability of neoliberal globalization.

Conclusion

This has not been a book about the role played by global corporations in respect of governance, although the potential for it was considered as a result of their private authority in Chapter 5. It has not been a book about the political power of "the" corporation, focusing on its organizational form, its legal construction, and the like, although this was touched on and flows from the discussion in Chapters 2 and 4 of global corporations' entanglement with states and embedding in different national institutional contexts. Nor has it been about the enduring role of states in regulating corporations, although this is suggested in the geographical patterns of trade, investment, production, and ownership and control presented in Chapter 3. Excellent books and studies have been referred to throughout that are more focused on areas such as these. This book complements them by focusing specifically on the *political power* possessed by *global* corporations, and how it may be best understood so that it may be analyzed. It therefore speaks to, and hopefully with, these other studies by providing stronger foundations for understanding the contours of the political power global corporations possess. The reason it has done so is because, as Culpepper (2011, 185) notes, "The study of business power is currently more neglected than it has been for the last half century." Reflecting on this statement, Bell (2012, 661) sees it as more accurate to say that "debates about business power ... did not wholly end but were deflected into wider debates about 'globalization' and related arguments about how the structures of global capitalism shape the capacities, resources, and even the ideologies of actors."

Instead of going somewhat missing in the abstractions inherent in the course that the debates have taken, and in what amounts to a states-versus-markets account, with more focus on the states and *a priori* assumptions about the markets, global corporations should be central to understanding where political power and influence reside in today's world. Global economic processes as embodied in global corporations are neither about markets nor about competition. They are about control, leverage, relationships, strategic decision making, and the creation of discourses conducive to enhancing material interests. They are about political power exercised by global corporations as political actors. Focusing on global corporations as key actors driving change in an economically interconnected world speaks truth to power more accurately than pronouncements of the inevitable death or diminishment of the state on the altar of global market forces. The latter view has led many to see states as having no alternative but to embrace market imperatives. In reality, it is the market that has also been "killed" by global corporations.

Studying the reality of global corporations based in, and operating from, economically powerful states also means rejecting the notion that we have a world characterized by market-focused firms versus national interest-focused governments. This has led many with a critical perspective on economic relations to believe a "fight" is going on. The reality is that both are often "dancing" instead. Analyzing this dance in which they are engaged calls for an actor-centered perspective that focuses on the corporations and the governments of nations where they are headquartered, for it is from their home bases that global corporations still substantially derive their power. As such, their enduring embeddedness in distinct national contexts for material and institutional reasons remains important for understanding the intersection of national and corporate interests in world affairs. Economically powerful states are potentially empowered through their global corporations. It is therefore virtually impossible to disentangle their interests in developing policies and the outcomes that result. The complexity of the relationship between the two should be the focus for analysis.

Ultimately, we should engage in fewer theoretical abstractions. We know the global corporations' names, we know the states in which they are headquartered, and we know the states in which they invest and operate. We need to have a better idea of what they do, as well as how and why they do it, and therefore to make them the subject of political analysis.

NOTES

1 Introduction: The Global Corporate Takeover

1 By way of historical comparison, much Cold War science fiction imagined an expansive, cosmopolitan future in which the solar system or galaxy was colonized (e.g., the works of Isaac Asimov and Arthur C. Clarke), with this threatened by repressive regimes and the potential for nuclear annihilation (e.g., Walter M. Miller's *A Canticle for Leibowitz* and John Wyndham's *The Chrysalids*).
2 Later, he also adopted the geographical analogy that, due to globalization, "the world is flat" (Friedman 2005).
3 Based on this definition, "a company where 70% of their sales are generated in Asia would not be considered a global MNE even though they might have significant operations in more than one country, but one where 30% of sales are from each of Asia, Africa and Europe would be considered a global MNE" (*Financial Times*, n.d.)
4 Even with the result of the UK's Brexit referendum, it remains hard to find an example of another entity that involves the supranational sharing of sovereignty to the extent of the EU encompassing a shared currency and monetary policy, judicial and regulatory functions, an elected parliament, and so on. The World Trade Organization is often seen as a weaker example of supranationalism, given its quasi-judicial function in settling trade disputes. See Kahler and Lake (2009) for a broader discussion.
5 Although to be completely accurate, he later said that despite the title of his 1971 book being *Sovereignty at Bay*, he had been unfairly associated

with the prediction that MNEs were destroying the state (Vernon 1981). In fact, he had been focusing specifically on the global spread of US enterprises, and the manner in which this may serve the interests of the US as much as it undermines the sovereignty of other states.

6 This list is compiled on the basis of their annual revenues.
7 It might be noted that a list which included financial corporations would have contained banking and insurance companies such as AXA Group (revenues of US$154 billion, greater than Hungary's GDP) and JP Morgan Chase (revenues of US$98billion, around the same as the Slovak Republic's GDP). The reason they were not included is because they do not strictly make sales in the same manner as nonfinancial corporations. Instead, they generate revenues. Therefore, while some lists include them together, such as the Forbes Global 2000 (2015), they are not strictly comparable on the same basis.
8 Its 2013 consolidated budget of CHF197,203,900 converted at a 2013 yearly average of CHF1=US$1.079397, using http://www.usforex.com/forex-tools/historical-rate-tools/yearly-average-rates.
9 This list is compiled on the basis of their stock market capitalization.
10 This calculation treats the top 100 corporations as a group, calculating their transnationality based on the sum of their assets, sales, and employment.
11 This calculation again treats the top 100 corporations as a group, calculating their transnationality based on the sum of their assets, sales, and employment.

2 Theorizing Global Corporations' Power

1 Today these are the board members and shareholders of corporations, increasingly one and the same (e.g., see Lazonick and O'Sullivan 2000; Lazonick 2014).
2 It should be noted that neither do scholars like Linda Weiss. She does not actually say in any of her writing that either the entwinement of global and national networks, or of the states and corporations that comprise them, must imply mutual support. Even so, for me intertwinement conjures images that suggest this—e.g., of a "rope" or a "net." Recognizing the pervasive yet messy nature of the relationship, I prefer "entanglement."
3 For a summary of the regulatory measures introduced, see US Senate Commission on Banking, Housing, and Urban Affairs (n.d.).
4 The American Bankers Association describes itself as "the united voice of America's hometown bankers—small, regional and large banks that together employ more than 2 million people, hold more than $15 trillion in assets, safeguard $11 trillion in deposits and extend more than $8 trillion in loans" (see http://www.aba.com/About/Pages/default.aspx). The

Financial Services Roundtable represents "the leading banking, insurance, asset management, finance and credit card companies in America" (see http://fsroundtable.org/about-fsr/), and lists eighty-six of these on its "FSR Members" page at http://fsroundtable.org/members/. The Securities Industry and Financial Markets Association has a membership "ranging from the largest global financial players to independent, small firms," a list of which may be seen at http://www.sifma.org/member-directory/.

5 The IPC was formed in 1986, and over the following decade included Bristol-Myers, DuPont, FMC Corporation, General Electric, General Motors, Hewlett-Packard, IBM, Johnson and Johnson, Merck, Monsanto, Pfizer, Rockwell International, Warner Communications, Digital Equipment Corporation, CBS, Procter and Gamble, and TimeWarner (Sell 2003, 96, and Braithwaite and Drahos 2000, 71).

6 CFCs were used as propellants in spray cans as well as in air conditioning systems. The major producers included DuPont, Allied Chemical, ICI, Atochem, and Hoechst.

3 Geographical Concentration

1 South Korea and the Netherlands, rather than India and Sweden, are in the top ten for the Fortune Global 500. South Korea and Taiwan, rather than Sweden and Switzerland, made the top ten for the Forbes Global 2000.

2 This is particularly the case for where they wield their instrumental power, given that it involves interactions between corporate and state office holders. It may have some bearing on where they exercise their structural and discursive power as well.

3 UNCTAD (2013b) defines FDI stocks as the value of the share of associate and subsidiary enterprises' capital and reserves (including retained profits) attributable to their parent enterprise. In other words, they represent the net assets controlled by a corporation outside its home state: total assets minus total liabilities plus the net indebtedness of the associate or subsidiary enterprise to the parent corporation. For a branch of the corporation abroad, it is the value of fixed assets plus current assets and investments minus amounts due to the parent corporation and liabilities to third parties. Therefore, a state's inward FDI stock represents investments by parent enterprises headquartered in other states, while a state's outward FDI stock represents the converse: investments by its parent enterprises in other states.

4 The one exception to this is the US in 2000. Of course, there may be other exceptions in other years, given that only three are shown here for comparative purposes, but the tendency seems to exist nonetheless.

5 UNCTAD (2013c) defines FDI flows as the net sales of shares and loans to the parent enterprise plus the parent enterprise's share of affiliate's

reinvested earnings plus total net intra-company loans provided by the parent enterprise. For a branch of an enterprise abroad, FDI flows consist of the increase in reinvested earnings plus the net increase in funds received from the parent enterprise. Therefore, inward FDI flows represent movements in investment funds in and out of a state by parent enterprises headquartered in another state, while a state's outward FDI flows represent the converse: movements in investment funds by its parent enterprises to other states.

4 National Institutional Embeddedness

1 South Africa is now usually added to this group so that it is known as the BRICS, rather than BRICs. However, South Africa's shrinking GDP, including as a percentage of global GDP, and much smaller economy by comparison to the others make it problematic to consider it an emerging market economy in the same way as the others. For example, South Africa's GDP in 2011 was US$417 billion (0.57 percent of global GDP) by comparison to China's GDP of 7.3 trillion (10 percent of global GDP). By 2015, South Africa's economy had contracted to US$324 billion (0.43 percent of global GDP), whereas China's had grown to US$11.2 trillion (15 percent of global GDP). In fact, based on its performance as measured by growth and share of global GDP, it would make more sense to include Nigeria rather than South Africa in the group (Bishop 2016, 3). Therefore, it is omitted here.
2 They are referred to as such largely because they are English-speaking and share common cultural traditions and histories.
3 It may be noted that a similar desire was earlier expressed in Hall (1999).
4 Albeit marginally, so it may be more accurate to say that they have maintained barriers to entrepreneurship.

5 Private Authority and the Potential for Private Governance

1 In actual fact, Gramscians would probably agree with this on the basis that the dominant (i.e., hegemonic) discourses reflect the structural basis for the class relations underpinning capitalism.
2 Related to these, there is a third incentive for global corporations whose operations must be geographically specific, such as mining companies. For them, these two broad incentives are crucial in demonstrating they should be permitted a "social license to operate" where their facilities are located (Burke 1999; Dashwood 2007).

3 Their book won the International Studies Association's 2012 Best Book Award.
4 It may also be noted that the institutional complementarity they analyze between the national and international levels is analogous to the rationale for why the institutions that produce states' varieties of capitalism give rise to categories, rather than individual cases, at the national level—i.e., they likewise serve stakeholders' interests.
5 Strictly speaking, it is not the case that the law in all states requires this. Even so, publicly listed corporations are legally required to act in their shareholders' interests, and their interests are often taken as being served by maximizing profitability and paying dividends.
6 In the same year Shell was also implicated in the execution of a Nigerian activist and eight of his colleagues, known as "the Ogoni Nine."
7 Utting discusses the manner in which a normative shift toward ecological modernization as a dominant discourse in environmental politics has occurred, with this led by corporations that stressed their embrace of environmental concern rather than using instrumental and structural power to oppose regulation.
8 The Fortune 500 World's Most Admired Companies ranks corporations on the basis of management quality; quality of products/services offered; innovativeness; value as a long-term investment; soundness of financial position; ability to attract, develop, and retain talent; community responsibility; wise use of corporate assets; and effectiveness in conducting a global business (Fortune 2015c). The Soft Power 30 ranks states on the basis of their political institutions; extent of their cultural appeal; strength of their diplomatic network; global reputation of their higher education system; attractiveness of their economic model; and digital engagement with the world (McClory 2015, 46).
9 In 2017, Amazon purchased Whole Foods Market, so this characterization of the company may no longer be the case in future.
10 On this latter point, it may be noted that US Bancorp is categorized by Fortune as a "superregional" US bank rather than a "megabank" (Fortune 2015c).
11 Less conservative estimates suggest they may be as high as US$650 billion (Crivelli et al. 2016).
12 Like any global survey there are also limitations, such as differing interpretations of the same question depending on social and cultural factors, whether or not the sample may be said to be representative of national values, and the context and timing surrounding the questions asked.
13 The question they answered is: "I am going to name a number of organizations. For each one, could you tell me how much confidence you have in them: is it a great deal of confidence, quite a lot of confidence, not very much confidence, or none at all?"

6 Conclusion: Three Implications

1 Although, as shown in Chapter 3, this is more accurately a national capitalist class. The transnationality of their interests expressed through the global corporations they control is more accurate.
2 "Geocentrism" refers to a corporation that has a global approach to its management, one that does not arise from a national basis for strategizing but from whatever best serves business interests. In other words, a globalist account of corporate decision making and identity. "Ethnocentricism," as the name suggests, involves organizational forms based on ethnicity, with norms and patterns of behavior based on this. Between the two, another possibility is "polycentrism," in which different strategies are adopted depending on the states in which a corporation invests and has operations (Perlmutter 1969; see also Bartlett and Beamish 2010).

REFERENCES

Abrams, R. (2016). Mastercard-Visa Settlement with Retailers Is Overturned. *New York Times*, 30 June, http://www.nytimes.com/2016/07/01/business/mastercard-visa-settlement-with-retailers-is-overturned.html?_r=0, accessed 25 August 2016.

Adams, S. (2012). Apple's New Foxconn Embarrassment. *Forbes*, 12 September, http://www.forbes.com/sites/susanadams/2012/09/12/apples-new-foxconn-embarrassment/#103b24a28ae6, accessed 6 September 2016.

Adler, E. (1997). Seizing the Middle Ground: Constructivism in World Politics. *European Journal of International Relations* 3, no. 3, 319–363.

Aggarwal, V. K., and Evenett, S. J. (2014). Do WTO Rules Preclude Industrial Policy? Evidence from the Global Economic Crisis. *Business and Politics* 16, no. 4, 481–509.

Aldrich, H. E. (1999). *Organizations Evolving*. London: Sage.

Allard, T. (2014). Global Tax Avoidance: A Trillion Dollar Evil. *Sydney Morning Herald*, 21 February, http://www.smh.com.au/business/global-tax-avoidance–a-trillion-dollar-evil-20140221-337u1.html, accessed 14 May 2015.

Altman, R. (2009). The Great Crash: A Geopolitical Setback for the West. *Foreign Affairs* 88, no. 1, 2–14.

Amable, B. (2000). Institutional Complementarity and Diversity of Social Systems of Innovation and Production. *Review of International Political Economy* 7, no. 4, 645–687.

Amable, B. (2003). *The Diversity of Modern Capitalism*. Oxford: Oxford University Press.

Amable, B., and Palombarini, S. (2009). A Neorealist Approach to Institutional Change and the Diversity of Capitalism. *Socio-economic Review* 7, no. 1, 123–143.

Americans for Financial Reform (2015). Wall Street Money in Washington, 18 March, http://ourfinancialsecurity.org/blogs/wp-content/ourfinancialsecurity.

org/uploads/2014/12/Wall-Street-Money-Final-March-2015.pdf, accessed 20 July 2015.

Amin, A., and Palan, P. (2001). Towards a Non-Rationalist International Political Economy. *Review of International Political Economy* 8, no. 4, 559–577.

Amit, R., Ding, Y., Villalonga, B., and Zhang, H. (2010). The Role of Institutional Development in the Prevalence and Value of Family Firms. *HBS Working Papers*, 10–103.

Amoore, L. (2006). Making the Modern Multinational. In May, C. (ed.), *Global Corporate Power*. Boulder, CO: Lynne Rienner Publishers.

Andersen, J., Ikenberry, G. J., and Risse, T. (eds.) (2008). *The End of the West? Crisis and Change in the Atlantic Order*. Ithaca, NY: Cornell University Press.

Anon (2011). The Dwindling Allure of Building Factories Offshore. *The Economist*, 12 May, http://www.economist.com/node/18682182?story_id=18682182, accessed 25 May 2011.

Anon (2012). The Visible Hand. *The Economist*, 12 January, http://www.economist.com/node/21542931, accessed 30 March 2016.

Anon (2013). Apple's International Structure. *New York Times*, http://www.nytimes.com/interactive/2013/05/21/business/apples-international-structure.html?ref=business&_r=0, accessed 14 May 2015.

Anon (2015). Apple Bans "Bonded Servitude" for Factory Workers. *BBC News*, 12 February, http://www.bbc.com/news/technology-31438699, accessed 7 June 2017.

Anon (2016a). Too Much of a Good Thing. *The Economist*, 26 March, http://www.economist.com/news/briefing/21695385-profits-are-too-high-america-needs-giant-dose-competition-too-much-good-thing, accessed 7 April 2016.

Anon (2016b). Special Report: Companies. *The Economist*, 17–23 September.

Aoki, M., Jackson, G., and Miyajima, H. (2007). *Corporate Governance in Japan: Institutional Change and Organizational Diversity*. Oxford: Oxford University Press.

Bachrach, P., and Baratz, M. (1962). Two Faces of Power. *American Political Science Review* 56, no. 4, 947–952.

Bakan, J. (2005). *The Corporation: The Pathological Pursuit of Profit and Power*. London: Constable and Robinson.

Bakir, C. (2015). Bargaining with Multinationals: Why State Capacity Matters. *New Political Economy* 20, no. 1, 63–84.

Banks Around the World (2015). *Top 100 Banks in the World*, http://www.relbanks.com/worlds-top-banks/assets, accessed 2 February 2016.

Barkan, J. (2013). *Corporate Sovereignty: Law and Government under Capitalism*. Minneapolis: University of Minnesota Press.

Barnett, M., and Duvall, R. (2005). Power in International Politics. *International Organization* 59, no. 1, 39–75.

Barnett, M., and Duvall, R. (2005). Power in Global Governance. In Barnett, M., and Duvall, R. (eds.), *Power in Global Governance*. Cambridge: Cambridge University Press.

Barnett, M., and Finnemore, M. (2004). *Rules for the World: International Organizations in Global Politics*. Ithaca, NY: Cornell University Press.

Bartlett, C. A., and Beamish, P. W. (2010). *Transnational Management: Text, Cases, and Readings in Cross-Border Management*, 6th ed. Boston: McGraw-Hill.

Bauer, S., Steinar, A., and Biermann, F. (2012). International Bureaucracies. In Bierman, F., and Pattberg, P. (eds.), *Global Environmental Governance Reconsidered*. Cambridge, MA: MIT Press.

Beck, T., Kunt, D., and Levine, R. (2005). *Bank Concentration and Fragility: Impact and Mechanics*. The National Bureau of Economic Research. Working Paper 11500, http://www.nber.org/papers/w11500, accessed 10 June 2014.

Beder, S. (2002). *Global Spin: The Corporate Assault on Environmentalism*. Foxhole: Green Books.

Beeson, M. (2009). Trading Places? China, the United States and the Evolution of the International Political Economy. *Review of International Political Economy* 16, no. 4, 729–741.

Bell, S. (2012). The Power of Ideas: The Ideational Shaping of the Structural Power of Business. *International Studies Quarterly* 56, no. 4, 661–673.

Bell. S. (2013). How Governments Mediate the Structural Power of International Business. In Mikler, J. (ed.), *The Handbook of Global Companies*. Oxford: Wiley Blackwell.

Bell, S., and Hindmoor, A. (2009). *Rethinking Governance: The Centrality of the State in Modern Societies*. Cambridge: Cambridge University Press.

Berger, S. (1996). Introduction. In Berger, S., and Dore, R. (eds.), *National Diversity and Global Capitalism*. Ithaca, NY: Cornell University Press.

Bernstein, S., and Cashore, B. (2007). Can Non-state Global Governance Be Legitimate? An Analytical Framework. *Regulation and Governance* 1, no. 4, 347–371.

Bhagwati, J. (2004). *In Defense of Globalisation*. Oxford: Oxford University Press.

Bianco, M. (2010). Corporate Governance in China: A Changing Model? Presented at the Banca d'Italia Workshop on the Chinese Economy. Venice, 25–27 November.

Bishop, M. (2016). *Rethinking the Political Economy of Development Beyond "The Rise of the BRICS,"* SPERI Paper No.30, http://speri.dept.shef.ac.uk/wp-content/uploads/2016/07/Beyond-the-Rise-of-the-BRICS.pdf, accessed 17 August 2016.

Block, F. (2011). Innovation and the Hidden Hand of Government. In Block, F., and Keller, M. R. (eds.), *State of Innovation: The US Government's Role in Technology Development*. Boulder, CO: Paradigm Publishers.

Block, F., and Keller, M. R. (2009). Where Do Innovations Come From? Transformations in the US Economy, 1970–2006. *Socio-economic Review* 7, no. 3, 459–83.

Blyth, M. (2002a). *Great Transformations: Economic Ideas and Institutional Change in the Twentieth Century*. Cambridge: Cambridge University Press.

Blyth, M. (2002b). Book Review: Varieties of Capitalism: The Institutional Foundations of Comparative Advantage. *West European Politics* 25, no. 4, 238–239.

Blyth, M. (2003a). Same as It Never Was: Temporality and Typology in the Varieties of Capitalism. *Comparative European Politics* 1, no. 2, 215–225.

Blyth, M. (2003b). Structures Do Not Come with an Instruction Sheet: Interests, Ideas, and Progress in Political Science. *Perspectives in Politics* 1, no. 4, 695–706.

Blyth, M. (2016). Global Trumpism: Why Trump's Victory Was 30 Years in the Making and Why It Won't Stop Here. *Foreign Affairs*, 15 November, https://www.foreignaffairs.com/articles/2016-11-15/global-trumpism, accessed 21 November 2016.

Bonturi, M., and Fukasaku, K. (1993). Globalisaton and Intra-firm Trade: An Empirical Note. *OECD Economic Studies* 20, Spring, 145–159.

Boyer, R. (1996). The Convergence Hypothesis Revisited: Globalization but Still the Century of Nations? In Berger, S., and Dore, R. (eds.), *National Diversity and Global Capitalism*. Ithaca, NY: Cornell University Press.

Braithwaite, J. (2008). *Regulatory Capitalism: How It Works, Ideas for Making It Work Better*. Cheltenham: Edward Elgar.

Braithwaite, J., and Drahos, P. (2000). *Global Business Regulation*. Cambridge: Cambridge University Press.

Breslin, S. (2012). Government-Industry Relations in China: A Review of the Art of the State. In Walter, A., and Zhang, X. (eds.), *East Asian Capitalism: Diversity, Continuity and Change*. Oxford: Oxford University Press.

Broome, A. (2014). *Issues and Actors in the Global Political Economy*. Houndmills, Basingstoke: Palgrave Macmillan.

Brown, B., and Perry, S. (1994). Removing the Financial Performance Halo from Fortune's "Most Admired" Companies. *Academy of Management Journal* 37, no. 5, 1347–1359.

Bryant, R. L., and Bailey, S. (1997). *Third World Political Ecology*. London: Routledge.

Burke, P. L. (1999). Embedded Private Authority: Multinational Enterprises and the Amazonian Indigenous Peoples Movement in Ecuador. In Cutler, A. C., Haufler, V., and Porter, T. (eds.), *Private Authority and International Affairs*. Albany: State University of New York Press.

Büthe, T., and Mattli, W. (2011). *The New Global Rulers: The Privatization of Regulation in the World Economy*. Princeton, NJ: Princeton University Press.

Cahill, D. (2009). Is Neoliberalism History? *Social Alternatives* 28, no. 1, 12–16.

Cahill, D. (2014). *The End of Laissez Faire? On the Durability of Embedded Neoliberalism*. Cheltenham: Edward Elgar.

Callaghan, M. (2015). Why a "Google Tax" Is Not the Answer to Corporate Tax Avoidance. *Lowy Interpreter*, http://www.lowyinterpreter.org/post/2015/04/13/Why-the-UK-Google-tax-is-not-the-answer-to-corporate-tax-avoidance.aspx?COLLCC=3861547897&, accessed 22 May 2015.

Camfferman, K., and Zeff, S. (2007). *Financial Reporting and Global Capital Markets: A History of the International Accounting Standard Committee 1973–2000*. Oxford: Oxford University Press.

Carpenter, D., and Moss, D. A. (eds.) (2014). *Preventing Regulatory Capture: Special Interest Influence and How to Limit It*. Cambridge: Cambridge University Press.

Cartwright, M. (2011). *Globalization and Comparative Capitalism: The Industrial Relations of Volkswagen and Ford in South African Export Zones*. Honors thesis, https://ses.library.usyd.edu.au/handle/2123/8280, accessed 24 November 2015.

Cashore, B. W. (2002). Legitimacy and the Privatization of Environmental Governance: How Non-state Market-driven (NSMD) Governance Systems Gain Rule-making Authority. *Governance* 15, no. 4, 503–529.

Cashore, B. W., Auld, G., and Newsom, D. (2004). *Governing through Markets: Forest Certification and the Emergence of Non-State Authority*. New Haven, CT: Yale University Press.

Cerny, P. (2000). Political Globalization and the Competition State. In Stubbs, R., and Underhill, G. (eds.), *Political Economy and the Changing Global Order*. Oxford: Oxford University Press.

Cerny, P. (2010). The Competition State Today: From Raison Détat to Raison du Monde. *Policy Studies* 31, no. 1, 5–21.

CFR.org staff (2015). *The Credit Rating Controversy*, CFR Backgrounders. Council on Foreign Relations, http://www.cfr.org/financial-crises/credit-rating-controversy/p22328, accessed 15 October 2016.

Chandler, A. D. Jr. (1977). *The Visible Hand: The Managerial Revolution in American Business*. Cambridge, MA: Harvard University Press.

Chang, H. (2002). *Kicking Away the Ladder*. London: Anthem.

Chang, H. (2008). *Bad Samaritans: The Myth of Free Trade and the Secret History of Capitalism*. New York: Bloomsbury Press.

Chen, G., Firth, M., and Xu, L. (2009). Does the Type of Ownership Control Matter? Evidence from China's Listed Companies. *Journal of Banking and Finance* 33, no. 1, 171–181.

Chen, M. X., Otsuki, T., and Wilson, J. S. (2006). Do Standards Matter for Export Success? *World Bank Policy Research Paper*, no. 3809. January, http://dx.doi.org/10.1596/1813-9450-3809.

Christodoulou, M. (2011). UK Auditors Criticized on Bank Crisis. *Wall Street Journal*, 30 March, https://www.wsj.com/articles/SB10001424052748703806304576232231353594682, accessed 8 June 2017.

Clapp, J. (1998). The Privatization of Global Environmental Governance: ISO 14000 and the Developing World. *Global Governance* 4, no. 3, 295–316.

Clapp, J. (2005). Transnational Corporations and Global Environmental Governance. In Dauvergne, P. (ed.), *Handbook of Global Environmental Politics*. Cheltenham: Edward Elgar.

Clapp, J., and Fuchs, D. (2009). Agrifood Corporations, Global Governance and Sustainability: A Framework for Analysis. In Clapp, J., and Fuchs, D.

(eds.), *Corporate Power in Global Agrifood Governance*. Cambridge, MA: MIT Press.

Clark, I. (1999). *Globalization and International Relations Theory*. Oxford: Oxford University Press.

Coates, D. (2002). Book Review: Varieties of Capitalism: The Institutional Foundations of Comparative Advantage. *American Political Science Review* 96, no. 3, 661–662.

Coburn, E. (2011). Resisting Neoliberal Capitalism: Insights from Marxist Political Economy. In Teeple, G., and McBride, S. (eds.), *Relations of Global Power: Neoliberal Order and Disorder*. Toronto: University of Toronto Press.

Coen, D. (2009). Business Lobbying in the European Union. In Coen, D., and Richardson, J. (eds.), *Lobbying the European Union: Institutions, Actors and Issues*. Oxford: Oxford University Press.

Cooper, H., and Savage, C. (2008). A Bit of "I Told You So" Outside World Bank Talks. *New York Times*, 10 October. http://www.nytimes.com/2008/10/11/business/11scene.html?_r=0, accessed 17 August 2015.

Corfield, J. (2013). Procter and Gamble Inc. In Salinger, L. M. (ed.), *Encyclopedia of White Collar and Corporate Crime*, 2nd ed. Thousand Oaks, CA: Sage.

Corrigan, M., and Modrak, A. (2010). Australia. In Low, M. (ed.), *Getting the Deal Through: Cartel Regulation, Getting the Fine Down in 42 Jurisdictions Worldwide*. London: Law Business Research, https://www.claytonutz.com/ArticleDocuments/178/Getting-The-Deal-Through-Cartel-Regulation-Australia-2010.pdf.aspx?Embed=Y, accessed 16 August 2016.

Cox, R. W. (1987). *Production, Power and World Order: Social Forces in the Making of History*. New York: Columbia University Press.

Cox, R. W. (1996). Social Forces, States and World Orders: Beyond International Relations Theory. In Cox, R. W., and Sinclair T. J. (eds.), *Approaches to World Order*. Cambridge: Cambridge University Press.

Crane, A. (2008). *Corporate Social Responsibility in Global Context*, 2nd ed. Los Angeles: Sage.

Crane, A., Matten, D., McWilliams, A., Moon, J., and Siegel, D. S. (eds.) (2009). *The Oxford Handbook of Social Responsibility*. Oxford: Oxford University Press.

Crivelli, E., De Mooij, R., and Keen, M. (2016). Base Erosion, Profit Shifting and Developing Countries. *FinanzArchiv: Public Finance Analysis* 72, no. 3, 268–301.

Crouch, C. (2004). *Post-Democracy*. Cambridge: Polity Press.

Crouch, C. (2005). Models of Capitalism. *New Political Economy* 10, no. 4, 339–456.

Crouch, C. (2011). *The Strange Non-Death of Neoliberalism*. Cambridge: Polity Press.

Culpepper, P. D. (2011). *Quiet Politics and Business Power: Corporate Control in Europe and Japan*. Cambridge: Cambridge University Press.

References 159

Curtis, P. (2011). Will David Cameron's Veto Protect the City? *The Guardian*, 13 December, https://www.theguardian.com/politics/reality-check-with-polly-curtis/2011/dec/12/debt-crisis-conservatives, accessed 2 November 2016.

Cutler, A. C. (2002). Private Regimes and Inter-Firm Cooperation. In Hall, R. B., and Biersteker, T. J. (eds.), *The Emergence of Private Authority in Global Governance*. Cambridge: Cambridge University Press.

Cutler, A. C. (2003). *Private Power and Global Authority: Transnational Merchant Law in the Global Political Economy*. Cambridge: Cambridge University Press.

Cutler, A. C., Haufler, V., and Porter, T. (eds.) (1999a). *Private Authority and International Affairs*. Albany: State University of New York Press.

Cutler, A. C., Haufler, V., and Porter, T. (1999b). The Contours and Significance of Private Authority in International Affairs. In Cutler, A. C., Haufler, V., and Porter, T. (eds.), *Private Authority and International Affairs*. Albany: State University of New York Press.

Cutler, A.C. Haufler, V., and Porter, T. (1999c). Private Authority and International Affairs. In Cutler, A. C., Haufler, V. and Porter, T. (eds.), *Private Authority and International Affairs*. Albany: State University of New York Press.

Dahl, R. (1957). The Concept of Power. *Behavioral Science* 2, 201–215.

Dashwood, H. S. (2007). Canadian Mining Companies and Corporate Social Responsibility: Weighing the Impact of Global Norms. *Canadian Journal of Political Science* 40, no. 1, 129–156.

Dauvergne, P. (2016). *Environmentalism of the Rich*. Cambridge, MA. MIT Press.

Davies, A. (2015). CSG Industry Hires Well-Connected Staffers. *Sydney Morning Herald*, 25 May. http://www.smh.com.au/nsw/csg-industry-hires-wellconnected-staffers-20150524-gh2rg3.html, accessed 22 July 2015.

Davies, W. (2016). The New Neoliberalism. *New Left Review* 101, September/October, 121–134.

Davis, A. K., Guenther, D. A., Krull, L. K., and Williams, B. M. (2016). Do Socially Responsible Firms Pay More Taxes? *Accounting Review* 91, no. 1, 47–68.

Davis, K., and Blomstrom, R. (1966). *Business and Its Environment*. New York: McGraw-Hill.

Dicken, P. (1998). *Global Shift: Transforming the World Economy*, 3rd ed. London: Paul Chapman Publishing.

Dicken, P. (2007). *Global Shift: Mapping the Changing Contours of the World Economy*, 5th ed. London: Sage.

Dicken, P. (2010). *Global Shift: Mapping the Changing Contours of the Global Economy*, 6th ed. London: Sage.

Dicken, P. (2015). *Global Shift: Mapping the Changing Contours of the World Economy*, 7th ed. New York: Guilford Press.

Dobbs, R., Koller, T., Ramaswamy, S., Woetzel, J., Manyika, J., Krishnan, R., and Andreula, N. (2015). *Playing to Win: The New Global Competition for Corporate Profits.* McKinsey Global Institute, http://www.mckinsey.com/business-functions/strategy-and-corporate-finance/our-insights/the-new-global-competition-for-corporate-profits, accessed 8 September 2016.

Dore, R. (1997). The Distinctiveness of Japan. In Crouch, C., and Streeck, W. (eds.), *Political Economy of Modern Capitalism: Mapping Convergence and Diversity.* London: Sage.

Dore, R. (2000a). *Stock Market Capitalism: Welfare Capitalism: Japan and Germany versus the Anglo Saxons.* Oxford: Oxford University Press.

Dore, R. (2000b). Will Global Capitalism be Anglo-Saxon Capitalism? *New Left Review* 6, 101–119.

Dore, R., Lazonick, W., and O'Sullivan, M. (1999). Varieties of Capitalism in the Twentieth Century. *Oxford Review of Economic Policy* 15, no. 4, 102–120.

Doremus, P. N., Keller, W. W., Pauly, L. W., and Reich, S. (1999). *The Myth of the Global Corporation.* Princeton, NJ: Princeton University Press.

Drezner, D. W. (2001). Globalization and Policy Convergence. *International Studies Review* 3, no. 1, 53–78.

Drezner, D. W. (2007). *All Politics Is Global: Explaining International Regulatory Regimes.* Princeton, NJ: Princeton University Press.

Drucker, P. F. (2011). *The Frontiers of Management.* Abingdon: Routledge.

Eden, L., Lenway, S., and Schuler, D. (2005). From the Obsolescing to the Political Bargaining Model. In Grosse, R. (ed.), *International Business and Government Relations in the 21st Century.* Cambridge: Cambridge University Press.

Elbra, A. (2014). Interests Need Not Be Pursued If They Can Be Created: Private Governance in African Gold Mining. *Business and Politics* 16, no. 2, 247–266.

Elbra, A. (2016). *Governing African Gold Mining: Private Governance and the Resource Curse.* Houndmills, Basingstoke: Palgrave Macmillan.

Elbra, A., and Mikler, J. (2017). Paying a "Fair Share": Multinational Corporations' Perspectives on Taxation. *Global Policy* 8, no. 2, 181–190.

Ernst, D. (2004). Global Production Networks in East Asia's Electronics Industry and Upgrading Perspectives in Malaysia. In Yusuf, S., Altaf, M., and Nabeshima, K. (eds.), *Global Production Networking and Technological Change in East Asia.* Washington, DC, and Oxford: World Bank and Oxford University Press.

Esping-Andersen, G. (1990). *The Three Worlds of Welfare Capitalism.* Cambridge: Polity Press.

European Commission (2011). *Antitrust: Commission Fines Producers of Washing Powder €315.2 million in Cartel Settlement Case,* 13 April. Press Release Database, IP/11/473, http://europa.eu/rapid/press-release_IP-11-473_en.htm, accessed 16 August 2016.

Evans, P. (1995). *Embedded Autonomy: States and Industrial Transformation.* Princeton, NJ: Princeton University Press.

Falkner, J. (2008). *Business Power and Conflict in International Environmental Politics.* Houndmills, Basingstoke: Palgrave Macmillan.

Fichtner, J. (2016). Perpetual Decline or Persistent Dominance? Uncovering Anglo-America's True Structural Power in Global Finance. *Review of International Studies*, First View, doi:10.1017/S0260210516000206.

Fields, K. (2012). Not of a Piece: Developmental States, Industrial Policy, and Evolving Patterns of Capitalism in Japan, Korea, and Taiwan. In Walter, A., and Zhang, X. (eds.), *East Asian Capitalism: Diversity, Continuity and Change*. Oxford: Oxford University Press.

Financial Times (2016), *FT Global 500 2015*, www.ft.com/ft500, accessed 5 June 2016.

Financial Times (n.d.). *Definition of Global Multinational Enterprises*, http://lexicon.ft.com/Term?term=global-multinational-enterprises, accessed 28 October 2016.

Finnemore, M., and Sikkink, K. (1998). International Norm Dynamics and Political Change. *International Organization* 52, no. 4, 887–917.

Finnemore, M., and Sikkink, K. (2001). Taking Stock: The Constructivist Research Program in International Relations and Comparative Politics. *Annual Review of Political Science 2001* 4, 391–416.

Fioretos, O. (2001). The Domestic Sources of Multilateral Preferences: Varieties of Capitalism in the European Community. In Hall, P. A., and Soskice, D. (eds.), *Varieties of Capitalism: The Institutional Foundations of Comparative Advantage*. Oxford: Oxford University Press.

Fligstein, N., and Zhang, J. (2011). A New Agenda for Research on the Trajectory of Chinese Capitalism. *Management and Organization Review* 7, no. 1, 39–62.

Forbes Global 2000 (2015). *The World's Biggest Public Companies*, http://www.forbes.com/global2000/list/, accessed 11 November 2015.

Fortune (2015a). *Fortune Global 500*, http://fortune.com/global500/, accessed 11 November 2015.

Fortune (2015b). *How to Become the World's Most Admired Company*, http://fortune.com/video/2015/02/19/how-to-become-the-worlds-most-admired-company/, accessed 2 February 2015.

Fortune (2015c). *World's Most Admired Companies 2015*, http://fortune.com/worlds-most-admired-companies/2015/, accessed 31 July 2015.

Fortune (2015d). *World's Most Admired Companies Ranked by Key Attributes*, http://fortune.com/2015/02/19/wmac-ranked-by-key-attribute/, accessed 24 February 2016.

Frank, A. G. (1978). *Dependent Accumulation and Underdevelopment*. London: Macmillan.

Friedman, M. (1970). The Social Responsibility of Business Is to Increase Profits. *New York Times Magazine*, 13 September.

Friedman, T. (2000). *The Lexus and the Olive Tree*, rev. ed. London: HarperCollins.

Friedman, T. (2005). *The World Is Flat: A Brief History of the Twenty-First Century*. New York: Farrar, Strauss and Giroux.

Fryxell, G. E., and Wang, J. (1994). The Fortune Corporate "Reputation" Index: Reputation for What? *Journal of Management* 20, no. 1, 1–14.

Fuchs, D. (2005). Commanding Heights? The Strength and Fragility of Business Power in Global Politics. *Millennium: Journal of International Studies* 33, no. 3, 771–801.

Fuchs, D. (2007). *Business Power in Global Governance*. Boulder, CO: Lynne Rienner Publishers.

Fuchs, D., and Lederer, M. M. (2007). The Power of Business. *Business and Politics* 9, no. 3, 1–17.

Fukuyama, F. (1992). *The End of History and the Last Man*. New York: Avon Books.

Galbraith, J. K. (1958). *The Affluent Society*. London: Hamish Hamilton.

Galbraith, J. K. (1977). The Bimodal Image of the Modern Economy: Remarks upon Receipt of the Veblen-Commons Award. *Journal of Economic Issues* 11, no. 2: 189–200.

Geppert, M., and Dörrenbächer, C. (2011). Politics and Power in the Multinational Corporation: An Introduction. In Dörrenbächer, C., and Geppert, M. (eds.), *Politics and Power in the Multinational Corporation: The Role of Institutions, Interests, and Identities*. Cambridge: Cambridge University Press.

Giddens, A. (2009). *The Politics of Climate Change*. Cambridge: Polity Press.

Gilpin, R. (1987). *The Political Economy of International Relations*. Princeton, NJ: Princeton University Press.

Goldstein, A. (2007). *Multinational Companies from Emerging Economies: Composition, Conceptualization and Direction in the Global Economy*. Houndmills, Basingstoke: Palgrave Macmillan.

Goldstein, A. (2013a). The Political Economy of Global Business: The Case of the BRICs. *Global Policy* 4, no. 1, 162–172.

Goldstein, A. (2013b). Big Business in the BRICs. In Mikler, J. (ed.), *The Handbook of Global Companies*. Oxford: Wiley Blackwell.

Goodin, R., Headey, B., Muffels, R., and Dirven, H. J. (1999). *The Real Worlds of Welfare Capitalism*. Cambridge: Cambridge University Press.

Goodin, R. E. (2003). Choose Your Capitalism? *Comparative European Politics* 1, no. 2, 203–213.

Gotsi, M., and Wilson, A. M. (2001). Corporate Reputation: Seeking a Definition. *Corporate Communications: An International Journal* 6, no. 1, 24–30.

Gourevitch, P., and Shinn, J. (2005). *Political Power and Corporate Control: The New Global Politics of Corporate Governance*. Princeton, NJ: Princeton University Press.

Gravelle, J. G. (2015). *Tax Havens: International Tax Avoidance and Evasion*. Washington, DC: Congressional Research Services.

Green, J. F. (2013). *Rethinking Private Authority: Agents and Entrepreneurs in Global Environmental Governance*. Princeton, NJ: Princeton University Press.

Hale, T., Held, D., and Young, K. (2013). *Gridlock: Why Global Cooperation Is Failing When We Need It Most*. Cambridge: Polity Press.

Hall, J. (1993). Ideas and the Social Sciences. In Goldstein, J., and Keohane, R. (eds.), *Ideas and Foreign Policy: Beliefs, Institutions, and Political Change.* Ithaca, NY: Cornell University Press.

Hall, P. A. (1993). Policy Paradigms, Social Learning, and the State: The Case of Economic Policymaking in Britain. *Comparative Politics* 25, no. 3, 275–296.

Hall, P. A. (1999). The Political Economy of Europe in an Era of Interdependence. In Kitschelt, H., Lange, P., Marks, G., and Stephens, J. (eds.), *Continuity and Change in Contemporary Capitalism.* Cambridge: Cambridge University Press.

Hall, P. A. (2007). The Evolution of Varieties of Capitalism in Europe. In Hancké, B., Rhodes, M., and Thatcher, M. (eds.), *Beyond Varieties of Capitalism: Contradictions, Complementarities and Change.* Oxford: Oxford University Press.

Hall, P. A., and Gingerich, D. W. (2009). Varieties of Capitalism and Institutional Complementarities in the Political Economy. *British Journal of Political Science* 39, no. 3, 449–482.

Hall, P. A., and Soskice, D. (eds.) (2001a). *Varieties of Capitalism: The Institutional Foundations of Comparative Advantage.* Oxford: Oxford University Press.

Hall, P. A., and Soskice, D. (2001b). An Introduction to Varieties of Capitalism. In Hall, P. A., and Soskice, D. (eds.), *Varieties of Capitalism: The Institutional Foundations of Comparative Advantage.* Oxford: Oxford University Press.

Hall, P. A., and Soskice, D. (2003). Varieties of Capitalism and Institutional Change: A Response to Three Critics. *Comparative European Politics* 1, no. 2, 241–250.

Hall, P. A., and Thelen, K. (2009). Institutional Change in Varieties of Capitalism. *Socio-economic Review* 7, no. 1, 7–34.

Hall, R., and Biersteker, T. J. (eds.) (2002a). *The Emergence of Private Authority in Global Governance.* Cambridge: Cambridge University Press.

Hall, R. B., and Biersteker, T. J. (2002b). The Emergence of Private Authority in the International System. In Hall, R. B., and Biersteker, T. J. (eds.), *The Emergence of Private Authority in Global Governance.* Cambridge: Cambridge University Press.

Hall, T., and Biersteker, T. J. (2002c). Private Authority as Global Governance. In Hall, R. B., and Biersteker, T. J. (eds.), *The Emergence of Private Authority in Global Governance.* Cambridge: Cambridge University Press.

Halper, S. (2010). *The Beijing Consensus: How China's Authoritarian Model Will Dominate the Twenty-first Century.* New York: Basic Books.

Hamilton, C. (2007). *Scorcher: The Dirty Politics of Climate Change.* Melbourne: Black Inc. Agenda.

Hamilton, D. S., and Quinlan, J. P. (eds.) (2005). *Deep Integration: How Transatlantic Markets Are Leading Globalization.* Washington, DC, and Brussels: Center for Transatlantic Relations and Center for European Policy Studies.

Hampden-Turner, C., and A. Trompenaars (1993). *The Seven Cultures of Capitalism: Value Systems for Creating Wealth in the United States, Japan, Germany, France, Britain, Sweden, and the Netherlands*. New York: Currency Doubleday.

Hancké, B. (ed.) (2009). *Debating Varieties of Capitalism: A Reader*. Oxford: Oxford University Press.

Harrod, J. (2006). The Century of the Corporation. In May, C. (ed.), *Global Corporate Power*. Boulder, CO: Lynne Rienner Publishers.

Harvey, D. (2005). *A Brief History of Neoliberalism*. Oxford: Oxford University Press.

Haufler, V. (1997). *Dangerous Commerce: Insurance and the Management of International Risk*. Ithaca, NY: Cornell University Press.

Haufler, V. (2000). Private Sector International Regimes. In Higgott, R., Underhill, G., and Bieler, A. (eds.), *Non-state Actors and Authority in the Global System*. London: Routledge.

Haufler, V. (2001). *A Public Role for the Private Sector: Industry Self-Regulation in a Global Economy*. Washington, DC: Carnegie Endowment for International Peace.

Haufler, V. (2006). Global Governance and the Private Sector. In May, C. (ed.), *Global Corporate Power*. Boulder, CO: Lynne Rienner Publishers.

Hay, C. (2005). Two Can Play at That Game … or Can They? Varieties of Capitalism, Varieties of Institutionalism. In Coates, D. (ed.), *Varieties of Capitalism, Varieties of Approaches*. Houndmills, Basingstoke: Palgrave Macmillan.

Hay, C. (2006). Constructivist Institutionalism. In Moran, M., Rein, M., and Goodin, R. E. (eds.), *The Oxford Handbook of Political Institutions*. Oxford: Oxford University Press.

Hay, C., and Marsh, D. (2000). Introduction: Demystifying Globalization. In Hay, C., and Marsh, D. (eds.), *Demystifying Globalization*. Houndmills, Basingstoke: Palgrave Macmillan.

Hayward, J. (1995). *Industrial Enterprise and Economic Integration: From National to International Champions in Western Europe*. Oxford: Oxford University Press.

Healey, J. R. (2013). Government Sells Last of Its GM Shares. *USA Today*, 10 December, http://www.usatoday.com/story/money/cars/2013/12/09/government-treasury-gm-general-motors-tarp-bailout-exit-sale/3925515/, accessed 18 January 2016.

Heidenreich, M. (2012). The Social Embeddedness of Multinational Companies: A Literature Review. *Socio-economic Review* 10, no. 3, 549–579.

Heires, M. (2008). The International Organization for Standardization (ISO). *New Political Economy* 13, no. 3, 357–367.

Held, D., and McGrew, A. (eds.) (2002). *Governing Globalization: Power, Authority, and Global Governance*. Cambridge: Polity Press.

Held, D., and McGrew, A. (eds.) (2003). *The Global Transformations Reader*. Cambridge: Polity Press.

Held, D., McGrew, A., Goldblatt, D., and Perraton, J. (1999). *Global Transformations*. Cambridge: Polity Press.

Helleiner, E. (2002). Economic Nationalism as a Challenge to Economic Liberalism? Lessons from the 19th Century. *International Studies Quarterly* 46, no. 3, 307–29.

Helleiner, E., and Pickel, A. (eds.) (2005). *Economic Nationalism in a Globalizing World*. Ithaca, NY: Cornell University Press.

Hollingsworth, J. (1997). Continuities and Changes in Social Systems of Production: The Cases of Japan, Germany, and the United States. In Hollingsworth, J., and Boyer, R. (eds.), *Contemporary Capitalism: The Embeddedness of Institutions*. Cambridge: Cambridge University Press.

Howell, C. (2003). Varieties of Capitalism: And Then There was One? *Comparative Politics* 36, no. 1, 103–124.

Hymer, S. (1972). The Multinational Corporation and the Law of Uneven Development. In Bhagurat., J. (ed.), *Economics and World Order from the 1970s to the 1990s*. New York: Collier Macmillan.

ICANN (2016). *Welcome to ICANN!*, https://www.icann.org/resources/pages/welcome-2012-02-25-en, accessed 19 August 2016.

ICANN GAC (2016). *Governmental Advisory Committee*, https://gacweb.icann.org/display/gacweb/Governmental+Advisory+Committee, accessed 19 August 2016.

ICC (2016a). The Merchants of Peace. *International Chamber of Commerce*, http://www.iccwbo.org/about-icc/history/, accessed 29 August 2016.

ICC (2016b). A Word from our Secretary General. *International Chamber of Commerce*, http://www.iccwbo.org/about-icc/, accessed 29 August 2016.

ICC (2016c). Governance. *International Chamber of Commerce*, http://www.iccwbo.org/about-icc/governance/, accessed 29 August 2016.

ICC (2016d). ICC International Court of Arbitration. *International Chamber of Commerce*, http://www.iccwbo.org/about-icc/organization/dispute-resolution-services/icc-international-court-of-arbitration/, accessed 29 August 2016.

IDC (2015). *Smartphone Vendor Market Share, Q1 2015*, http://www.idc.com/prodserv/smartphone-market-share.jsp, accessed 20 July 2015.

IEA (2008). CO_2 *Emissions from Fuel Combustion: 2008 Edition*. Paris: International Energy Agency.

Ihlen, O. (2009). Business and Climate Change: The Climate Response of the World's 30 Largest Corporations. *Environmental Communication: A Journal of Nature and Culture* 3, no. 2, 244–262.

IMF (2012). *Global Financial Stability Report: Restoring Confidence and Progressing Reforms*. October 2012. Washington, DC: IMF, http://www.imf.org/external/pubs/ft/gfsr/2012/02/pdf/text.pdf, accessed 10 June 2014.

IMF (2015). *World Economic Outlook Database: April 2015 Edition*, http://www.imf.org/external/pubs/ft/weo/2015/01/weodata/index.aspx, accessed 12 January 2016.

ISO (2016a). ISO Members, *ISO*, http://www.iso.org/iso/home/about/iso_members.htm?membertype=membertype_MB, accessed 22 August 2016.

ISO (2016b). United States (ANSI), *ISO*, http://www.iso.org/iso/home/about/iso_members/iso_member_body.htm?member_id=2188, accessed 22 August 2016.

Iversen, T., and Pontusson, J. (2000). Comparative Political Economy: A Northern European Perspective. In Iversen, T., Pontusson, J., and Soskice, D. (eds.), *Unions, Employers, and Central Banks: Macroeconomic Coordination and Institutional Change in Social Market Economies*. New York: Cambridge University Press.

Jackson, G., and Deeg, R. (2008). Comparing Capitalisms: Understanding Institutional Diversity and Its Implications for International Business. *Journal of International Business Studies* 39, no. 4, 540–561.

Jackson, K. T. (2004). *Building Reputational Capital: Strategies for Integrity and Fair Play That Improve the Bottom Line*. Oxford: Oxford University Press.

Jacoby, S. M. (2005). *The Embedded Corporation: Corporate Governance and Employment Relations in Japan and the United States*. Princeton, NJ: Princeton University Press.

Johal, S., Moran, M., and Williams, K. (2015). Power, Politics and the City of London after the Great Financial Crisis. *Government and Opposition* 49, no. 3, 400–425.

Johnson, C. (1995). *Japan: Who Governs? The Rise of the Developmental State*. New York: Norton.

Johnston, D. C. (2014). How Google and Apple Make Their Taxes Disappear. *Newsweek*, 14 December, http://www.newsweek.com/2014/12/26/how-google-and-apple-make-their-taxes-disappear-291571.html, accessed 15 May 2015.

Jones, G. (2006). The Rise of Corporate Nationality. *Harvard Business Review* 84, no. 10, 20–22.

Jones, O. (2014). *The Establishment and How They Get Away With It*. London: Allen Lane.

Jordana, J., and Levi-Faur, D. (eds.) (2004). *The Politics of Regulation: Institutions and Regulatory Reforms for the Age of Governance*. Cheltenham: Edward Elgar.

Kahancová, M. (2007). *Corporate Values in Local Contexts: Work Systems and Workers' Welfare in Western and Eastern Europe*. Max Planck Institute for the Study of Societies, MPIfG working paper 07/1.

Kahler, M., and Lake, D. A. (2009). Economic Integration and Global Governance: Why So Little Supranationalism? In Mattli, W., and Woods, N. (eds.), *The Politics of Global Regulation*. Princeton, NJ: Princeton University Press.

Kaletsky, A. (2010). *Capitalism 4.0*. London: Bloomsbury.

Kalleberg, A. (2009). Precarious Work, Insecure Workers: Employment Relations in Transition. *American Sociological Review* 74, February, 1–22.

Kang, N., and Moon, J. (2012). Institutional Complementarity between Corporate Governance and Corporate Social Responsibility: A Comparative Institutional Analysis of Three Capitalisms. *Socio-economic Review* 10, no. 1, 85–108.

Karliner, J. (1997). *The Corporate Planet: Ecology and Politics in the Age of Globalization.* San Francisco: Sierra Club.
Keck, M., and Sikkink, K. (1998). *Activists beyond Borders.* Ithaca, NY: Cornell University Press.
Keck, M., and Sikkink, K. (1999). Transnational Advocacy Networks in International and Regional Politics. *International Social Science Journal* 51, March, 89–101.
Kelly, D., and Amburgey, T. L. (1991). Organizational Inertia and Momentum: A Dynamic Model of Strategic Change. *Academy of Management Journal* 34, no. 3, 591–612.
Kim, S-Y. (2013). East Asian Developmental States and Global Companies as Partners of Techno-Industrial Competitiveness. In Mikler, J. (ed.), *The Handbook of Global Companies.* Oxford: Wiley Blackwell.
Kindleberger, C. (1969). *American Business Abroad: Six Lectures on Direct Investment.* New Haven, CT: Yale University Press.
Kitching, G. (2001). *Seeking Social Justice through Globalization: Escaping a Nationalist Perspective.* University Park: Pennsylvania State University Press.
Kogut, B. (2005). Learning, or the Importance of Being Inert: Country Imprinting and International Competition. In Ghoshal, S., and Westney, D. E. (eds.), *Organization Theory and the Multinational Corporation*, 2nd ed. Houndmills, Basingstoke: Palgrave Macmillan.
Kolleck, N. (2013). How Global Companies Wield Their Power: The Discursive Shaping of Sustainable Development. In Mikler, J. (ed.), *The Handbook of Global Companies.* Oxford: Wiley Blackwell.
Kollman, K. (2008). The Regulatory Power of Business Norms: A Call for a New Research Agenda. *International Studies Review* 10, no. 3, 397–419.
Koppell, J. G. (2010). *World Rule: Accountability, Legitimacy, and the Design of Global Governance.* Chicago: University of Chicago Press.
Korten, D. (2015). *When Corporations Rule the World*, 3rd ed. Oakland: Berrett-Koehler Publishers.
Koske, I., Wanner, I., Bitetti, R., and Barbiero, O. (2015). The 2013 Update of the OECD's Database on Product Market Regulation: Policy Insights for OECD and Non-OECD Countries, *OECD Economics Department Working Papers*, no. 1200, OECD Publishing. http://dx.doi.org/10.1787/5js3f5d3n2vl-en, accessed 22 February 2016.
Kumar, N., and Wright, O. (2012). Google Boss: I'm Very Proud of Our Tax Avoidance Scheme. *The Independent*, 13 December, http://www.independent.co.uk/news/uk/home-news/google-boss-im-very-proud-of-our-tax-avoidance-scheme-8411974.html, accessed 21 April 2017.
Lagarde, C. (2014). *Economic Inclusion and Financial Integrity: An Address to the Conference on Inclusive Capitalism*, 27 May. London. International Monetary Fund, http://www.imf.org/external/np/speeches/2014/052714.htm, accessed 20 August 2014.
Lang, A., Ronit, K., and Schneider, V. (2008). From Simple to Complex: An Evolutionary Sketch of Theories of Business Association. In

Grote, J. R., Lang, A., and Schneider, V. (eds.), *Organized Business Interests in Changing Environments*. Houndmills, Basingstoke: Palgrave Macmillan.

Langley, P. (2015). *Liquidity Lost: The Governance of the Global Financial Crisis*. Oxford: Oxford University Press.

Lawrence, A., Weber, J., and Post, J. (2005). *Business and Society: Stakeholders, Ethics, Public Policy*, 11th ed. New York: McGraw-Hill.

Lazonick, W. (2014). The Big Idea: Profits without Prosperity. *Harvard Business Review* September, 46–55.

Lazonick, W., and O'Sullivan, M. (2000). Maximizing Shareholder Value: A New Ideology for Corporate Governance. *Economy and Society* 29, no. 1, 13–35.

Lazonick, W., and O'Sullivan, M. (2004). Mazimizing Shareholder Value: A New Ideology for Corporate Governance. In Clarke, T. (ed.), *Theories of Corporate Governance: The Philosophical Foundations of Corporate Governance*. London: Routledge.

LeBaron, G. (2014). Subcontracting Is Not Illegal, but Is It Unethical? Business Ethics, Forced Labour, and Economic Success. *Brown Journal of World Affairs* 20, no. 2, 237–249.

Leonard, H. J. (1988). *Pollution and the Struggle for World Product: Multinational Corporations, Environment, and International Comparative Advantage*. Cambridge: Cambridge University Press.

Levitin, A. J. (2007). Payment Wars: The Merchant-Bank Struggle for Control of Payment Systems. *Stanford Journal of Law, Business and Finance* 12, no. 2, 425–485.

Levitt, T. (1983). The Globalization of Markets. *Harvard Business Review* 61, no. 3, 92–102.

Levy, D. L., and Egan, D. (1998). Capital Contests: National and Transnational Channels of Corporate Influence on the Climate Change Negotiations. *Politics and Society* 26, no. 3, 337–362.

Levy, D. L., and Newell, P. J. (2002). Business Strategy and International Environmental Governance: Towards a Neo-Gramscian Synthesis. *Global Environmental Politics* 2, no. 4, 84–101.

Levy, D., and Rothenberg, S. (2002). Heterogeneity and Change in Environmental Strategy: Technological and Political Responses to Climate Change in the Global Automobile Industry. In Hoffman, A., and Ventresc, M. (eds.), *Organizations, Policy, and the Natural Environment: Institutional and Strategic Perspectives*. Stanford, CA: Stanford University Press.

Lindblom, C. (1977). *Politics and Markets*. New York: Basic Books.

Lipset, S. (1983). *Political Man: The Social Basis of Politics*. London: Heinemann.

Liu, G. S., and Sun, P. (2005). The Class of Shareholdings and Its Impacts on Corporate Performance: A Case of State Shareholding Composition in Chinese Public Corporations. *Corporate Governance: An International Review* 13, no. 1, 46–59.

Louis, M., and Ruwet, C. (2016). Representatives from Within: A Comparison between the ILO and the ISO. *Globalizations*, doi: 10.1080/14747731.2016.1201327.

Lowi, T. J. (2001). Our Millennium: Political Science Confronts the Global Corporate Economy. *International Political Science Review* 22, no. 2, 131–150.

Lukes, S. (1974). *Power: A Radical View*. London: Palgrave Macmillan.

Lukes, S. (2005). *Power: A Radical View*, 2nd ed. Houndmills, Basingstoke: Palgrave Macmillan.

Luttwak, E. (1999). *Turbo Capitalism: Winners and Losers in the Global Economy*. New York: HarperCollins.

Mahoney, J., and Thelen, K. (2010). A Theory of Gradual Institutional Change. In Mahoney, J., and Thelen, K. (eds.), *Explaining Institutional Change: Ambiguity, Agency and Power*. New York: Cambridge University Press.

Mann, M. (1993). *The Sources of Social Power. Volume II: The Rise of Classes and Nation-States*. Cambridge: Cambridge University Press.

Mann, M. (1997). Has Globalisation Ended the Rise and Rise of the Nation-State? *Review of International Political Economy* 4, no. 3, 472–496.

Mann, M. (2000). *Globalisation and Modernity*. Unpublished manuscript. Department of Sociology, UCLA.

Mann, M. (2004). The First Failed Empire of the 21st Century. *Review of International Studies* 30, no. 4, 631–653.

March, J., and Olsen, J. (1989). *Rediscovering Institutions. The Organizational Basis of Politics*. New York: Free Press.

March, J., and Olsen, J. (1998). The Institutional Dynamics of International Political Orders. *International Organization* 52, no. 4, 943–969.

Margolis, J. D., and Walsh, J. P. (2001). *People and Profits? The Search for a Link Between a Company's Social and Financial Performance*. Mahwah: Lawrence Erlbaum Associates.

Marsh, D. (2009). Keeping Ideas in Their Place: In Praise of Thin Constructivism. *Australian Journal of Political Science* 44, no. 4, 679–696.

Martell, L. (2007). The Third Wave in Globalization Theory. *International Studies Review* 9, no. 2, 173–196.

Marx, K. (2007 [1867]). *Capital: A Critique of Political Economy. Volume I, Part II: The Process of Capital Accumulation*. New York: Cosimo Classics.

Marx, K., and Engels, F. (1967 [1848]). *The Communist Manifesto*. Harmondsworth: Penguin.

Marzinotto, B. (2002). Book Review: Varieties of Capitalism: The Institutional Foundations of Comparative Advantage. *Review of International Affairs* 78, no. 3, 631–632.

Mattli, W., and Woods, N. (2009). In Whose Benefit? Explaining Regulatory Change in Global Politics. In Mattli, W., and Woods, N. (eds.), *The Politics of Global Regulation*. Princeton, NJ: Princeton University Press.

May, C. (2006). Introduction. In May, C. (ed.), *Global Corporate Power*. Boulder, CO: Lynne Rienner Publishers.

McAlinden, S. P., and Menk, D. M. (2013). *The Effect on the US Economy of the Successful Restructuring of General Motors*. Center for Automotive Research, file:///C:/Users/jmik3038/Downloads/the_effect_final.pdf, accessed 18 January 2016.

McClory, J. (2015). *The Soft Power 30: A Global Ranking of Soft Power*. London: Portland Communications, http://softpower30.portland-communications.com/, accessed 22 February 2016.

McFarland, A. (2004). *Neopluralism: The Evolution of Political Process Theory*. Lawrence: University Press of Kansas.

McGregor, R. (2010). *The Party: The Secret World of China's Communist Rulers*. London: Penguin.

Melo, T., and Garrido-Morgado, A. (2012). Corporate Reputation: A Combination of Social Responsibility and Industry. *Corporate Social Responsibility and Environmental Management* 19, no. 1, 11–31.

Micklethwait, J., and Wooldridge, A. (2003). *The Company: A Short History of a Revolutionary Idea*. London: Phoenix.

Mikler, J. (2008). Sharing Sovereignty for Global Regulation: The Cases of Fuel Economy and Online Gambling, *Regulation and Governance* 2, no. 4, 383–404.

Mikler, J. (2009). *Greening the Car Industry: Varieties of Capitalism and Climate Change*. Cheltenham: Edward Elgar.

Mikler, J. (2011). Sharing Sovereignty for Policy Outcomes. *Policy and Society* 30, no. 3, 151–160.

Mikler, J. (2012). The Illusion of the Power of Markets. *Journal of Australian Political Economy* 68, 41–61.

Mikler, J. (2014). (Multi?)national Corporations and the State in Established Economies. In Nölke, A. (ed.), *Multinational Corporations from Emerging Markets: State Capitalism 3.0*. Houndmills, Basingstoke: Palgrave Macmillan.

Mikler, J., and Harrison, N. (2013). Climate Innovation: Australian Corporate Perspectives on the Role of Government. *Australian Journal of Politics and History* 59, no. 3, 414–428.

Miller, D., and Chen, M. J. (1994). Sources and Consequences of Competitive Inertia: A Study of the US Airline Industry. *Administrative Science Quarterly* 39, no. 1, 1–23.

Mitchell, David (2014). *Thinking About It Only Makes It Worse: And Other Lessons from Modern Life*. London: Guardian Faber Publishing.

Molina, O., and Rhodes, M. (2007). Conflict, Complementarities and Institutional Change in Mixed Market Economies. In Hancke, B., Rhodes, M., and Thatcher, M. (eds.), *Beyond Varieties of Capitalism: Contradictions, Complementarities and Change*. Oxford: Oxford University Press.

Moran, M. (2008). Representing the Corporate Elite in Britain: Capitalist Solidarity and Capitalist Legacy. In Savage, M., and Williams, K. (eds.), *Remembering Elites*. Oxford: Blackwell.

Myers, C. (2013). *Corporate Social Responsibility in the Consumer Electronics Industry: A Case Study of Apple Inc.*, Georgetown University. Edmund A.

Walsh School of Foreign Service, http://lwp.georgetown.edu/wp-content/uploads/Connor-Myers.pdf, accessed 7 September 2016.

Newell, P. (2000). *Climate for Change: Non-state Actors and the Global Politics of the Greenhouse*. Cambridge: Cambridge University Press.

Newell, P., and Levy, D. L. (2006). The Political Economy of the Firm in Global Environmental Governance. In May, C. (ed.), *Global Corporate Power*. London: Lynne Rienner Publishers.

NEXTera Energy (2016). http://www.nexteraenergy.com/index.shtml, accessed 6 August 2016.

Nolan, P. (2007). *Capitalism and Freedom: The Contradictory Character of Globalisation*. London: Anthem Press.

Nolan, P., Sutherland, D., and Zhang, J. (2002). The Challenge of the Global Business Revolution. *Contributions to Political Economy* 21, no. 1, 91–110.

Nölke, A. (2010a). A "BRIC"-Variety of Capitalism and Social Inequality: The Case of Brazil. *Revista a Estudos e Pesquisassobre as Américas* 4, no. 1, 1–14.

Nölke, A. (2010b). The Politics of Accounting Regulation: Responses to the Subprime Crisis. In Helleiner, E. (ed.), *Global Finance in Crisis: The Politics of International Regulatory Change*. New York: Routledge.

Nölke, A. (2012). The Rise of the "B(R)IC-Variety of Capitalism": Toward a New Phase of Organized Capitalism. In Overbeek, H., and van Apeldoorn, B. (eds.), *Neoliberalism in Crisis*. Basingstoke and New York: Palgrave Macmillan.

Nölke, A. (2014). Private Chinese Multinationals and the Long Shadow of the State. In Nölke, A. (ed.), *Multinational Corporations from Emerging Markets: State Capitalism 3.0*. Houndmills, Basingstoke: Palgrave Macmillan.

North, D. (1990). *Institutions, Institutional Change and Economic Performance*. Cambridge: Cambridge University Press.

Nye, J. S. (2004a). *Soft Power: The Means to Succeed in World Politics*. New York: Public Affairs.

Nye, J. S. (2004b). Soft Power and American Foreign Policy. *Political Science Quarterly* 119, no. 2, 255–270.

O'Callaghan, T. (2007). Disciplining Multinational Enterprises: The Regulatory Power of Reputation Risk. *Global Society* 21, no. 1, 95–117.

O'Callaghan, T. (2016). *Reputation Risk and Globalization: Exploring the Idea of a Self-Regulating Corporation*. Cheltenham: Edward Elgar.

O'Callaghan, T., and Vivoda, V. (2013). How Global Companies Make National Regulations. In Mikler, J. (ed.), *The Handbook of Global Companies*. Oxford: Wiley Blackwell.

O'Neill, K. (2009). *The Environment and International Relations*. Cambridge: Cambridge University Press.

O'Rourke, J., and Collins, S. (2008). *Managing Conflict and Workplace Relationships*, 2nd ed. Mason: South-Western Cengage Learning.

Oatley, T., Winecoff, W. K., Danzman, S. B., and Pennock, A. (2013). The Political Economy of Global Finance: A Network Model. *Perspectives on Politics* 11, no. 1, 133–153.

OECD (2011). *Bank Competition and Financial Stability*. http://www.oecd.org/finance/financial-markets/48501035.pdf, accessed 10 June 2014.

OECD (2014a). Concentration of the Banking Sector: Assets of Three Largest Banks as a Share of Assets of All Commercial Banks, percent, 2011, *OECD Economic Surveys: Netherlands 2014*, http://10.1787/eco_surveys-nld-2014-graph31-en, accessed 10 June 2014.

OECD (2014b). *OECD International Direct Investment Statistics 2014*, OECD Publishing, http://www.oecd-ilibrary.org/finance-and-investment/oecd-international-direct-investment-statistics-2014_idis-2014-en, accessed 24 November 2015.

OECD (2015). *Reforms to the International Tax System for Curbing Avoidance by Multinational Enterprises*, http://www.oecd.org/tax/oecd-presents-outputs-of-oecd-g20-beps-project-for-discussion-at-g20-finance-ministers-meeting.htm, accessed 13 July 2016.

OECD (2016a). *Tax on Corporate Profits*, https://data.oecd.org/tax/tax-on-corporate-profits.htm, accessed 18 January 2017.

OECD (2016b). *Tax Revenue*, https://data.oecd.org/tax/tax-revenue.htm, accessed 18 January 2017.

OECD (2016c). *Tax on Personal Income*, https://data.oecd.org/tax/tax-on-personal-income.htm, accessed 18 January 2017.

OECD (2016d). *Social Security Contributions*, https://data.oecd.org/tax/social-security-contributions.htm, accessed 18 January 2017.

OECD (2016e). *Tax on Payroll*, https://data.oecd.org/tax/tax-on-payroll.htm, accessed 18 January 2017.

OECD (2016f). *Tax on Property*, https://data.oecd.org/tax/tax-on-property.htm, accessed 18 January 2017.

OECD (2016g). *Tax on Goods and Services*, https://data.oecd.org/tax/tax-on-goods-and-services.htm, accessed 18 January 2017.

OECD (2016h). Strictness of Employment Protection Legislation: Individual and Collective Dismissals, *OECD Employment and Labour Market Statistics* (database), doi: 10.1787/lfs-data-en, accessed 22 February 2016.

OECD (2016i). Economy Wide Regulation, *OECD Product Market Regulation Statistics* (database), doi: 10.1787/pmr-data-en, accessed 22 February 2016.

Office of the United States Trade Representative (2016). *TPP: Made in America*, https://ustr.gov/tpp/#strategic-importance, accessed 7 November 2016.

Official Journal of the European Union (2015). *Regulation (EU) 2015/751 of the European Parliament and of the Council of 29 April 2015 on Interchange Fees for Card-based Payment Transactions*, 19 May, L123/1, http://eur-lex.europa.eu/legal-content/EN/TXT/PDF/?uri=CELEX:32015R0751&from=EN, accessed 7 December 2016.

Ohmae, K. (1990). *The Borderless World: Power and Strategy in the Interlinked Economy*. London: Collins.

OICA (2014). *Motor Vehicle Production by Manufacturer: World Ranking of Manufacturers*, http://www.oica.net/wp-content/uploads//Ranking-2014-Q4-Rev.-22-July.pdf, accessed 12 January 2016.

Olsen, J. P. (2009). Change and Continuity: An Institutional Approach to Institutions of Democratic Government. *European Political Science Review* 1, no. 1, 3–32.

OpenSecrets.org (2015a). American Bankers Association, http://www.opensecrets.org/lobby/clientsum.php?id=D000000087&year=2015, accessed 15 January 2016.

OpenSecrets.org (2015b). Financial Services Roundtable, http://www.opensecrets.org/lobby/clientsum.php?id=D000021984&year=2015, accessed 15 January 2016.

OpenSecrets.org (2015c). Securities Industry and Financial Markets Association, http://www.opensecrets.org/lobby/clientsum.php?id=D000000229&year=2015, accessed 15 January 2016.

OpenSecrets.org (2015d), JP Morgan Chase and Co, http://www.opensecrets.org/orgs/lobby.php?id=D000000103, accessed 15 January 2016.

Orsini, A. (2011). Thinking Transnationally, Acting Individually: Business Lobby Coalitions in International Environmental Negotiations. *Global Society* 25, no. 3, 311–329.

Ostry, J. D., Loungani, P., and Furceri, D. (2016). Neoliberalism: Oversold? *Finance and Development*, June, 38–41.

Ougaard, M. (2006). Instituting the Power to Do Good? In May, C. (ed.), *Global Corporate Power*. Boulder, CO: Lynne Rienner Publishers.

Oxfam (2016). *Broken at the Top: How America's Dysfunctional Tax System Costs Billions in Corporate Tax Dodging*. Oxfam America, http://www.oxfamamerica.org/static/media/files/Broken_at_the_Top_FINAL_EMBARGOED_4.12.2016.pdf, accessed 11 May 2016.

Ozawa, T. (2014). Multinationals as an Instrument of Catch-Up Industrialization: Understanding the Strategic Links between State and Industry in Emerging Markets. In Nölke, A. (ed.), *Multinational Corporations from Emerging Markets: State Capitalism 3.0*. Houndmills, Basingstoke: Palgrave Macmillan.

Palan, R., and Wigan, D. (2014). Herding Cats and Taming Tax Havens: The US Strategy of "Not In My Backyard." *Global Policy* 5, no. 3, 334–343.

Palmberg, E. (2012). TPP: The Insider List. *Sojourners*, 29 June, https://sojo.net/articles/insider-list, accessed 15 December 2015.

Panetta, F., Faeh, T., Grande, G., Ho, C., King, M., Levy, A., Signoretti, F. M., Taboga, M., and Zaghini, A. (2009). *BIS No.48: An Assessment of Financial Sector Rescue Programmes*. In BIS Papers. Basel: Switzerland, http://www.bis.org/publ/bppdf/bispap48.pdf, accessed 3 November 2016.

Panic, M. (1995). The Bretton Woods System: Concept and Practice. In Michie, J., and Smith, J. G. (eds.), *Managing the Global Economy*. Oxford: Oxford University Press.

Parkinson, J., Gamble, A., and Kelly, G. (eds.) (2000). *The Political Economy of the Company*. Oxford: Hart Publishing.

Parvin, P. (2007). *Friend or Foe? Lobbying in British Democracy*. London: Hansard Society, http://www.hansardsociety.org.uk/wp-content/uploads/

2012/10/Friend-or-Foe-Lobbying-in-British-Democracy-2007.pdf, accessed 11 August 2015.

Patnaik, A. K. (1988). Gramsci's Concept of Common Sense: Towards a Theory of Sabaltern Consciousness in Hegemony Processes. *Economic and Political Weekly* 23, no. 5, 2–10.

Pauly, L., and Reich, S. (1997). National Structures and Multinational Corporate Behavior: Enduring Differences in the Age of Globalization. *International Organization* 51, no. 1, 1–30.

Pearse, G. (2007). *High and Dry*. Camberwell: Viking/Penguin.

Peck, J., and Zhang, J. (2013). A Variety of Capitalism … with Chinese Characteristics? *Journal of Economic Geography* 13, no. 3, 357–396.

Perlmutter, H. (1969). The Tortuous Evolution of Multinational Enterprises. *Columbia Journal of World Business* 4, no. 1, 9–18.

Picketty, T. (2013). *Capital in the Twenty-first Century*. Cambridge, MA: Belknap Press of Harvard University Press.

Pontusson, J. (2005). *Inequality and Prosperity: Social Europe versus Liberal America*. Ithaca, NY: Cornell University Press.

Porter, T. (1993). *States, Markets and Regimes in Global Finance*. New York: St. Martin's Press.

Porter, T. (1999). Hegemony and the Private Governance of International Industries. In Cutler, A. C., Haufler, V., and Porter, T. (eds.), *Private Authority and International Affairs*. Albany: State University of New York Press.

Porter, T., and Brown, S. (2013). Why, When, and How Global Companies Get Organized. In Mikler, J. (ed.), *The Handbook of Global Companies*. Oxford: Wiley Blackwell.

Porter, T., and Ronit, K. (2006). Self-regulation as Policy Process: The Multiple and Criss-Crossing Stages of Private Rule-making. *Policy Sciences* 39, no. 1, 41–72.

Portland Communications (2015). Index Results. *The Soft Power 30*, http://softpower30.portland-communications.com/ranking/#2015, accessed 22 February 2016.

Price, R., and Reus-Smit, C. (1998). Dangerous Liaisons? Critical International Relations Theory and Constructivism. *European Journal of International Relations* 4, no. 3, 259–294.

Protess, B. (2011). Wall Street Continues to Spend Big on Lobbying. *New York Times*, 1 August, http://dealbook.nytimes.com/2011/08/01/wall-street-continues-to-spend-big-on-lobbying/, accessed 2 July 2014.

PwC (2016). *Making a Difference: Global Annual Review 2016*. https://www.pwc.com/gx/en/annual-review/2016/pwc-global-annual-review.pdf, accessed 8 June 2017.

Pye, L., and Pye, M. (1985). *Asian Power and Politics: The Cultural Dimension of Authority*. Cambridge, MA: Belknap Press of Harvard University Press.

Ramamurti, R. (2001). The Obsolescing Bargaining Model: MNC-Host Developing Country Relations Revisited. *Journal of International Business Studies* 32, no. 1, 23–39.

Ricardo, D. (1962 [1821]). *The Principles of Political Economy and Taxation.* London: Dent.
Riegels, C. (2014). *The IBC Act—the Building of a Nation*, http://print.harneys.com/files/the-ibc-act-the-building-of-a-nation-(2).pdf, accessed 24 November 2015.
Robinson, W., and Harris, J. (2000). Towards a Global Ruling Class? Globalization and the Transnational Capitalist Class. *Science and Society* 64, no. 1, 11–54.
Rodrik, D. (2001). Trading in Illusions. *Foreign Policy* 123, March/April, 54–62.
Ronit, K., and Schneider, V. (1997). Organisierte Interessen in Nationalen und Supranationalen Politokologien: Ein Vegleich der G7 Lander mit der Europaischen Union, in von Alemann, U., and Wessels, B. (eds.), *Verbande in Vergleihender Perpektiv.* Berlin: Edition Sigma.
Royal Dutch Shell (2008). *Brent Spar Dossier.* http://www.shell.co.uk/sustainability/decommissioning/brent-spar-dossier/_jcr_content/par/textimage.stream/1426853000847/6b0c52ecc4c60be5fa8e78ef26c4827ec4da3cd3cd73747473b4fc60f4d12986/brent-spar-dossier.pdf, accessed 25 August 2016.
Rudd, K. (2009). The Global Financial Crisis. *The Monthly* 42, February, 20–29.
Ruggie, J. G. (1992). Multilateralism: The Anatomy of an Institution. *International Organisation* 46, no. 3, 561–598.
Ruggie, J. G. (1998). What Makes the World Hang Together? Neo-utilitarianism and the Social Constructivist Challenge. *International Organization* 52, no. 4, 855–885,
Rugman, A. (2000). *The End of Globalization.* London: Random House Business Books.
Rugman, A. (2005). *The Regional Multinationals: MNEs and "Global" Strategic Management.* Cambridge: Cambridge University Press.
Rugman, A. (ed.) (2007). *Regional Aspects of Multinationality and Performance.* Bingley: Emerald.
Rugman, A., and Collinson, S. (2004). The Regional Nature of the World's Automotive Sector. *European Management Journal* 22, no. 5, 471–482.
Rugman, A., and Girod, S. (2003). Retail Multinationals and Globalization: The Evidence is Regional. *European Management Journal* 21, no. 1, 24–37.
Rugman, A., and Verbeke, A. (2009). Location, Competitiveness, and the Multinational Enterprise. In Rugman, A. (ed.), *The Oxford Handbook of International Business*, 2nd ed. Oxford: Oxford University Press.
Schmidpeter, R., and Stehr, C. (2015). A History of Research on CSR in China: The Obstacles for the Implementation of CSR in Emerging Markets. In Schmidpeter, R., Lu, H., Stehr, C., and Huang, H. (eds.), *Sustainable Development and CSR in China: A Multi-Perspective Approach.* Springer International Publishing.
Schmidt, V. (2002). *The Futures of European Capitalism.* Oxford: Oxford University Press.

Scholte, J. A. (2002). Civil Society and Democracy in Global Governance. *Global Governance* 8, no. 3, 281–304.
Scholte, J. A. (2005). *Globalisation: A Critical Introduction*, 2nd ed. Houndmills, Basingstoke: Palgrave Macmillan.
Scholte, J. A. (2011). Global Governance, Accountability and Civil Society. In Scholte, J.A. (ed.), *Building Global Democracy: Civil Society and Accountable Global Governance*. Cambridge: Cambridge University Press.
Schwartz, H. (2000). *States versus Markets*, 2nd ed. Houndmills, Basingstoke: Macmillan.
Sell, S. (1999). Multinational Corporations as Agents of Change: The Globalization of Intellectual Property Rights. In Cutler, A. C., Haufler, V., and Porter, T. (eds.), *Private Authority and International Affairs*. Albany: State University of New York Press.
Sell, S. (2003). *Private Power, Public Law: The Globalization of Intellectual Property Rights*. Cambridge: Cambridge University Press.
Sell, S. (2009). Corporations, Seeds, and Intellectual Property Rights Governance. In Clapp, J., and Fuchs, D. (eds.), *Corporate Power in Global Agrifood Governance*. Cambridge, MA: MIT Press.
Sharman, J. C. (2006). *Havens in a Storm: The Struggle for Global Tax Regulation*. Ithaca, NY: Cornell University Press.
Sidel, R. (2016). Battle over Cards Heats Up as Court Rejects Visa, MasterCard Deal with Retailers. *Wall Street Journal*, 30 June, http://www.wsj.com/articles/visa-mastercard-class-action-settlement-rejected-by-u-s-court-1467300658, accessed 25 August 2016.
Siffert, N. F., and Souza e Silva, C. (1999). *Large Companies in the 1990s: Strategic Responses to a Scenario of Change*. Rio de Janeiro: Banco Nacional de Desenvolvimento Econômico e Social.
Sklair, L. (2001). *The Transnational Capitalist Class*. Oxford: Blackwell.
Smith, A. (2003 [1776]). *The Wealth of Nations*. New York: Bantam Classic.
Staples, C. L. (2007). Board Globalisation in the World's Largest TNCs 1993–2005. *Corporate Governance* 15, no. 2, 311–321.
Starrs, S. (2013). American Economic Power Hasn't Declined—It Globalized! Summoning the Data and Taking Globalization Seriously. *International Studies Quarterly* 57, no. 4, 817–830.
Statista (2015). *Global Smartphone Shipments from 2009 to 2014 (in million units)*. http://www.statista.com/statistics/271491/worldwide-shipments-of-smartphones-since-2009/, accessed 20 July 2015.
Statista (2016). *Global Operating Systems Market Share for Desktop PCs, from January 2012 to July 2016*, http://www.statista.com/statistics/218089/global-market-share-of-windows-7/, accessed 10 August 2016.
Strange, S. (1996). *The Retreat of the State: The Diffusion of Power in the World Economy*. Cambridge: Cambridge University Press.
Strange, S. (1997). The Future of Global Capitalism; or Will Divergence Persist Forever? In Crouch, C., and Streeck, W. (eds.), *Political Economy of Modern Capitalism: Mapping Convergence and Diversity*. London: Sage.

Strange, S. (1988). *States and Markets: An Introduction to International Political Economy*. London: Pinter Publishers.
Streeck, W. (1997). German Capitalism: Does It Exist? Can It Survive? In Crouch, C., and Streeck, W. (eds.), *Political Economy of Modern Capitalism: Mapping Convergence and Diversity*. London: Sage.
Streeck, W. (2001). Introduction: Explorations into the Origins of Nonliberal Capitalism in Germany and Japan. In Streeck, W., and Yamamura, K. (eds.), *The Origins of Nonliberal Capitalism: Germany and Japan in Comparison*. Ithaca, NY: Cornell University Press.
Streeck, W. (2009). *Re-forming Capitalism: Institutional Change in the German Political Economy*. Oxford: Oxford University Press.
Streeck, W., and Yamamura, K. (eds.) (2001). *The Origins of Nonliberal Capitalism: Germany and Japan in Comparison*. Ithaca, NY: Cornell University Press.
Streeck, W., and Yamamura, K. (eds.) (2003). *The End of Diversity? Prospects for German and Japanese Capitalism*. Ithaca, NY: Cornell University Press.
Suchman, M. C. (1995). Managing Legitimacy: Strategic and Institutional Approaches. *Academy of Management Review* 20, no. 3, 571–610.
Tait, N., and Wilson, J. (2011). P&G and Unilever Fined for Price Fixing, 13 April. *Financial Times*, http://www.ft.com/cms/s/0/e0e21f9a-65b3-11e0-baee-00144feab49a.html#axzz4HS1Dthqa, accessed 17 August 2016.
Tam, G. F. (2010). Foxconn Factories are Labor Camps: Report. *South China Morning Post*, 11 October, http://www.scmp.com/article/727143/foxconn-factories-are-labour-camps-report, accessed 7 September 2016.
Teeple, G., and McBride, S. (eds.) (2011). *Relations of Global Power: Neoliberal Order and Disorder*. Toronto: University of Toronto Press.
Thatcher, M. (2007). *Internationalisation and Economic Institutions*. Oxford: Oxford University Press.
Thompson, G. (2003). Globalisation as the Total Commercialisation of Politics? *New Political Economy* 8, no. 3, 401–408.
Thurbon, E. (2016). *Developmental Mindset: The Revival of Financial Activism in South Korea*. Ithaca, NY: Cornell University Press.
Tiberghien, Y. (2007). *Entrepreneurial States: Reforming Corporate Governance in France, Japan and Korea*. Ithaca, NY: Cornell University Press.
Tienhaara, K. (2014). Corporations: Business and Industrial Influence. In Harris, P. G. (ed.), *Routledge Handbook of Global Environmental Politics*. Abingdon: Routledge.
Tienhaara, K., Orsini, A., and Falkner, R. (2012). Global Corporations. In Bierman, F., and Pattberg, P. (eds.), *Global Environmental Governance Reconsidered*. Cambridge, MA: MIT Press.
UK Public Accounts Committee on Tax Avoidance–Google (2015). http://www.publications.parliament.uk/pa/cm201314/cmselect/cmpubacc/112/11202.htm, accessed 22 May 2015.
UNCTAD (2008). *World Investment Report: Transnational Corporations and the Infrastructure Challenge*. New York: United Nations Conference

on Trade and Development, http://unctad.org/en/Docs/wir2008overview_en.pdf, accessed 19 January 2015.

UNCTAD (2011). *World Investment Report 2011*. Web Table 34: Number of Parent Corporations and Foreign Affiliates, by Region and Economy 2010, http://unctad.org/Sections/dite_dir/docs/WIR11_web%20tab%2034.pdf, accessed 20 July 2015.

UNCTAD (2013a). *World Investment Report 2013*. Web Table 28: The World's Top 100 Non-Financial TNCs. Ranked by Foreign Assets 2012, http://unctad.org/Sections/dite_dir/docs/WIR2013/WIR13_webtab28.xls, accessed 7 August 2015.

UNCTAD (2013b), *FDI Stock*. http://unctad.org/en/Pages/DIAE/FDI%20Statistics/FDIStock.aspx, accessed 17 November 2015.

UNCTAD (2013c), *FDI Flows*. http://unctad.org/en/Pages/DIAE/FDI%20Statistics/FDIFlows.aspx, accessed 17 November 2015.

UNCTAD (2013d). *World Investment Report 2013*. Annex Table 30: The Top 50 Financial TNCs Ranked by Geographical Spread Index 2012, http://unctad.org/en/pages/DIAE/World%20Investment%20Report/Annex-Tables.aspx, accessed 4 March 2014.

UNCTAD (2014a). *World Investment Report 2014*. Web Table 28: The World's Top 100 Non-Financial TNCs. Ranked by Foreign Assets 2013, http://unctad.org/Sections/dite_dir/docs/WIR2014/WIR14_tab28.xls, accessed 20 October 2015.

UNCTAD (2014b). *World Investment Report 2014*. Web Table 29: The World's Top 100 Non-Financial TNCs from Developing and Transition Economies. Ranked by Foreign Assets 2012, http://unctad.org/Sections/dite_dir/docs/WIR2014/WIR14_tab29.xls, accessed 20 October 2015.

UNCTAD (2014c). *World Investment Report 2014*. Web Table 10: Value of Cross-Border M&As by Region/Economy of Purchaser 1990–2013, http://unctad.org/Sections/dite_dir/docs/WIR2014/WIR14_tab10.xls, accessed 20 October 2015.

UNCTAD (2014d). *World Investment Report 2014*. Web Table 9: Value of Cross-Border M&As by Region/Economy of Seller 1990–2013, http://unctad.org/Sections/dite_dir/docs/WIR2014/WIR14_tab09.xls, accessed 20 October 2015.

UNCTAD (2014e). *World Investment Report 2014*. Web Table 3: FDI Inward Stock, by Region and Economy 1990–2013, http://unctad.org/Sections/dite_dir/docs/WIR2014/WIR14_tab03.xls, accessed 20 October 2015.

UNCTAD (2014f). *World Investment Report 2014*. Web Table 4: FDI Outward Stock, by Region and Economy 1990–2013, http://unctad.org/Sections/dite_dir/docs/WIR2014/WIR14_tab04.xls, accessed 20 October 2015.

UNCTAD (2014g). *World Investment Report 2014*. Web Table 1: FDI Inflows, by Region and Economy 1990–2013, http://unctad.org/Sections/dite_dir/docs/WIR2014/WIR14_tab01.xls, accessed 20 October 2015.

UNCTAD (2014h). *World Investment Report 2014*. Web Table 2: FDI Outflows, by Region and Economy 1990–2013, http://unctad.org/Sections/dite_dir/docs/WIR2014/WIR14_tab02.xls, accessed 20 October 2015.

UNEP (2002). *Industry as a Partner for Sustainable Development—10 Years after Rio: The UNEP Assessment.* www.uneptie.org/Outreach/wssd/contributions/publications/pub_global.htm, accessed 13 June 2003.

UNEP and ACEA (2002). *Industry as a Partner for Sustainable Development: Automotive.* http://www.unepti.e.org/outreach/wssd/docs/sectors/final/automotive.pdf, accessed 14 May 2003.

United Nations (2012). *Regular Budget 2012–2013.* http://www.un.org/en/hq/dm/pdfs/oppba/Regular%20Budget.pdf, accessed 9 March 2016.

US Securities and Exchange Commission (2012). *Annual Report on Nationally Recognized Statistical Rating Organizations.* https://www.sec.gov/divisions/marketreg/ratingagency/nrsroannrep1212.pdf, accessed 15 August 2016.

US Senate Commission on Banking, Housing and Urban Affairs (n.d.). *Brief Summary of the Dodd-Frank Wall Street Reform and Consumer Protection Act.* http://www.banking.senate.gov/public/_files/070110_Dodd_Frank_Wall_Street_Reform_comprehensive_summary_Final.pdf, accessed 20 July 2015.

US Senate Committee on Homeland Security and Governmental Affairs (2013). Subcommittee to Examine Offshore Profit Shifting and Tax Avoidance by Apple Inc. http://www.hsgac.senate.gov/subcommittees/investigations/media/subcommittee-to-examine-offshore-profit-shifting-and-tax-avoidance-by-apple-inc., accessed 21 May 2015.

Utting, P. (2002). *The Greening of Business in Developing Countries: Rhetoric, Reality and Prospects.* London: Zed Books.

van Ham, P. (2002). Branding Territory: Inside the Wonderful Worlds of PR and IR Theory. *Millennium: Journal of International Studies* 31, no. 2, 249–269.

van Ham, P. (2008). Place Branding: The State of the Art. *The Annals of the American Academy of Political and Social Science* 616, no. 1, 126–149.

van Veen, K., and Elbertsen, E. (2008). Governance Regimes and National Diversity in Corporate Boards: A Comparative Study of Germany, the Netherlands and the United Kingdom. *Corporate Governance* 16, no. 5, 386–399.

van Veen, K., and Marsman, I. (2008). How International Are Executive Boards of European MNCs? National Diversity in 15 European Countries. *European Management Journal* 26, 188–198.

Vernon, R. (1971). *Sovereignty at Bay: The Multinational Spread of US Enterprise.* New York: Basic Books.

Vernon, R. (1977). *Storm over the Multinationals: The Real Issues.* Cambridge, MA: Harvard University Press.

Vernon, R. (1981). Sovereignty at Bay: Ten Years After. *International Organization* 35, Summer, 517–529.

Viner, J. (1948). Power versus Plenty as Objectives of Foreign Policy in the Seventeenth and Eighteenth Centuries. *World Politics* 1, no. 1, 1–29.

Vitols, S. (2001). Varieties of Corporate Governance: Comparing Germany and the UK. In Hall, P. A., and Soskice, D. (eds.), *Varieties of Capitalism: The Institutional Foundations of Comparative Advantage.* Oxford: Oxford University Press.

Vogel, D. (1995). *Trading Up: Consumer and Environmental Regulation in the Global Economy*. Cambridge, MA: Harvard University Press.

Vogel, D. (2005). *The Market for Virtue: The Potential and Limits of Corporate Social Responsibility*. Washington, DC: Brookings Institute Press.

Vogel, D. (2010). Taming Globalization? Civil Regulation and Corporate Capitalism. In Coen, D., Grant, W., and Wilson, G. (eds.), *The Oxford Handbook of Business and Government*. Oxford: Oxford University Press.

Vogel, S. (1996). *Freer Markets, More Rules: Regulatory Reform in Advanced Industrial Countries*. Ithaca, NY: Cornell University Press.

Vogel, S. (2001). The Crisis of German and Japanese Capitalism: Stalled on the Road to the Liberal Market Model? *Comparative Political Studies* 34, no. 10, 1103–1133.

Vormedal, I. (2008). The Influence of Business and Industry NGOs in the Negotiation of the Kyoto Mechanisms: The Case of Carbon Capture and Storage in the CDM. *Global Environmental Politics* 8, no. 4, 36–65.

Voss, H. (2013). The Global Company. In Mikler, J. (ed.), *The Handbook of Global Companies*. Oxford: Wiley Blackwell.

Wade, R. (2003). What Strategies Are Viable for Developing Countries Today? The World Trade Organization and the Shrinking of "Development Space." *Review of International Political Economy* 10, no. 4, 621–644.

Wade, R. (2010). Is the Globalization Consensus Dead? *Antipode* 41, no. S1, 141–165.

Wallerstein, I. (1984). *The Politics of the World Economy: The States, the Movements and the Civilizations*. Cambridge: Cambridge University Press.

Wallerstein, I. (2004). *World Systems Analysis: An Introduction*. New York: Basil Blackwell.

Walmart (2013). *Walmart 2103 Annual Report*. http://c46b2bcc0db5865f5a76-91c2ff8eba65983a1c33d367b8503d02.r78.cf2.rackcdn.com/88/2d/4fdf67184a359fdef07b1c3f4732/2013-annual-report-for-walmart-stores-inc_130221024708579502.pdf, accessed 18 April 2017.

Walmart (2017). *Apply to Be a Supplier*. http://corporate.walmart.com/suppliers/apply-to-be-a-supplier, accessed 18 April 2017.

Walter, A., and Zhang, X. (eds.) (2012a). *East Asian Capitalism: Diversity, Continuity and Change*. Oxford: Oxford University Press.

Walter, A., and Zhang, X. (2012b). Debating East Asian Capitalism: Issues and Themes. In Walter. A., and Zhang, X. (eds.), *East Asian Capitalism: Diversity, Continuity and Change*. Oxford: Oxford University Press.

Wank, D. (1998). *Commodifying Chinese Communism: Business, Trust and Politics in a South Coast City*. Cambridge: Cambridge University Press.

Watson, M. (2003). Ricardian Political Economy and the "Varieties of Capitalism" Approach: Specialization, Trade and Comparative Institutional Advantage. *Comparative European Politics* 1, no. 2, 227–240.

Watson, M. (2008). Theoretical Traditions in Global Political Economy. In Ravenhill, J. (ed.), *Global Political Economy*, 2nd ed. Oxford: Oxford University Press.

WBCSD (2002). *The Business Case for Sustainable Development.* file:///C:/Users/jmik3038/Downloads/BusinessCaseForSD-MakingDiffTowardsJohannesburgSummit.pdf, accessed 29 August 2016.
WBCSD (2016). *Business Solutions for a Sustainable World.* http://www.wbcsd.org/about/organization.aspx, accessed 29 August 2016.
Weber, S. (2001). Introduction. In Weber, S. (ed.), *Globalization and the European Political Economy.* New York: Columbia University Press.
Weidenbaum, M. (2004). *Business and Government in the Global Marketplace,* 7th ed. Upper Saddle River: Prentice Hall.
Weil, N. (1998). New US Policy Turns Net Governance Over to the Private Sector. *SunWorld,* June 1998, http://sunsite.uakom.sk/sunworldonline/swol-06-1998/swol-06-ntia.html, accessed 19 August 2016.
Weisman, J., and Lipton, E. (2015). In New Congress, Wall St. Pushes to Undermine Dodd-Frank Reform. *New York Times,* 13 January, http://www.nytimes.com/2015/01/14/business/economy/in-new-congress-wall-st-pushes-to-undermine-dodd-frank-reform.html, accessed 20 July 2015.
Weiss, L. (1998). *The Myth of the Powerless State.* Cambridge: Polity Press.
Weiss, L. (2003). Introduction: Bringing Domestic Institutions Back In. In Weiss, L. (ed.), *States in the Global Economy: Bringing Domestic Institutions Back In.* Cambridge: Cambridge University Press.
Weiss, L. (2006). Infrastructural Power, Economic Transformation, and Globalization. In Hall, J. A., and Schroeder, R. (eds.), *An Anatomy of Power: The Social Theory of Michael Mann.* Cambridge: Cambridge University Press.
Weiss, L. (2010). The State in the Economy: Neoliberal or Neoactivist? In Morgan, G., Campbell, J. L., Crouch, C., Pedersen, O. K., and Whitley, R. (eds.), *The Oxford Handbook of Comparative Institutional Analysis.* Oxford: Oxford University Press.
Weiss, L. (2014). *America Inc.: Innovation and Enterprise in the National Security State.* Ithaca, NY: Cornell University Press.
Weiss, L., and Hobson, J. M. (1995). *States and Economic Development: A Comparative Historical Analysis.* Cambridge: Polity Press.
Wendt, A. (1999). *Social Theory of International Politics.* Cambridge: Cambridge University Press.
Whitley, R. (1999). *Divergent Capitalisms: The Social Structuring and Change of Business Systems.* Oxford: Oxford University Press.
Whitley, R. (2009). The Multinational Company as a Distinct Organizational Form. In Collinson, D., and Morgan, G. (eds.), *Images of the Multinational Firm.* Chichester: Wiley and Sons.
Whole Foods Market (2016). *Company Info,* http://www.wholefoodsmarket.com/company-info, accessed 6 August 2016.
Wilks, S. (1990). The Embodiment of Industrial Culture in Bureaucracy and Management. In Clegg, S., and Redding, S. (eds.), *Capitalism in Contrasting Cultures.* Berlin: Walter de Gruyter.
Wilks, S. (2013). *The Political Power of the Business Corporation.* Cheltenham: Edward Elgar.

Wilks-Heeg, S., Blick, A., and Crone, S. (2012). *How Democratic is the UK? The 2012 Audit*. Liverpool: Democratic Audit, http://democracyuk-2012.democraticaudit.com/, accessed 20 July 2015.

Winnett, R., Porter, A., Conway, E., and Swaine, J. (2009). G20 Summit: Gordon Brown Unveils $1.1 Trillion Global Recession Fightback. *The Telegraph*, 2 April, http://www.telegraph.co.uk/finance/g20-summit/5094824/G20-summit-Gordon-Brown-unveils-1.1trn-global-recession-fight-back.html, accessed 10 June 2014.

Wolf, M. (2004). *Why Globalisation Works*. New Haven, CT: Yale University Press.

Woo-Cumings, M. (ed.) (1999). *The Developmental State*. Ithaca, NY: Cornell University Press.

Woods, N. (2006). *The Globalizers: The IMF, the World Bank and Their Borrowers*. Ithaca, NY: Cornell University Press.

World Bank (2002). *Global Economic Prospects and the Developing Countries 2002*. Washington, DC: World Bank, http://www.worldbank.org/content/dam/Worldbank/GEP/GEParchives/GEP2002/310436360_20050012014722.pdf, accessed 14 August 2015.

World Bank (2016). *Gross Domestic Product 2015*. World Development Indicator Database, 11 October, http://databank.worldbank.org/data/download/GDP.pdf, accessed 1 November 2016.

World Values Survey (2015). *World Values Survey (2005–2009): Crossings by Country*. Study # 906-WVS2005, v.2015.04.18, http://www.worldvaluessurvey.org/WVSDocumentationWV5.jsp, accessed 18 March 2016.

Wright, C., and Rwabizambuga, A. (2006). Institutional Pressures, Corporate Reputation, and Voluntary Codes of Conduct: An Examination of the Equator Principles. *Business and Society Review* 111, no. 1, 89–117.

WTO (n.d.). *What Is the WTO?* https://www.wto.org/english/theWTO_e/whatis_e/whatis_e.htm, accessed 5 June 2017.

WTO (2011). As Trade Changes Rapidly, You Must Help Guide WTO, Lamy Tells Global Business, *WTO News: Speeches—DG Pascal Lamy*, 12 May, http://www.wto.org/english/news_e/sppl_e/sppl192_e.htm, accessed 16 May 2011.

WTO (2016), WTO Secretariat Budget for 2013–14. *The WTO: Secretariat and Budget*, https://www.wto.org/english/thewto_e/secre_e/budget_e.htm, accessed 15 January 2016.

Xia, J., Boal, K., and Delios, D. (2009). When Experience Meets National Institutional Environmental Change: Foreign Entry Attempts of US Firms in the Central and Eastern European Region. *Strategic Management Journal* 30, no. 12, 1286–1309.

Zadek, S. (2007). *The Civil Corporation: The New Economy of Corporate Citizenship*, 2nd ed. London: Earthscan.

Zadek, S. (2013). Will Business Save the World? In Mikler, J. (ed.), *The Handbook of Global Companies*. Oxford: Wiley Blackwell.

INDEX

accountancy firms
   "Big Four" 106, 107
   standards 112
actor-centered analysis 3–4, 6, 31, 40–5
Adams, S. 116
Africa 68
agriculture, sustainable 124
Algeria 8
Amazon, tax minimization arrangements 125, 142
American Bankers Association 36
Amoore, L. 106
Android operating system 41
anti-cartel regulations 109
Apple 8, 41, 43, 134
   suicides and exploitation of workers 116–17, 141
   tax minimization arrangements 125–6, 142
Apple Operations International 125–6
arbitration, rules of 111
Asia 64, 66
Atwood, Margaret, *Maddadam* 1
austerity policies 38, 42, 126
Australia 37, 40, 42, 48, 64, 79

Austria 77
authoritarianism 7
authority
   concept of 103
   diffusion from national governments 2
   hybrid forms of 16–17, 120
   and power 120
   and standardization 105–6
   see also private authority
automobile industry 40, 41–2, 117

Bachrach, P. 40
Bank of International Settlements 42
banks
   assets of global 42–3
   bailouts 42, 138
   lobbying by 36, 38, 48
   loss of discursive legitimacy 48
   transnationality of world 59
Baratz, M. 40
Beeson, M. 96
"Beijing Consensus" 96
Belgium 69
Bell, S. 34, 115, 145
Bermuda, as tax haven 125

bicycle production   113
Biersteker, T.J.   120
Block, F.   18
Blyth, M.   46, 86, 135
boards of directors   37
  nationality of members   60, 63
bourgeoisie see capitalist class
Braithwaite, J.   16, 140
brands   121
  and corporate social responsibility (CSR)   103–4
Brazil   62, 64, 68, 94, 96
  see also BRICs
Brecher, Jeremy   18
Breslin, S.   95
Bretton Woods Institutions   26, 51, 138
Brexit   135
BRICs (Brazil, Russia, India, China)   17, 21, 66, 100–1, 139
  community attitudes to corporations   127, 128
  greenhouse gas emissions   142
  state control compared with industrialized states   96–8 (Table 4.3)
  state-corporation relations   75, 94–9, 100–1
British Virgin Islands   64–6, 68
Brown, Gordon   48
"business integrity thesis"   47–8
business power   145
business systems
  national   77
  "obsolescing bargain model"   108
Büthe, T.   112

C&A   117
Cahill, D.   15, 136
Cameron, David   38
Canada   42, 79, 129
capital
  reputational   47–8
  transnational   44–5

capitalism
  Anglo-Saxon form   78, 79, 93, 107, 129
  comparative literature   78–9, 86
  convergence on neoliberal form   75–6, 86, 87–8, 91–4, 99
  evolution of national systems   85–94
  "ideal types"   78
  "inclusive"   136
  laissez-faire   2, 3, 48
  "mega-corporate"   134, 140
  state-led   78, 94, 95–9, 101, 107, 139
  and tax strategies   126
  US model   77–9, 84, 129, 139
  see also shareholder capitalism; varieties of capitalism (VOC)
capitalist class
  national   60
  relations underpinning globalization   2, 26–7, 71
  transnational   27, 28, 52, 60, 134–5
Caribbean states   12, 13
cartels   108–10
Cashore, B.W.   115
Cerny, P.   44, 53
Chandler, A. D. Jr.   8
Chang, H.   46, 138
Chartered Institute of Public Relations (UK)   36
Chen, G.   101
Chile   68
China   18, 56, 62, 113, 125
  employment conditions   116
  FDI   64, 66, 68, 70
  greenhouse gas emissions   142
  as headquarters of global corporations   21, 54–8, 60–1, 70, 137, 139
  leadership and political power of corporations   75, 96, 98
  soft power   121–2

state capitalism   94–9, 101, 129, 139
  see also BRICs
chlorofluorocarbons (CFCs)   39
Christian Aid   126
Citibank   117
civil society   4, 114
class relations   77
  global and governments   27
  Marxist   26–7, 28
Clayton Utz   110
climate change   37, 135, 141–2
  international agreements   38, 40, 111, 142
Clinton, Bill   6, 135
Coates, D.   86
Coen, D.   39
Cold War   2, 26, 48, 136
collusion, and coordination   108–10, 133–4
communitarianism   81–2
community attitudes   127–9
competition   7, 43–4, 131, 133–4
  at national level   134
  between suppliers   134
  control rather than   7–8, 20, 109, 131, 133–5
Confucius Institutes   122
consent, manufactured   46, 120–1
constructivism   23, 33, 46–7, 50
consumers
  activism   117–18
  illusion of choice   41, 105–6, 133, 141
  interests of   11–12, 115–16, 144
  protection   36, 118
control   7–8, 20, 40–5, 49, 52–3, 62, 70, 131, 133–5, 145
Cook, Tim   116
coordinated market economies (CMEs)   78–100
  compared with liberal market economies (LMEs)   78–85 (Table 4.1), 88, 91–4 (Table 4.2), 96–8 (Table 4.3)

coordination services firms   106–7
corporate social responsibility (CSR)   21–2, 47–8, 84, 104, 108, 140–1, 143
  and brand value   103–4
  community responsibility   123–4
  and profitability   115–20
  promoting and coordinating   111, 119–20
  questioned   118–20
  and reputation   47, 124–5, 126–9
  standards in   114
corporate-state relations   1–22, 32–3, 37–8
  de-territorialized   51–72
  and institutional contexts   21, 73–101
corporations
  as legal creations of states   32
  limited liability publicly listed   32, 37
  "publicization" of   32
corporatist states   77
credit rating agencies   106–7, 143
critical theory   25
Crouch, C.   8
Culpepper, P.D.   45, 145
Cutler, A.C.   103

Dahl, R.   35
Dauvergne, P.   117
Davies, A.   37
Davies, W.   136
Davis, A.K.   126
Deloitte   106
deregulation   2–3, 32, 82, 136
developmental state   18, 25, 29, 96
developing countries
  business and government relations   21
  deprived by OECD free trade agreements   18
  dominated by powerful states   25–6

186　Index

developing countries (cont.)
　and global supply chains　88, 114
　labor exploitation in　141
Dicken, P.　16, 28, 54
directors of corporations　37, 60, 63
discursive power　20, 22, 45–9, 111, 132, 143, 145
　and geographical concentration　56–7, 72
　and political legitimacy　24, 49, 102–4, 107, 115, 118–21, 127–30
　reputation and　119–20
discursive "veil"　12, 131, 135
Dodd-Frank Wall Street Reform and Consumer Protection Act (US 2010)　36
Dore, R.　82, 83, 90
DuPont　39

East Asian states　25, 51, 94, 96, 98, 107
　FDI stocks　64
　as headquarters of global corporations　55, 57, 58, 74, 137
economic geography　135
economic nationalism　24, 27
Economist, The　133, 135
economy, and politics　6, 16–17, 131
Elbra, A.　45, 121
elites　15, 26, 27–8
　national　60
　and norms　46
　political in business　37–8, 95, 98
　transnational　52
emerging market economies *see* BRICs
Engels, F., *Communist Manifesto*　27
entanglement *see* state-corporate relations
"entrepreneurialism"　133

environmental sustainability　18, 111, 118, 123–4, 135
　corporate lobbying　39–40
　and corporate risk　115–16
　and industry regulation　37, 81
　standards　114, 144
　and transnationality　19
Enyart, James　44
equality　77
Esping-Andersen, G.　77
"ethnocentrism"　139
Europe
　FDI flows　66, 70
　FDI stocks　64
　marine industry insurance　105
　mergers and acquisitions　63
　trade and investment　51
European Union (EU)　24
　anti-trust legislation　109–10
　capping of interchange fees　109
　car industry　42
　financial transactions tax proposed　38
　greenhouse gas emissions　142
　as headquarters of global corporations　21, 55–6, 57, 62, 74, 137
　lobbying　39
　as a "microcosm of globalization"　39
　nationality of board members　60
　regulation of global corporations　6, 87
　standard setting　112–13
Eurozone crisis　42
EY　106

Fichtner, J.　59
Fields, K.　53
financial flows, control of　52, 135
financial markets, LMEs compared with CMEs　79–81
financial sector
　global centers　59
　regulation of　36

rescue programs 42
standards 106, 107
Financial Services Roundtable 36
Finnemore, M 33, 46
Fitch Ratings 106
Fligstein, N. 98
Forbes Global 2000 companies 55, 56, 59
foreign direct investment (FDI) 17, 35
 flows 52, 54, 66–8 (Table 3.6), 79–80
 stocks 54, 63–6 (Table 3.5)
 stocks as a percentage of GDP in industrialized states 68–70 (Table 3.7)
 weaker states and 108, 135
Fortune Global 500 companies
 annual revenues 8, 55, 56, 59
 bi-national or regional 58
 professional services to 106
 World's Most Admired Companies 119, 121–2 (Table 5.1), 122–4 (Table 5.2)
Foxconn Technology 116
France 42, 48, 59, 64, 66, 68
 dirigiste model of capitalism 77, 78, 98
free market 2, 3, 6, 26, 28, 52, 81, 85, 139
 concept defunct 46, 48, 131, 133–6
free trade 35, 136
freedom
 of expression 122
 individual 7
Freeport Mining 117
Friedman, Milton 16
Friedman, Thomas 2–3
FT Emerging 500 corporations, headquarters 60–1 (Table 3.3)
FT Global 500
 banks 59

and foreign direct investment (FDI) 17
 headquarters of 55–6 (Table 3.1)
Fuchs, D. 20, 35, 39
Fukuyama, F. 2

G7 states, expenditure growth 12–13, 138
Galbraith, J.K. 11–12, 46
Gap 8, 117
General Agreement on Tariffs and Trade (GATT) 51
 see also World Trade Organization
General Motors 41, 42
geographical source of power 19, 21, 51–72, 102, 130, 131, 132, 137, 139
Germany 42, 59, 64, 66, 68, 69, 77
 capitalism in 76–7, 78, 79, 82–3, 84, 91
 Codetermination Act (1976) 83
Gibson, William, *Sprawl* 1
Giddens, A. 142
Gingerich, D.W. 91
Global Climate Coalition 40
global corporations
 defined 5, 6
 as market actors 6, 11–12, 26, 32, 136–7
 as anti-market actors 131, 136
 as national 53–4, 132, 140
 as political actors 4, 5–12, 20–2, 23–50, 34–5, 49–50, 51–4, 71, 75, 131–3, 145–6
 relations with home states 16–17, 22, 32–3, 50, 73–101, 138–9
 role of 3–4, 16–17, 52–3, 87–8
 self-regulation 20, 22, 47–8, 114–20, 120–9, 141, 143

global corporations (cont.)
  size 8–11 (Table 1.1), 41–3, 55–7, 133
  takeover 1–22, 24
  and tax avoidance 142–3
  threaten neoliberalism 2–3, 134, 136–7
global financial crisis (GFC) 138
  impact of 1, 12–15, 36, 38, 42, 48, 87, 91, 126
globalists 3, 28–31, 36, 52, 53–4, 75
globalization
  conceptualization waves 23, 25, 28–33, 50, 104
  "consensus" 52
  and evolution of national capitalist systems 74–5, 85–94
  and institutional contexts of global corporations 51, 139–40
  and IPE debates 24–35
  literature 3, 18, 20
  neoliberal 3, 11, 46–7, 135–6, 144
  "The dark lords of" 1
  "what states make of it" 76
Goldstein, A. 94, 98
Goodin, R. 87
Google 41, 43, 134
  tax minimization arrangements 125, 126, 127, 142
governance
  and discursive legitimacy 50
  failure of democratic 126
  markets or states 3, 58
  new forms of 120–9
  normatively appropriate 103
  potential for private 102–30
  private from private authority 111–14
  rational for private 114–20
  rationale for global 6, 118–20, 132, 143–4

governments
  business relations 37–8, 99–100, 145–6
  community attitudes to 127–9 (Table 5.3)
  and corporate taxation 12–16, 126
  democratically elected 143
  expenditure of G7 states (Fig. 1.1) 12–13
  and global class relations 27
  and global corporations 1, 6, 16–17, 22, 50, 81, 108
  and market forces 1–2, 76
Gramscianism 25, 180
greenhouse gas emissions 19, 39–40, 118, 142
"greenhouse mafia" 37, 40
Greenpeace 117
gross domestic product (GDP)
  compared with global corporations' sales 8–11
  and financial crisis 42
  total tax as a percentage of 14–15
  as value added measure 8

Haier 95
Hall, P.A. 91
  Varieties of Capitalism 74–5, 78, 86, 100
Hall, R. 120
Hampden-Turner, C. 84, 85
Harrod, J. 99
Harvey, D. 26
Haufler, V. 16
Hay, C. 20, 29
Hay Group 119
headquarter states 17–18, 70, 99, 132, 137–40, 145–6
  community attitudes to major companies 127–9 (Table 5.3)
  and coordination services firms 106–7

and corporate social
   responsibility 18, 140–4
identity of 21, 54–62, 60–1
national and global
   actors 55–62, 73–101
and soft power 121–2
transnationality of 58–62
Held, D. 28
Helleiner, Eric 27
Henkel 109–10
Hennes & Mauritz 117
Hindmoor, A. 115
Home Depot 117
Hong Kong 58, 62, 64, 66, 116
Huawei 95
human rights 118, 122
Hymer, Stephen 133
"hyperglobalists" 3

ideas
   "intersubjective" 33
   and political power 23–50
   the power of 33–5, 45–50, 86, 127–9
Ikea 117
India 55, 56, 62, 64, 68, 94, 96, 113
   see also BRICs
industrialized states
   community attitudes 127–9 (Table 5.3)
   institutional embedding in 74–5, 76–85
   LMEs compared with CMEs 91–3 (Table 4.2)
   state intervention compared with BRICs 96–8 (Table 4.3)
industry associations, and international standards 110–11, 143
industry policies 18, 27, 42, 53
inequality, growth of 27, 126, 134
infrastructural power 31, 138
institutional complementarity theory 113

institutional contexts
   and corporate-state relations 21, 24, 32, 54, 73–101, 102, 105–14, 132
   and globalization 85–94, 139–40, 145–6
   national 73–101
   and tax arrangements 125
institutions
   change as path-dependent 89–94
   continuity 86–9
   defined 46, 73, 100
   in developing states 96
   and political systems 73–4
   and "rules of thumb" 75, 102–3, 120–1, 129–30
instrumental power 20, 24, 35–40, 74, 132, 135, 143
   defined 35
   territorial nature of 40, 56–7, 72, 138
Intellectual Property Committee (IPC) 39
intellectual property rights 39
interests
   corporate or social 4, 18, 103–4, 140–1, 143–4
   elite 15, 27–8
   of global corporations 5, 15, 24, 115–20, 129–30, 135, 145
   individual 7
   and shared beliefs 33–5, 45–9
   shareholders 22, 144
   states and corporations 16–19, 52–3, 103–4
intergovernmental groups 40, 110–11
intersectoral links 43, 44, 133
International Accounting Standards Board 112
international agreements
   on climate change 38, 39, 142
   liberalism and 26, 94, 127
   on trade and investment 143–4

International Chamber of
    Commerce (ICC)   40,
    110–11
International Court of
    Arbitration   111
International Labor Organization
    (ILO)   141
international law   17
International Monetary Fund
    (IMF)   135–6, 144
International Organization for
    Standardization (ISO)   22,
    103, 112–14
international organizations   11, 40,
    52, 144
International Political Economy
    (IPE)   20, 23–50
    and conceptualization waves of
        globalization   28–31 (Table
        2.1)
    constructivist challenge to   23,
        33, 50
    and globalization debates   24–35,
        51
    traditions   23, 25–8, 50
international regimes,
    private   111–14
international relations   2, 11, 27,
    35, 121
international society   54
Internet Corporation for Assigned
    Names and Numbers
    (ICANN)   112
investment
    by subsidiaries of world banks   59
    liberalization   94
    national and regional   62–70, 70,
        71
    patterns   52, 54, 62, 108
    as a reflection of national
        economic power   68–70
    relations dominated by global
        corporations   41, 43–4
    and shareholder capitalism   79
    standards   112–14

invisible hand   7, 135
Ireland   68
    as tax haven   125–6
Italy   42, 77, 78

Japan   21, 42, 52, 56, 57, 59, 62,
    66, 68, 69, 137
    capitalism in   76, 79, 82, 83, 84,
        91
    community attitudes   127
    corporate taxes   13, 14
    greenhouse gas emissions   142
Johal, S.   48
joint-stock companies   7
Jones, G.   74
Jones, O.   26, 37
Jordana, J.   16
J. P. Morgan Chase   36

Kahancová, M.   88
Kang, N.   91
Keller, M. R.   18
Kolleck, N.   111, 119, 127
Korten, D.   4
KPMG   106

labor
    in automobile industry   41–2
    conditions   18, 83, 108, 135
    exploitative and forced   26,
        116–17, 141
    management relations   82–3
    standards   118, 144
    transnational   59–60, 62, 71
labor markets, LMEs compared
    with CMEs   82–3, 91–3
Lagarde, Christine   136
Lamy, Pascal   44
Latin America   12, 13, 64, 66, 68,
    70
law
    firms   106, 110
    influence of global corporations
        on   38
    international   17

national   107
public for the world   39, 115
LeBaron, G.   141
legitimacy   6, 20, 45, 144
  cognitive   46
  democratic   103
  discursive   20, 22, 24, 45–50, 73–4, 81, 102–4, 107, 115, 119–21, 127–30
  moral   45, 120
  perceptions of   22, 45–9, 118–20, 127–9
  pragmatic   45
  of private authority   21–2, 103–4, 132
Lehman Brothers   20
Lenovo   95
leverage   20, 24, 35, 45, 48, 49, 108, 145
Levi-Faur, D.   16
Levitt, T.   2
liberal democracy   31–2, 77
liberal market economies (LMEs)   78–100
  compared with coordinated market economies (CMEs)   78–85 (Table 4.1), 91–4 (Table 4.2), 96–8 (Table 4.3)
  convergence on   86, 87–8
  and shareholder capitalism   115, 129, 130, 142
liberalism   2, 6, 51
  classical   25
    IPE tradition   23, 26, 33, 36, 75, 76
liberalization   91–4
limited liability corporations   32
Liu, G.S.   95
lobbying   36–40, 50, 100, 102
Lukes, S.   45
Luxembourg   59, 68, 69

McGrew, A.   28
McKinsey Global Institute   133

Mahoney, J.   89
managed capitalism   78
management
  autonomy   99–100
  hierarchy of US corporations   8
  objectives of LMEs compared with CMEs   83–4
  regionally and nationally embedded   88, 94
  relations between workers and   82–3
  separation from ownership   7, 77
  standards in   114
  visible hand of   8
  see also senior management
management consultancy firms   106
Mann, M.   31, 72
manufacturing industry   82
Margolis, J.D.   119
market   46
  see also invisible hand
market capitalism   78
market capitalization   41, 43
market concentration, and geographical concentration   74, 139
market forces
  discourse of   47
  and governments   1–2, 76
  and market control   36, 52, 131, 143–4
  shaping or responding to   86–7, 135
market imperatives   2, 12, 81, 86
marketization   2, 3, 11
markets, versus states   1–3, 6–7, 76, 77, 81
Marsh, D.   20, 28
Marsman, I.   60
Martell, L.   28
Marx, Karl   134
  Communist Manifesto   27
Marxism   2, 15, 52, 134–5
  IPE tradition   23, 25, 26–7, 33, 44–5, 71, 75, 76, 102

Marzinotto, B. 86
Mastercard 109
Mattli, W. 38, 112
"mega-corporations" 16
members of parliament (MPs)
    as directors of corporations 37
    lobbying 37–8
mergers and acquisitions
    (M&As) 54, 60, 62–3, 66, 71
Mexico 64, 68
Micklethwait, J. 4 [?-e]
Microsoft 43
    operating system 105–6
mining 37–8, 40
Mitchell, David 47
monetary policies 18, 42
monopoly 7
Monsanto 44
Moody's 106
Moon, J. 91
moral issues 118–20
Moran, M. 37
multinational corporations
    (MNCs) 5, 132
    assets of top 100 US 52
    defined 5
    not global 137–40
    transnationality index (TNI) 19, 55–62
multinational enterprises
    (MNEs) 5

national economies, action to stabilize global economy 138
national identity 17–18, 19, 20–1, 24, 25–6, 31, 52–3, 131, 132, 137–40, 146
    and corporate interests 53–4, 88–9
national standards associations 112
nationality
    of corporate board members 59–60
    and institutional diversity 73–101
    and transnationality of top 100 corporations 57–60 (Table 3.2)
    and varieties of capitalism (VOC) 76–85
Nazism 76
nationalism 24, 29, 33, 96
IPE tradition 23, 24, 25–6, 33, 52–3, 71
neo-Marxism 25, 27, 52
neo-mercantilism 24
neo-nationalism 135
neoclassical economics 4
neoliberalism
    dominance in US 87–8
    evolution of 136
    inadequacy of 6, 131–2, 135–6
    inevitability of 2–3, 4, 46–7, 99, 136–7
    institutional embedding of 4, 25, 75
    and market-state relations 2–4, 26, 28, 52, 58
Nestlé 117
Netherlands 42, 59, 68, 78, 125
networks 31, 44, 107–8, 137
    banking 59
    captive 107–8
    hierarchical 107
    market-based 108
    modular 108
    of operations 5, 8, 43–4, 106–8, 134
    relational 108
"new world order" 48, 138
NEXTEra Energy 123, 124
Nike 8, 107, 117
Nolan, P. 7
Nölke, A. 95
non-government organizations
    (NGOs) 22, 41, 104, 117, 126
    community attitudes to 127–9 (Table 5.3)

norms
    and cognitive legitimacy 46, 127
    informal industry 105–6
    lifecycle 33–4 (Fig. 2.1), 46
    shaping and institutionalization
        of 24, 25, 33–5, 46–50,
        73–4, 86, 102–6, 119–20,
        129–30
North America
    FDI stocks 64, 70
    as headquarters of global
        corporations 51, 55, 57, 137
Nye, J.S. 120

O'Callaghan, T. 117
OECD states
    banks 41–2
    corporate taxes in 13–15
    free trade agreements 18, 43
    labor force 41
Ohmae, K. 2
oil and gas companies 37, 40
operations
    networks of 5, 8, 43–4, 106–8
    transnationality of 19
ownership 62, 70
    separated from management 7,
        77
Oxfam 126
Ozawa, T. 98

PanAm 20
Parvin, P. 36
Pauly, L. 77
policymaking
    and belief in globalization 46–7
    ideas shaping 46–7
    influence on 37–8, 40–5, 135,
        139
political economy 6, 140
    see also international political
        economy (IPE)
political power
    balancing global
        corporations' 22, 140–6

and FDI flows 69–70
and geographical factors 19,
    51–72
ideational basis of 23–50
perspective 4, 5–12
and private governance 102–30
see also legitimacy, discursive
politics, and economy 6, 16–17,
    136
Pontusson, J. 99
Portugal 8
power
    and authority 120
    hard 35
    of ideas 33–5
    institutionalization of perceived
        legitimate 48–9
    nature of 23
    patterns of national and regional
        economic 54–72
    soft 120–2
    three faces of 35–49
power relations 22, 32, 89–94,
    102–30, 133, 137–8, 145–6
private authority 102–30
    balanced against public good 16,
        120–9, 143–4
    definition 103
    forms of 104–14
    legitimacy of 21–2, 102–4, 130,
        139–44
    as moral authority 120
    and power relations 32, 102–30
    and private governance 111–20,
        132
    shaping market forces 135
    and social responsibility 140
private international
        regimes 111–14
privatization 2, 32, 136
Proctor and Gamble 109
product markets, LMEs compared
        with CMEs 81–2, 91–3
production
    capitalist mode of 26–7

production (cont.)
  capitalist relations of   31, 58, 71, 74, 100
  control by cartels   108–10
  control of means of   26–7, 44–5, 134, 135
production alliances   107–8
professional services firms   106, 139
profit maximization
  and corporate social responsibility (CSR)   115–20, 119–20, 143
  liberal accounts of   26, 79
  lobbying and   36–7
  mechanisms of   4
  and shareholders   83–4
profits, of global corporations   40–1, 70, 86
public good   7, 16, 27, 47–8, 81–2, 120–9, 143–4
  and corporate interests   118–20, 130
  perceptions of   127–9
public relations   36, 121
PwC   106

Qishan, Wang   48

re-embodyment   4–12, 131
re-territorialization   4, 5, 12–19, 20–1, 24, 51–72, 131, 140
Reagan, Ronald   135
regional identity   5, 18, 20–1, 24, 88–9, 131, 138
regulation (rules)   3, 6, 11, 16, 48, 75
  and cognitive legitimacy   46, 127–9
  financial sector in US   36
  influence of global corporations on   37–8, 129–30
  institutionalization by capitalist class   26–7
  preventing unwanted   48, 103–4, 118–19

prohibiting cartels   109
trade   44
transnational   38
and varieties of capitalism   87
see also self-regulation
Reich, S.   77
reputation
  "intermediaries"   106
  and social responsibility   47, 119–20, 123–4, 126–9
  and trust   47–8, 104, 117–18, 121, 127–9
research and development   18
responsibility   47–8
  see also corporate social responsibility (CSR)
Ricardo, D.   7
Riegels, Colin   68
Rio Tinto   117
Ronit, K.   39
Royal, Mark   119
Rudd, Kevin   48
Rugman, A.   58
Russia   62, 64, 68, 94
  see also BRICs

Samsung   41
Sarkozy, Nicolas   48
Saudi Arabia   56
Scandinavia   77
Schmidt, Eric   126
Schmidt, V.   78
Schneider, V.   39
Scholte, J.A.   28
science fiction   1, 27, 136
Securities Industry and Financial Market Association   36
self-regulation   20, 22, 47–8, 114–20, 120–9, 141, 143
senior management
  strategic planning   134
  and transnationality   54, 59–60
shareholder capitalism, and liberal market economy (LME)   79, 83–4, 142

shareholders
    activism 117–18, 141
    divorced from management
        control 7
    interests of 22, 103, 115, 144
Shell, Brent Spar 117–18, 141
Sikkink, K. 33, 46
Singapore 62, 64, 69
skeptics 28–31, 53–4
Sklair, L. 52
Smith, Adam 7, 25, 134, 135
    Wealth of Nations 16
"social capitalism" 48
social contract 82
social democracy 48, 77, 87
social responsibility *see* corporate
        social responsibility (CSR)
Soft Power 30, 121–2 (Table 5.1)
sole-traders 7
Soskice, D., *Varieties of
    Capitalism* 74–5, 78, 86,
    100
South Africa 150
South Korea 52, 56, 98, 121, 137
sovereignty
    concept of 6
    corporate 52, 140
    shared 6, 32, 50, 104–5, 129
    state 6, 12, 25, 53, 104, 137,
        140
    transformation of 32, 50
Spain 42
stakeholder capitalism 81, 83,
    99–100
Standard and Poor's 106
standardization 22, 103, 105, 107
standards
    influence of global corporations
        on 39, 108
    intellectual property 39
    international 112, 143
    and moral legitimacy 45–6
    national 112, 113
    organizations which set 111–14
Staples, C.L. 60

Starbucks 117
tax minimization
    arrangements 125, 142
Starrs, S. 138
state
    the demise of the 2, 12, 16
    relationships of LMEs compared
        with CMEs 84–5
    "second Great Transformation of
        the" 90–1
state capitalism 78, 95–9, 101, 107,
    139
state-corporate entanglement 4,
    16–17, 21, 22, 31, 32–3,
    35–50, 55, 141–4
    in BRICs 75, 94–9, 100–1
    and consent of citizens 121
    and evolution of national
        capitalist systems 85–94
    geographical
        concentration 51–72
    and institutional diversity 73–
        101, 114
states
    "competition" 44
    core and periphery 27, 71
    GDP compared with size of
        global corporations 8–11
    interactions with each other and
        non-state actors 28–33
    markets versus 1–3, 6–7, 12, 76,
        77, 81
    national interests of 25–6, 28,
        32–3
    neoliberal 32
    soft power for 120–1
    transformation of role 16–17,
        32–3, 53–5, 71–2, 90–1,
        104–5, 120
stock market 77
    capitalism (US) 77, 78, 79, 84,
        139
Strange, Susan 1–2, 72
strategic decision making 37–8,
    82–3, 134, 145

structural power 20, 24, 40–5, 52, 74, 102, 132, 135, 143
  and geographical concentration 56–7, 70–1, 72
Sub-Saharan Africa 12, 13
subcontractor relationships 107–8
subsidiaries, and tax arrangements 125–6
Sun, P. 95
supply chains, global 5, 8–11, 19, 41, 43–4, 134, 135
  and developing countries 88, 114
  and subcontracting conditions 107–8, 141
  and transnationality 19
Sweden 58, 78
Switzerland 42, 58, 68

Taiwan 52, 58, 62
Tax Justice Network 126
taxation
  avoidance 104, 124–7, 142–3
  on corporate profits 13–14 (Fig. 1.2)
  global rates of 13–15, 126, 144
  OECD share of 14–15 (Fig. 1.3)
  offshore havens 64–6, 125
  as percentage of GDP 14–15
technology 18, 81
Thatcher, Margaret, "TINA" principle 6
Thelen, K. 89
think tanks 26
Thompson, G. 8
Tiberghien, Y. 98
Tienhaara, K. 40
Tiffany and Co. 117
Toyota 41
trade
  dominance by global corporations 43–4, 52, 135
  intra-firm 107
  liberalization 94
  rules of 11, 52
  standards 112–14
Trade-Related Aspects of Intellectual Property Rights (TRIPs) 39
Trans-Pacific Partnership (TPP) agreement 53
transformationalists 28–31, 32, 50, 54, 104–5, 120
transnational capitalist class 28, 52, 60, 134
transnational corporations (TNCs) 5, 16, 54–62, 70, 132
transnationality 57–62, 63
transnationality index (TNI) (UNCTAD) 17–18, 19
  ratios 57
  states compared with corporations 69–70
  world's top 100 non-financial corporations 19, 57–8 (Table 3.2)
Trompenaars, A. 84, 85
Trump, Donald 53, 135
trust 96, 104, 117–18, 127–9
"turbo capitalism" 134
Turkey 62

Unilever 109
United Kingdom (UK)
  bank assets 43, 59
  bank bailouts 42, 48, 138
  business and political elites 37, 38
  commercial code 105
  employment protection 93
  FDI stocks 64, 68
  financial sector 36
  inquiries into Google's tax strategies 125
  liberal capitalism 78, 79, 93, 129
  mergers and acquisitions 63
  professional services firms 107
  senior managers 60

TNI of MNCs   19, 58
see also Brexit
United Nations Conference on Trade and Development (UNCTAD), transnationality index (TNI)   17–18, 94
United Nations Framework Convention on Climate Change   111
United Nations (UN)   111
   budget (2013)   11
United States (US)
   anti-trust legislation   109
   automotive industry   41–2
   bank assets   43, 59
   bank bailouts   42, 138
   corporate taxes   13–14
   Court of Appeals   109
   credit rating agencies   106
   FDI flows   66, 68, 69
   financial sector regulation   36
   greenhouse gas emissions   142
   as headquarters of global corporations   17, 21, 54, 55–7, 58, 62, 70, 74, 122, 137, 138–9
   managerial hierarchy   8, 60
   mergers and acquisitions   63
   National Standards Institute   112
   patent payments   39
   as a "security network state"   18
   stock market capitalism   77, 78, 79, 84, 129, 139
   structural power over global economy   87, 138–9
   tax avoidance   126
   TNI of MNCs   19
   US Trade Representative (USTR)   53

van Ham, P.   121
van Veen, K.   60
varieties of capitalism (VOC)   25, 48, 74–5, 78–94, 99–100, 139–40
   characterization of states   86, 94
   Europe compared with US   79–85, 113
   and nationality   76–85
Verbeke, A.   58
Vernon, R.   6, 137
Visa   109
Vogel, D.   117, 119
Vogel, S.   91
Freer Markets More Rules   3
Volkswagen   41
Voss, H.   58

Wade, R.   15, 51–2
Wallerstein, I., World Systems Theory   71
Walmart   8, 17–18
Walsh, J.P.   119
Walt Disney   123, 124
Walter, A.   95
Wank, D.   101
War on Want   126
Washington Consensus   15, 48, 87, 138
   or "Beijing Consensus"   96
Watson, M.   24
weaker states
   and multinational corporations   137, 138, 144
   and offering or withholding FDI   70, 135
Weiss, L.   15, 18, 31
welfare states, varieties of   77, 87
Whole Foods Market   123, 124, 181
Wilks, S.   54, 82, 136
Wilks-Heeg, S.   37
Williams, Jeff   116
Wolf, M.   88
Woods, N.   38
Wooldridge, A.   84
World Bank   48, 111, 144
World Business Council for Sustainable Development (WBCSD)   40, 111, 118

World Council   110–11
world economy   48, 59, 98, 133
World Systems Theory
    (Wallerstein)   25, 71
World Trade Organization
    (WTO)   44, 51, 87, 144
  budget (2013)   11
  Dispute Settlement Body   111
  lobbying   39
World Values Survey   127–9

World's Top 100 Non-financial
    Corporations
  from developing countries:
    nationality and
    transnationality   61 (Table 3.4)
  TNI of   19, 57–8 (Table 3.2)

Zadek, S.   119
Zhang, J.   98
Zhang, X.   95